The Campus History Series

APPALACHIAN STATE UNIVERSITY

On the Cover: The class of 1916 poses on the lawn next to the first administration building. The group of 28 students graduated at the July 11, 1916, commencement ceremony. In addition to the awarding of diplomas, the ceremony consisted of speeches, poetry reading, and music. (Courtesy of Appalachian State University Special Collections.)

The Campus History Series

APPALACHIAN STATE UNIVERSITY

PAMELA PRICE MITCHEM

ARCADIA PUBLISHING

ISBN 978-1-4671-2144-6

Published by Arcadia Publishing
Charleston, South Carolina

Printed in the United States of America

Library of Congress Catalog Card Number: 2013949417

For all general information, please contact Arcadia Publishing:
Telephone 843-853-2070
Fax 843-853-0044
E-mail sales@arcadiapublishing.com
For customer service and orders:
Toll-Free 1-888-313-2665

Visit us on the Internet at www.arcadiapublishing.com

For my daughter, Madeline

Contents

FOREWORD

You never really know a person until you hear about their family of origin and culture. So it is with a school. Like a person, it is a living entity. Appalachian began not as a state-mandated institution, but as the dream and labor of one family. My great-grandparents, Dauph and Lillie Dougherty, with Dauph's brother Blan, birthed this school and nurtured it through a brief childhood as Watauga Academy. Each one of this trio was teaching all day in that fall of 1899 in a borrowed building, after which Lillie cooked dinner while the brothers cut, sawed, and hauled wood from their family farm to construct the new Boone schoolhouse.

Daniel Baker Dougherty, their father, planted the seed, in his boys and in the community, that education would bring opportunity and a better life to this isolated part of North Carolina. Blan rode his horse all over the county as superintendent, befriending teachers and families in every tiny, one-room-schoolhouse community and earning their trust. Parents sent their young ones to board in Boone and attend the new school. Townspeople sacrificially gave, from 25¢ to $500 each, to enable this new venture to succeed. The gangly adolescence gained state support in 1903 to become Appalachian Training School. Young adulthood and maturity came with the credentials to certify teachers as a normal school and then its ultimate transition into a four-year college.

With total dedication and unwavering determination, Dauph, Lillie, and Blan steadfastly led Appalachian for a total of 123 years. And the Dougherty dream to give opportunity and a better life through education has grown and grown, expanding this year to nations and peoples all over the globe. Herein is a wonderful visual collection of the growing-up years of Appalachian. I trust you will enjoy getting to know ASU better!

—Doris Perry Stam

ACKNOWLEDGMENTS

This pictorial collection is not intended to be a definitive history of Appalachian State University. Instead, its purpose is to highlight the extensive and, in some instances, little-seen historical photographs in the university's collection. Because of the limitations of this approach, but also because any slim volume attempting to cover the whole of a university's history is bound to have its omissions, a number of significant people, campus structures, and memorable events may be missing. Neither can a selection of some 200-plus images adequately represent a collection that numbers more than 300,000. But this book does provide a broad-ranging, carefully chosen sampling of Appalachian's photograph archives for those who would like to dig deeper. It is my hope that it also proves satisfying to readers who are curious about or connected to the university.

Because this is a photographic history, not a scholarly one, there are no citations. All of the information collected for the book, however, came from the sources listed in the bibliography.

For those who would like to learn more about the university's story, or its relationship with the town of Boone, I can happily recommend a small handful of books, most of them generously illustrated: Ruby Lanier's *Blanford Barnard Dougherty, Mountain Educator* (1974); Doris Stam's *Mountain Educators: The Dougherty Family and the First Fifty Years of Appalachian* (2010); Ruth Currie's *Appalachian State University: The First Hundred Years* (1998); and Donna Warmuth's *Boone* (2003). I made every effort to avoid duplication of images, but, out of necessity, there is some small repetition, particularly in the early chapters.

I would also like to direct the reader to Appalachian's University Archives, which house thousands of materials documenting the university's history.

Thanks are due to Jim Jones and Doris Stam, both of whom generously agreed to read drafts of the manuscript. Their comments and suggestions were of great help to me, and they no doubt improved the book. I am grateful, too, for the longtime support of my colleagues in Special Collections. Unless otherwise noted, all images in this book are courtesy of Appalachian State University Special Collections.

INTRODUCTION

Like other universities of comparable age, Appalachian State University has undergone many changes in its dozen decades. What may be unique about its development, however, and about its story, is the setting. Boone, North Carolina, is known today as a destination for vacationers and sportsmen. It is a progressive, bustling town nestled among some of the highest mountains on the East Coast. But in the decades before and just after Appalachian's founding, it was a sparsely populated outpost in the Blue Ridge.

Early schools in the region were subscription-based, taught primarily by local ministers, and only met after the crops were gathered. Even after the state provided funding for public education, the mountain schools saw little benefit; they continued to suffer from a lack of oversight, inefficient management, and poor teacher pay.

In 1868, a new state constitution called for free public education to be provided for both white and black students. Since a portion of the funding for schools came from local taxes, the "Lost Provinces" of western North Carolina had some of the most poorly funded schools. As one of the "pauper counties," Watauga County had little industry and no railroad, which meant that it had few means to raise funds for public education. In the year that Appalachian was founded, 1899, there were nearly 5,000 children of school age in Watauga County, but figures indicate that far fewer were enrolled in school. The schools still had little oversight, and there were no requirements that teachers be trained.

During this time, Daniel Baker "D.B." Dougherty, a longtime Watauga County resident who was also the Boone postmaster, a justice of the peace, and the editor of the *Watauga Democrat*, took up the cause of education for the northwestern North Carolina counties. Dougherty had already used his influence at the local paper to encourage growth and development in the county, lobbying hard for the improvement of roads and the extension of the railroad to the mountains, but he knew that the area would not prosper unless its people were better educated. So he began to use his editorials to stir up interest in a new school. He also encouraged his two sons, who had been teaching at Holly Spring College in Tennessee, to start a school in Watauga County.

By 1899, the *Watauga Democrat* was reporting that "two educators of no small worth are thinking of opening a high grade school in Boone." On August 24, it was official: the school was to open, offering grammar, secondary, and two-year collegiate courses. The community raised $1,000 for construction, and land was donated by J.F. Hardin and Daniel Dougherty. School opened on Tuesday, September 5, 1899, in a borrowed building, the Three Forks Baptist Association's Boone Academy, which stood behind what is now the First Baptist Church and the Turchin Center. The Dougherty brothers, Blan and Dauph, taught the academic and collegiate courses, along with business, debate, and declamation, while Dauph's wife, Lillie, taught art and music. Tuition ranged from $1 to $3, with boarding opportunities available in the town.

By 1902, more than 100 pupils were enrolled in Watauga Academy, 90 percent of them adults. A teacher-training department was established, and free tuition was granted in exchange for a pledge to teach in the North Carolina schools for two years. Although enrollment grew steadily, the financial status of the academy rested on small tuition fees and modest public support. Dauph and Blan Dougherty knew that state funds would be necessary if their educational goals were to be met. After much lobbying of the state legislature, Blan Dougherty and local lawyer E.F. Lovill wrote a bill, introduced in the legislature by C.W. Newland, chairman of the judiciary committee, to make Watauga Academy a teacher-training school.

The Newland Bill was passed on March 9, 1903, clearing the way for Appalachian Training School. The bill provided an annual sum of $2,000 for maintenance and $1,500 for new buildings, on the condition that private contributions match public money dollar for dollar. But the location of the new school was yet to be determined. Several areas in the western North Carolina mountains voiced a desire to host the new institution, including Jefferson, in Ashe County; Globe Academy, in Caldwell County; Montezuma, in Mitchell County; and even Blowing Rock, Valle Crucis, and Shull's Mill, in Watauga County. After a vigorous campaign for local contributions, however, it was Boone's Watauga Academy that became Appalachian Training School, opening its doors on October 5, 1903, with six teachers and more than 300 students. Blan Dougherty was elected superintendent of the school in 1903, and Dauph became principal. Both brothers continued to teach, and Blan recruited students, campaigned for the school, and lobbied the legislature. He also served as superintendent of Watauga County Schools for 16 years, from 1899 to 1915.

In this early period, Appalachian Training School was essentially a regional high school that focused on teacher training. In 1917, however, the educational commission recognized the need for normal schools, which provided postsecondary teacher training. By 1921, Appalachian had begun offering a two-year normal school component, enlarging its academic departments and adding teachers to meet the state requirements. In 1925, the school's name was changed to Appalachian State Normal School (ASNS). Blan became president and Dauph business manager.

Dauph Dougherty died four years later, in 1929, but he lived long enough to hear the bell toll from Watauga Academy with the good news that the state had approved the school, now Appalachian State Teachers College (ASTC), as a four-year institution.

The 1930s brought the Great Depression, along with record-low enrollments and state-enforced cuts in appropriations; but under Blan Dougherty's leadership, the school continued to grow. New majors were added, and the Works Progress Administration (WPA) built faculty houses and a hospital (now Founders Hall). In 1942, after ASTC gained regional accreditation, graduate courses were offered. Just six years later, the school had a master's program in education.

Dr. Dougherty retired in 1955, at the age of 85, after 55 years at the helm of Appalachian. When William Plemmons became president that year, the campus consisted of 35 acres, and its enrollment was approximately 2,200. The faculty numbered just under 100.

The 1960s was a time of great change for the nation and for Appalachian. More students than ever enrolled at the school, and Appalachian saw its first African American graduate in 1968. Computer technology was ushered in on campus, with IBM processing equipment for computerized registration on campus.

Under Plemmons, Appalachian would add 24 campus buildings, establish new programs and colleges, bring in new faculty, increase enrollment, and institute the school's first long-range plan. The most noticeable change to occur under his administration, however, was in the school's name, which became Appalachian State University (ASU) in August 1967. By the end of his tenure, the campus had grown to more than 90 acres and 40 major buildings, and the number of faculty and students swelled to 300 and 6,000, respectively.

Dr. Herbert Walter Wey took over from Plemmons, and he provided a steady hand throughout the 1970s, a tumultuous time that saw student protests over world issues such as the Vietnam War and the environment. With a reputation as an educational consultant, Wey encouraged faculty to experiment with individualized instruction and team teaching. He led educational innovation on campus, creating independent study, interdisciplinary studies, the honors program, the internship program, Watauga College, Upward Bound, and new programs in teacher training. In an effort to get students more involved in the world, Appalachian established off-campus learning centers in New York City and Washington, DC.

In 1971, ASU joined the University of North Carolina System as one of the 16 (now 17) regional campuses, and President Wey became chancellor. Four years later, ASU shifted from the quarter system to semesters. The school pushed to expand offerings beyond education, adding degrees in technology and ecology. The College of Business was created, and in the late 1970s, women's studies and Appalachian studies were added to the curriculum. The changes helped grow the enrollment further, and it had passed 9,000 by the time Wey retired in 1979.

Taking the university into the 1980s and early 1990s was Dr. John Thomas. Chancellor Thomas utilized his background as a NASA engineer to facilitate improvements to technology at Appalachian. He led the construction of an underground coaxial cable system to computerize campus communications and run the energy management system. The campus enhanced distance education through computer technology that included a campus-wide computer network and a satellite to link to North Carolina public schools that provided educational programming. Also during this time, the university signed a faculty exchange with the Northeast Institute of Technology in Shenyang, China.

There were many other changes on campus in the 1980s. AppalCart began operation, and the Office of Residence Life was established, along with An Appalachian Summer Festival, the Kellogg Institute, the first doctoral program, and the Hayes School of Music. At the time of Dr. Thomas's retirement in 1993, Appalachian's enrollment had reached 11,650.

Dr. Francis T. "Frank" Borkowski became the fifth Appalachian State University chancellor on May 14, 1993, and promptly pursued his vision to bring the school into the 21st century. Under Dr. Borkowski's tenure, enrollment for Freshman Seminar increased and the Freshman Learning Communities Program received recognition and awards. Many advancements in student development, diversity, and cultural exchange were also made. A summer reading program was instituted in 1996, and five years later, in 2001, the university was named "College of the Year" by *Time* magazine. The early years of the new century also saw expansion of faculty and student exchange programs; the creation of the Appalachian Learning Alliance, which expanded distance education; the establishment of the Appalachian Energy Center; the founding of the GLBT Task Force; and the opening of the Turchin Center for the Visual Arts.

Chancellor Borkowski also made great strides in fund-raising, as the "Campaign for the Second Century" brought in $83 million. By the time Borkowski stepped down in 2003, several academic structures had been renovated and the campus had expanded, with a new science building, a convocation center, student apartments, and an alumni center.

Appalachian's sixth chancellor, Dr. Kenneth Edward Peacock, took the reins in 2004. Under Chancellor Peacock, the university has improved both retention and graduation rates, as well as the overall grade point average of incoming freshman; created the College of Health Sciences; and established the Appalachian Research Institute for Environment, Energy, and Economics (RIEEE). Peacock is also responsible for raising more than $53 million in private funding for the school and initiating more than $200 million in capital improvements. These include construction of the Athletics Center, Mountaineer Hall, the Student Recreation Center, Central Dining Hall, the new College of Education building, the Brad and Carole Wilson Honors and Engagement Community, the Beasley Media Complex, and a number of renovations and additions to structures on campus. Chancellor Peacock announced in April 2013 that he planned to step down after a search for a new chancellor had concluded. Dr. Sheri Noren Everts assumed the chancellor's position on July 1, 2014.

Thanks to the contributions of the chancellors, faculty, staff, students, and supporters over the 100-plus years of the school's history, Appalachian has grown to become the sixth-largest of the 17 UNC campus schools, with more than 17,000 students and 900 faculty members. Appalachian is widely known for the quality of its education and is consistently ranked among the top schools in the South.

One

The Early Years

This chapter covers the early history of Appalachian, and specifically the time before it became a four-year institution. This period, which includes the days of Watauga Academy (1899–1903), Appalachian Training School (1903–1925), and Appalachian State Normal School (1925–1929), is remembered chiefly for the strong leadership of the Doughertys, the school's cofounders. The chapter closes with the death of Dauph Dougherty in 1929.

Dr. Blan Dougherty's legacy is profound beyond his establishment and management of the school. He also pushed for change in Boone and Watauga County. An outspoken advocate for the building of roads to connect Boone to the North Carolina Piedmont and Tennessee, he was also largely responsible for the railroad coming to Boone in 1918. He was a tireless promoter of commerce, with a prophetic view of the importance of tourism and resorts to the area. Perhaps his greatest legacy, however, is the little-known Hancock Bill of Tax Equalization, which was passed in 1929 after 20 years of Dougherty's determined advocacy. Before the bill passed, citizens in poorer counties paid five times more in taxes for education than those in the 10 richest counties of North Carolina.

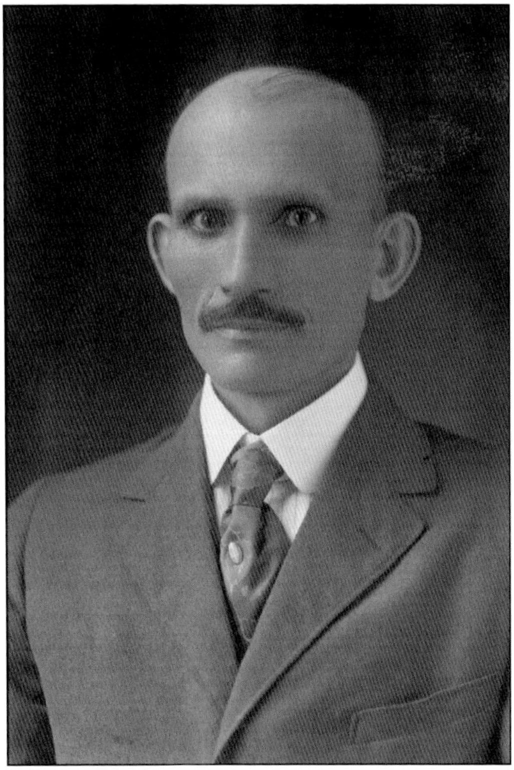

Dr. Blanford Barnard Dougherty, known as "Blan" or "B.B.," was born on March 11, 1869. He received bachelor's degrees from Carson-Newman College (1896) and the University of North Carolina at Chapel Hill (1899). Elon College would award him an honorary doctorate in 1926, and Wake Forest followed suit 10 years later, bestowing an honorary doctorate of education on Dougherty. He was cofounder, coprincipal, superintendent, and then president of Appalachian for 55 years.

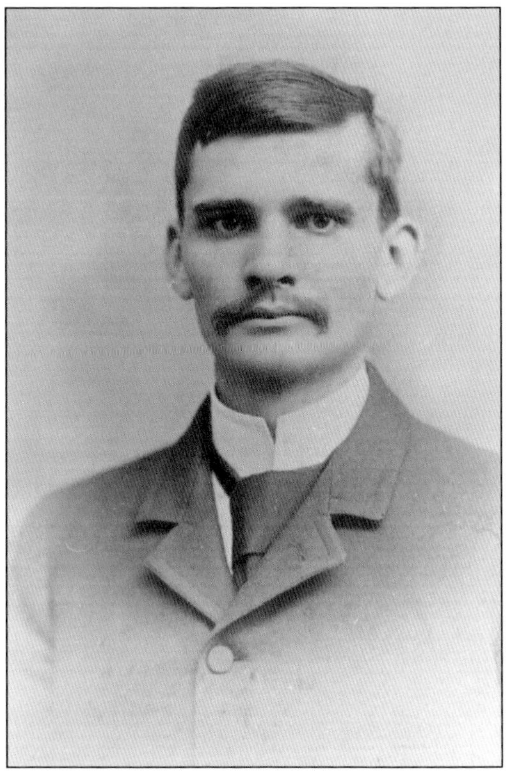

Dauphin Disco Dougherty, known as "D.D." or "Dauph," cofounded Watauga Academy with his brother Blan in 1899. Dauph graduated Wake Forest University with honors and taught mathematics and natural science at Holly Springs College in Butler, Tennessee. "Professor Dauph," as many called him, served as business manager and treasurer at Appalachian until his death in 1929. He married Lillie Shull of Butler, Tennessee, and they had five children together.

Lillie Shull Dougherty, Dauph's wife, is shown here at age 17. Born on January 16, 1875, to David and Martha Lewis Shull of Butler, Tennessee, Lillie was instrumental in establishing and managing Appalachian, serving as a music teacher and then as business manager and treasurer after her husband's death. She also founded the music department and a women's faculty group. Lillie Dougherty retired in 1938.

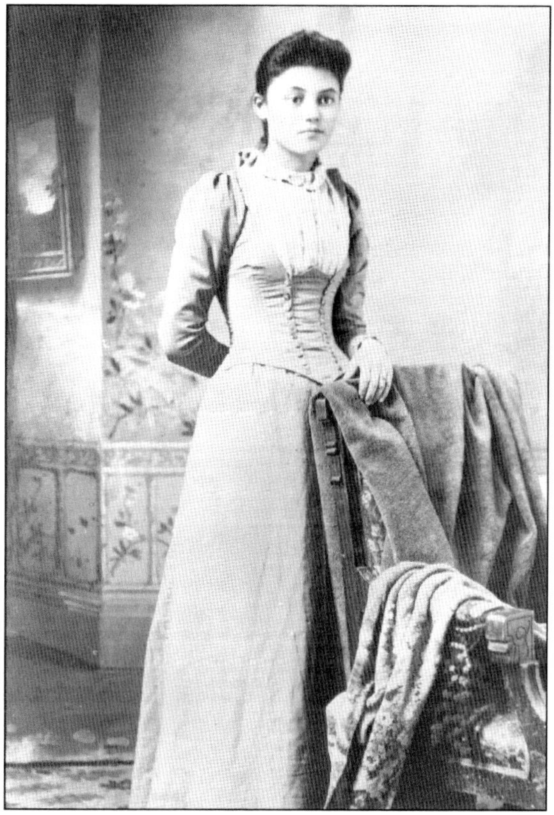

In this family photograph, Dauph and Lillie pose with their two oldest children, Clara Bartlett Dougherty (left), born in 1898, and Annie Lewis Dougherty (right), born in 1903. Dauphin Disco Dougherty and Lillie Shull were married on June 9, 1896. Professor Dauph initially taught math and science at Appalachian. Then, as business manager and treasurer, he did most of the purchasing and bookkeeping for the school and also managed the two school farms.

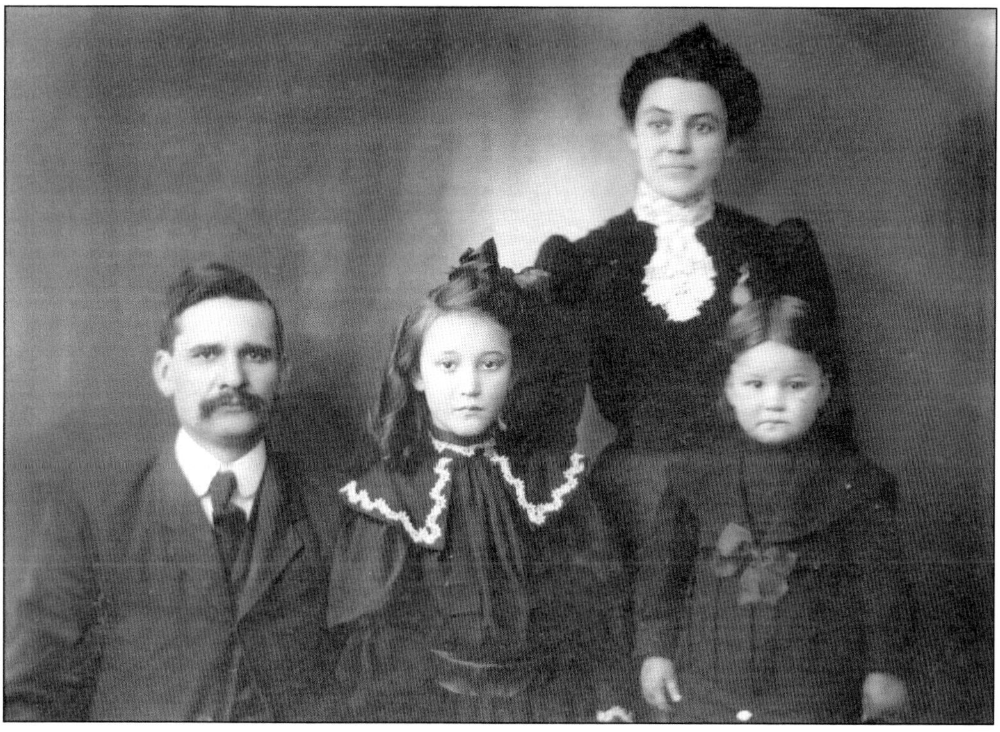

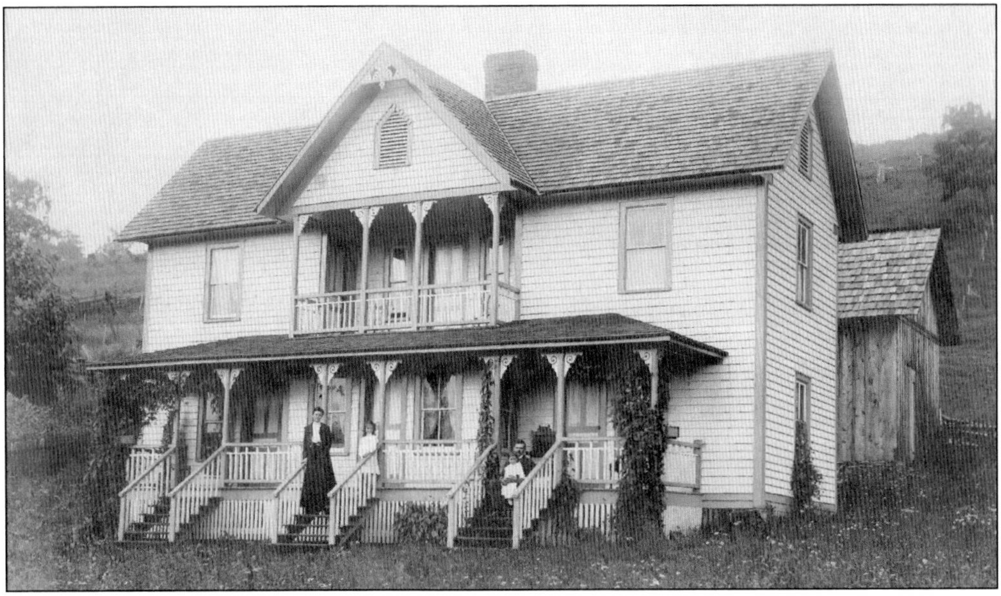

The Dougherty House, built in 1903, served as the home of Dauph Dougherty and his family, including his brother Blan. Many students also stayed with the Doughertys while attending Appalachian. The image above, from 1905, shows Lillie Dougherty and her oldest daughter Clara standing in front of the main entrance, with Dauph and daughter Annie on the right. The Dougherty House was located at the southern end (below) of what is now the Appalachian State campus, on Rivers Street across from Varsity Gymnasium, and it was a part of the campus until it was acquired by the Appalachian Heritage Museum in 1989. It now stands on Route 321 between Boone and Blowing Rock and is open to the public.

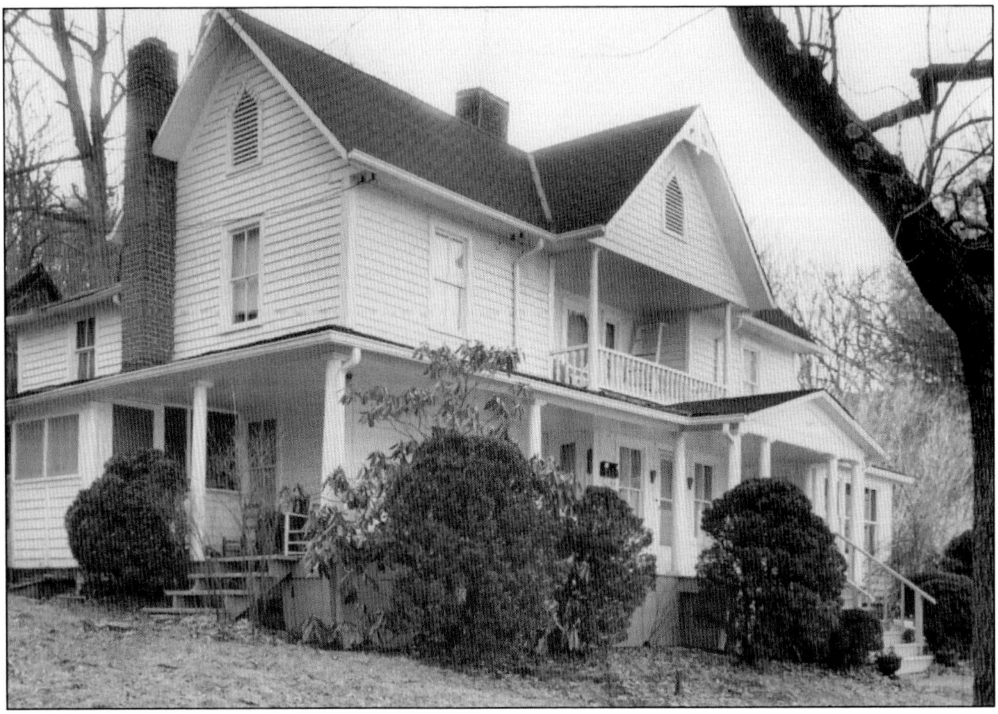

The image at right shows the southern (front) entrance to Watauga Academy, built in 1899. Below is the side view from the northwest. The academy was located on Appalachian Street, just south of I.G. Greer Hall. The only classroom and administrative building on campus, the structure was constructed using $1,000 from local donations. It included recitation rooms, a small library, a printing office, and a teachers' room, and it was later used as a Works Progress Administration school building before being renovated as a music hall in the late 1930s. It was destroyed, along with the science building, in a fire on November 22, 1946.

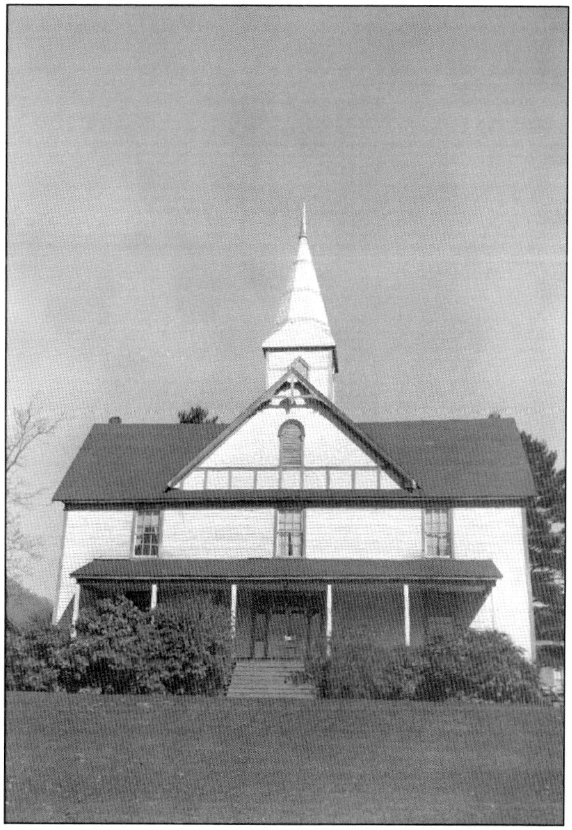

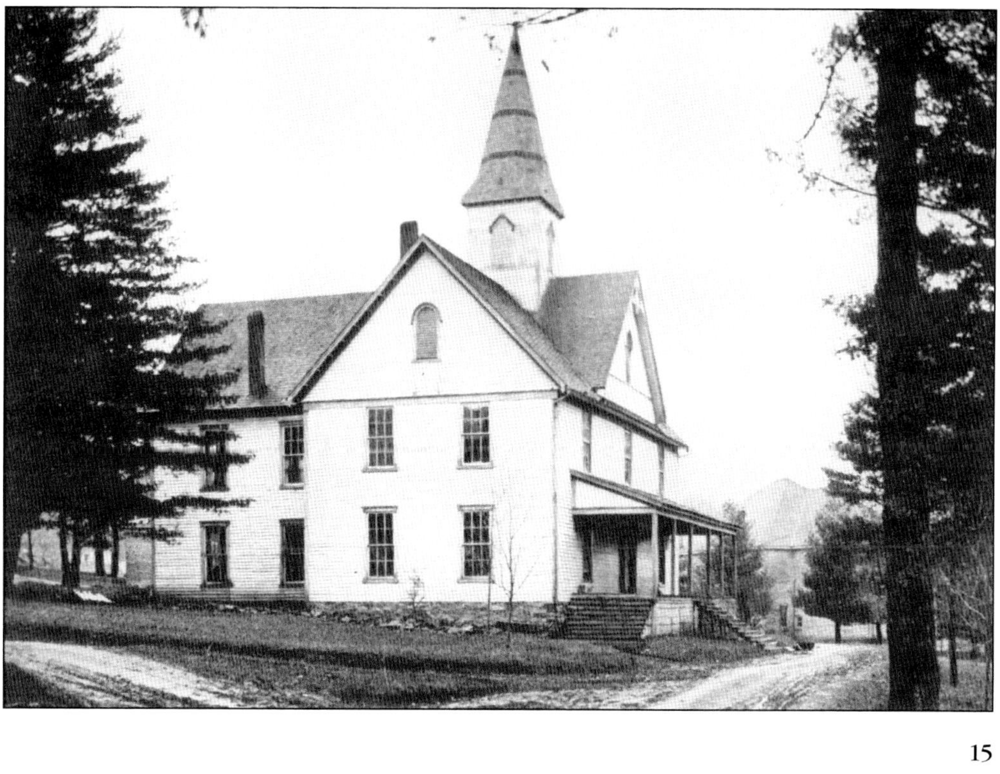

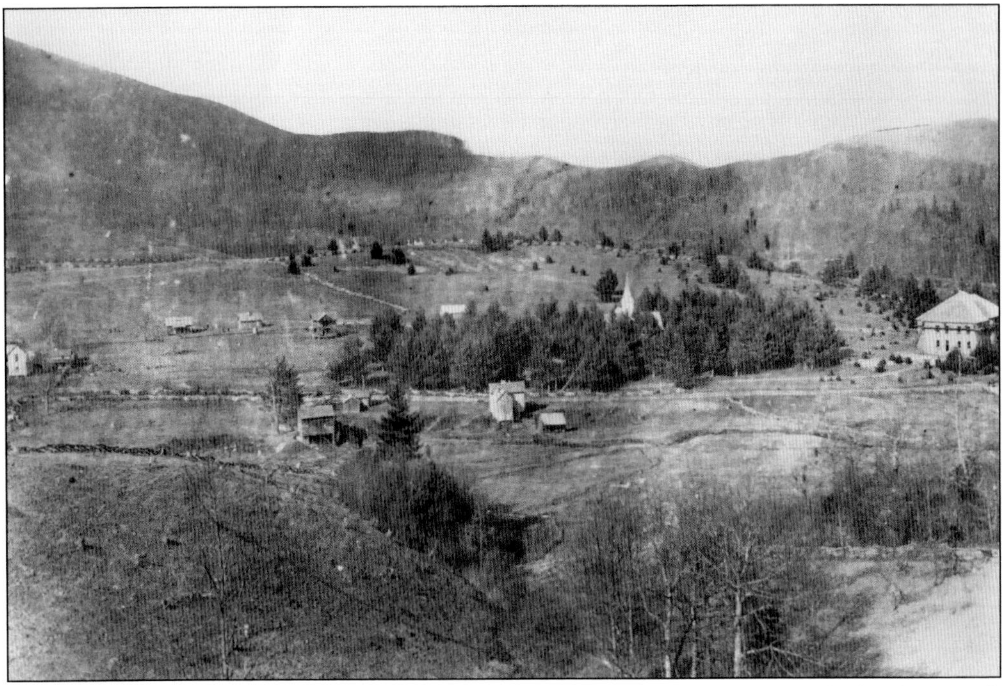

This is a 1903 photograph of campus. At the far left is the Cottrell House, which, along with the Stanbury House (center left, in the foreground), was where many students of the academy boarded. A portion of the administration building appears at the far right, and the steeple of Watauga Academy is visible in the wooded area.

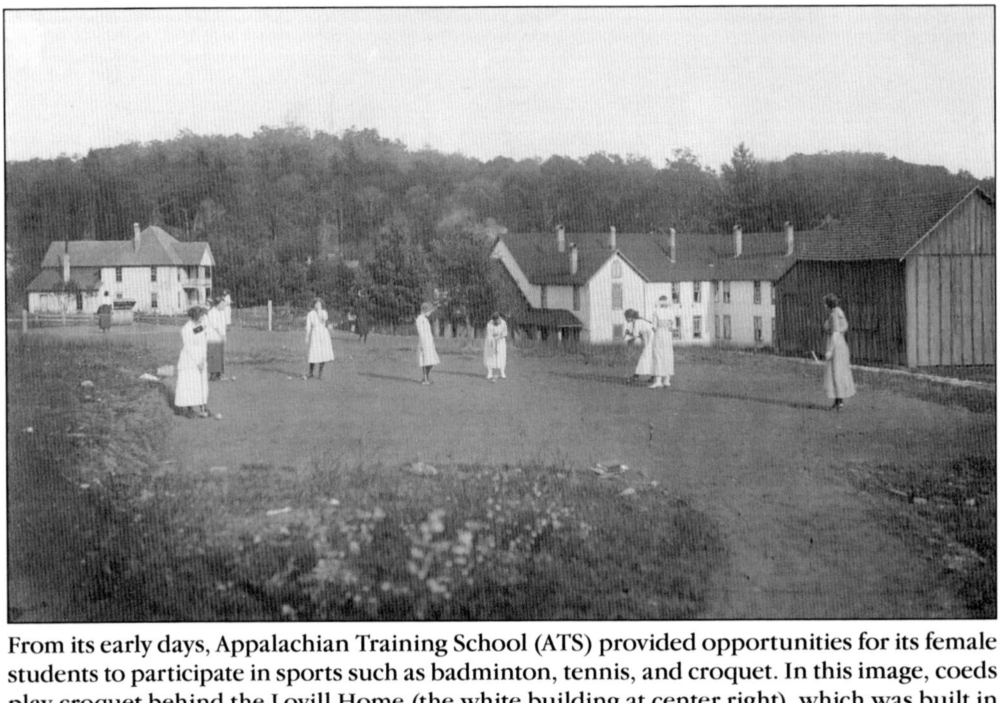

From its early days, Appalachian Training School (ATS) provided opportunities for its female students to participate in sports such as badminton, tennis, and croquet. In this image, coeds play croquet behind the Lovill Home (the white building at center right), which was built in 1906 and served as a women's dormitory.

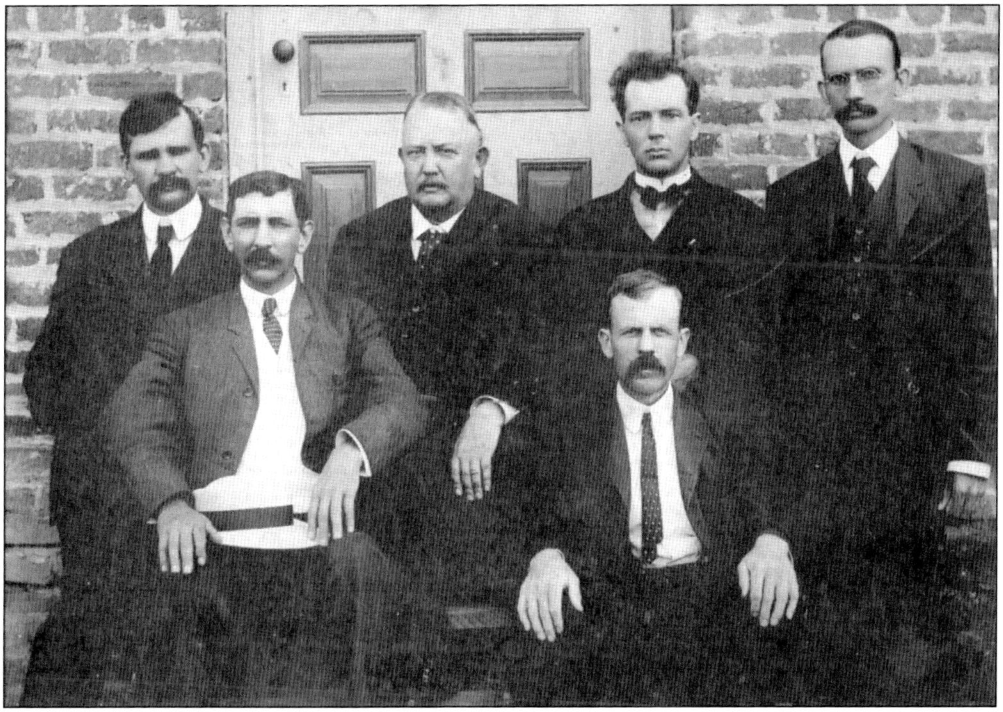

The 1906 Appalachian Training School faculty poses in front of the administration building. From left to right are (first row) Augustus Masters and W.J. White; (second row) Dauphin Disco Dougherty, coprincipal, teacher, and business manager; D.W. Read; Charles M. Dickson; and Blanford Barnard Dougherty, coprincipal, teacher, and county superintendent.

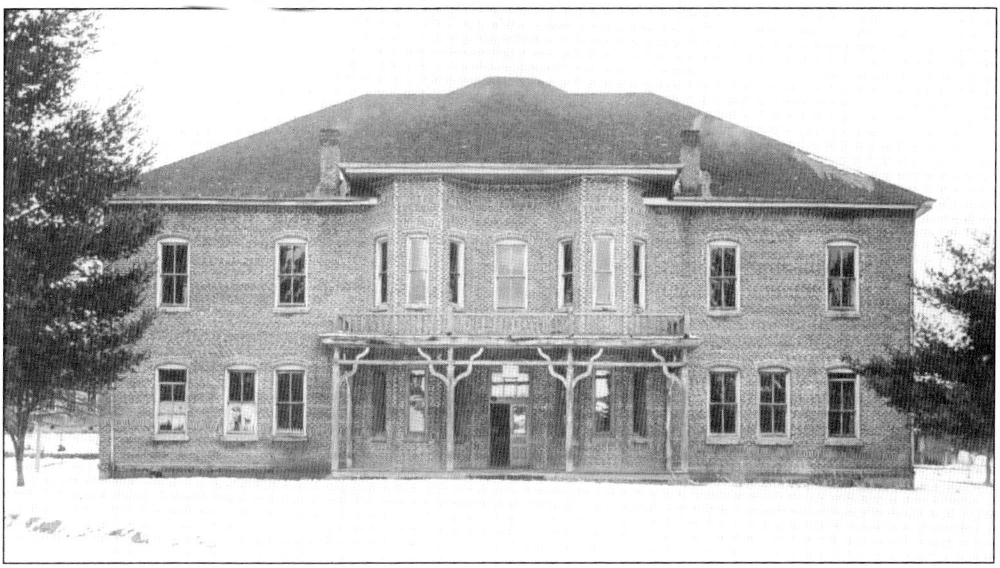

The first administration building, seen here, was erected in 1905 and sat in the location of the current administration building. It housed the administrative offices as well as classrooms and an auditorium. After the second administration building was completed in 1924, this structure was used for classroom space and then renovated in 1939 for the home economics department. It was finally razed in 1967.

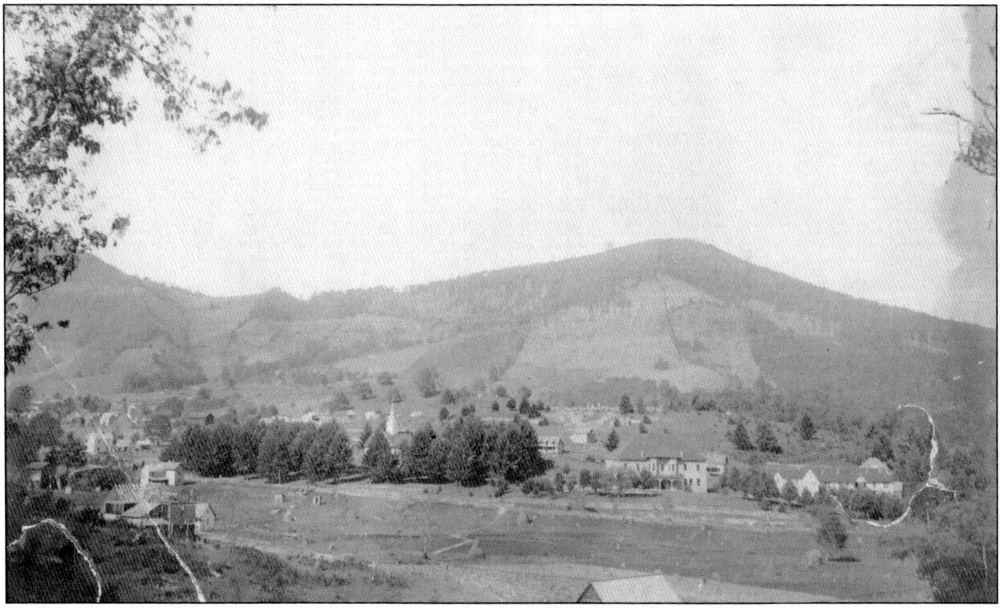

This photograph from around 1907 shows the first Lovill Home, a women's dormitory erected in 1906, to the right of the first administration building, constructed a year earlier. The steeple of the Watauga Academy building can be seen beyond the stand of trees at center left. In 1907, the campus sat on seven acres of land donated by the Dougherty brothers' father, Daniel Baker Dougherty, and J.F. Hardin.

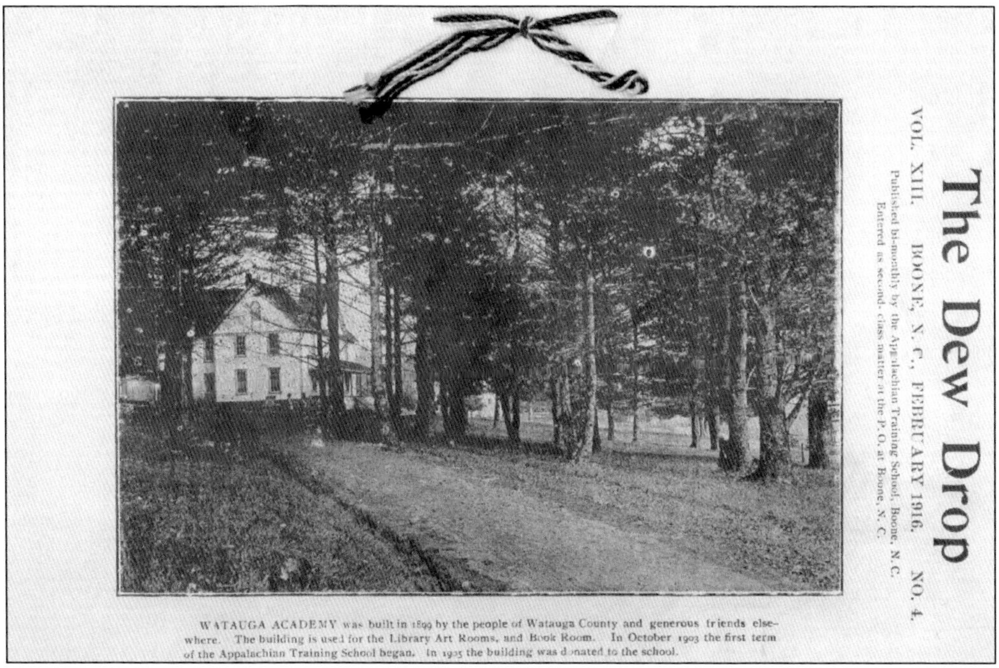

The *Dew Drop* was the college bulletin and newsletter from 1903 to 1929. It included course descriptions, building and grounds descriptions, announcements, lists of enrolled students, and sometimes photographs. After 1929, when the school became a four-year teachers college, the name *Dew Drop* was no longer used for the catalog.

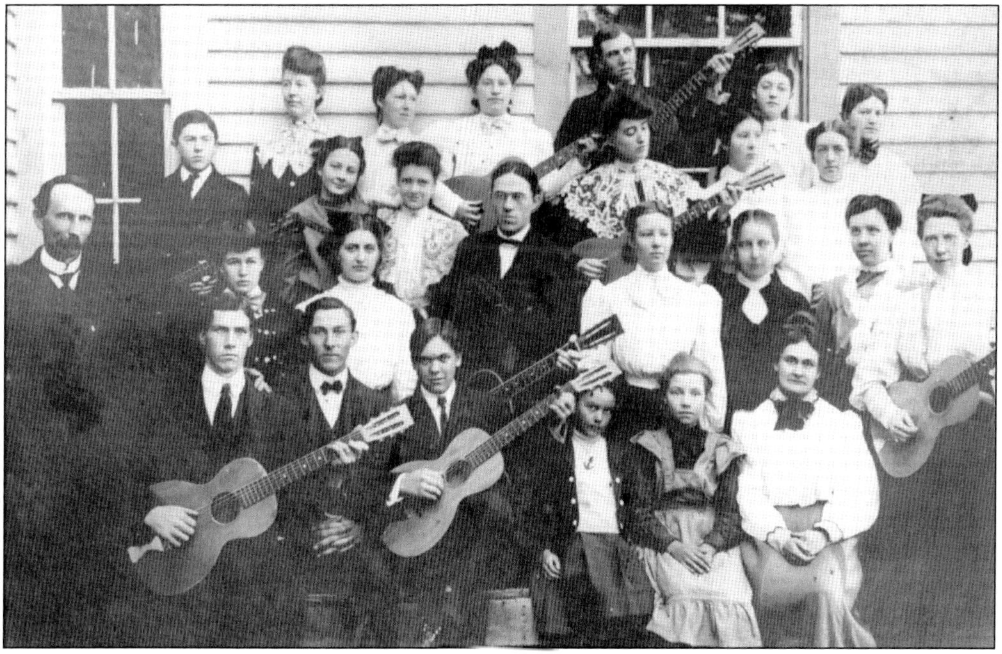

Appalachian Training School (ATS) students proudly display their musical instruments in this photograph from around 1910. The school's high school department offered courses in art, languages, and instrumental music. Lillie Shull Dougherty was the first music teacher. In addition to general music, she taught piano, guitar, and voice.

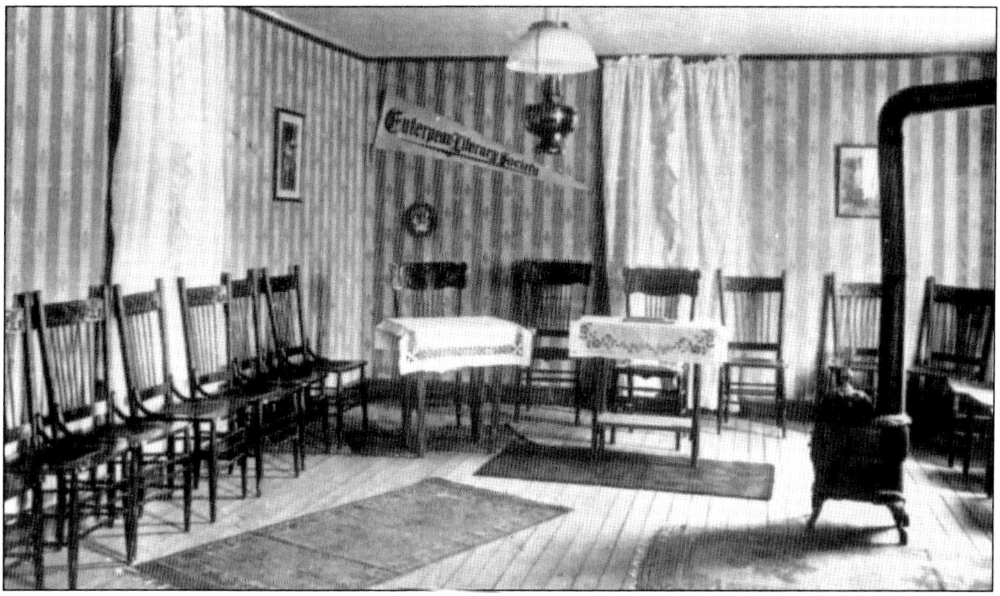

Literary societies have long been popular on college campuses, providing academic and social outlets for students. In 1910, Appalachian boasted four such organizations, two for men and two for women. That year's catalog, the *Dew Drop*, reported, "These societies aid very much in training their members in debate, declamation, and composition work." This photograph shows the recitation room of the Euterpean, a literary society for young women that met in Lovill Home, the women's dormitory.

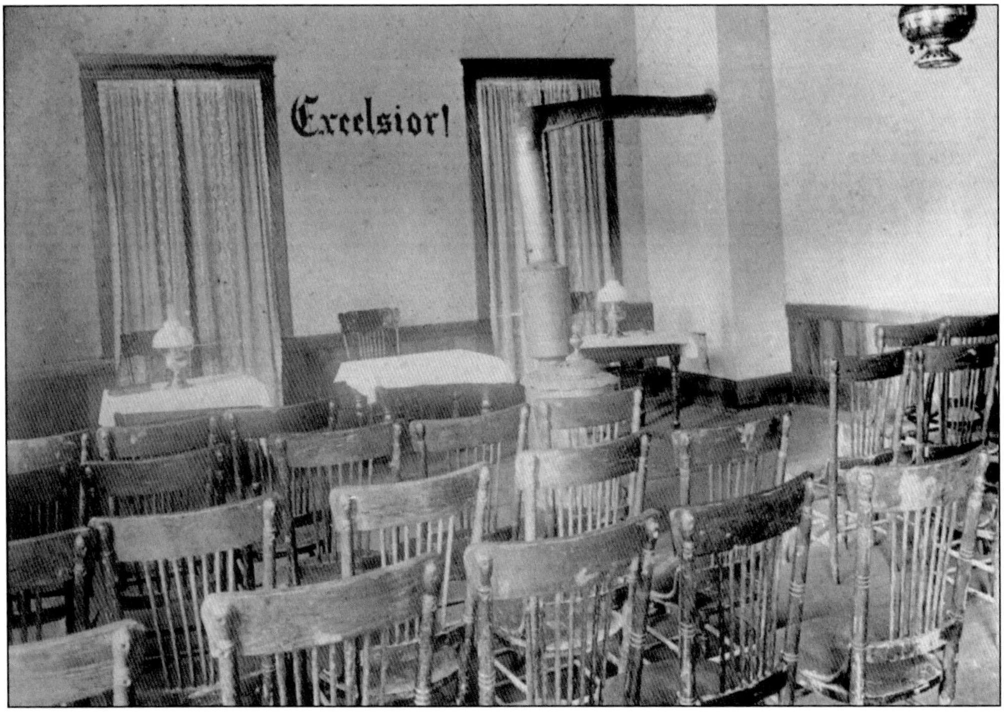

Recitations were not exclusive to the literary societies at Appalachian Training School; in fact, students were required to attend them daily, meeting in designated recitation rooms in Watauga Academy, the first administration building, and the science hall. These rooms doubled as meeting places for student literary societies. This 1910-era photograph shows a recitation room with "Excelsior!" (Latin for "ever upward") written on the wall.

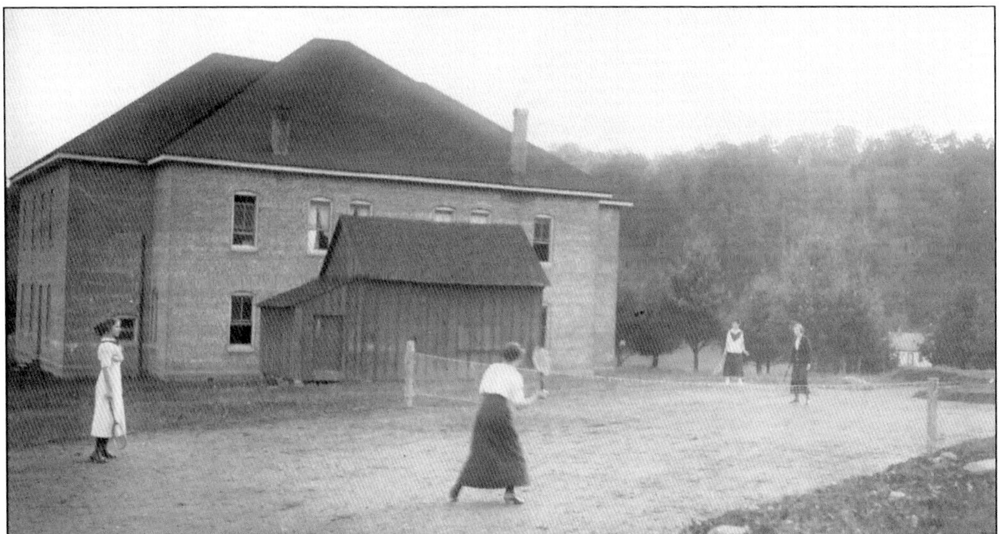

In this image from approximately 1910, women play badminton on a field behind the first administration building. Developed in the mid-1800s, badminton was quite popular for a time with both men and women. Along with tennis and croquet, it was also one of the few sports available to female students during the early years of the school.

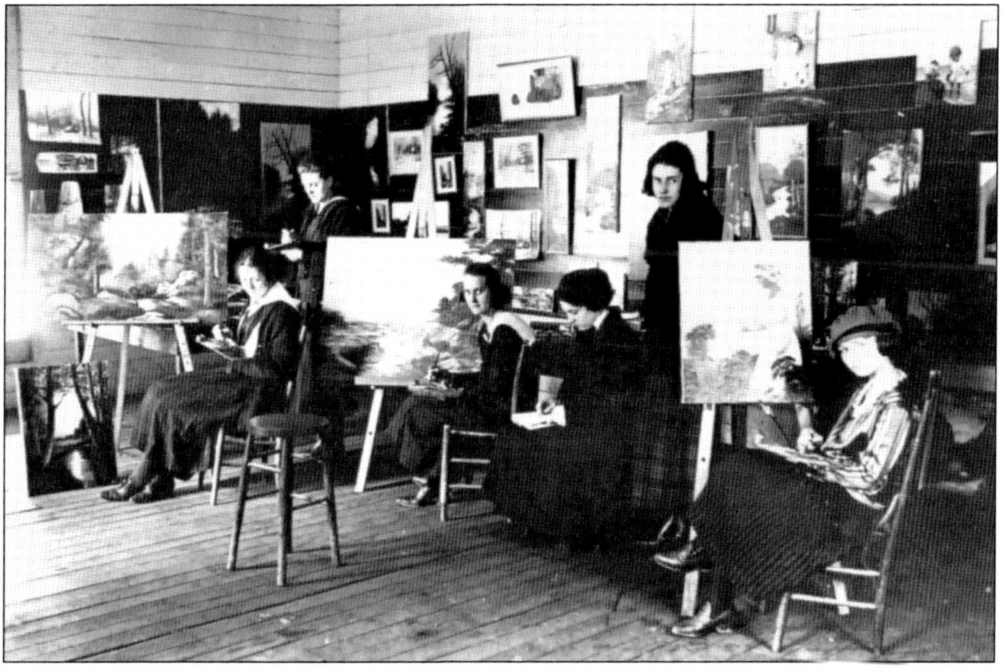

Here, coeds work on painting assignments. Art was a popular pursuit for Appalachian students. The first classes were held on the second floor of the Watauga Academy building, and by 1910, students could sign up for special courses that cost 25¢ per lesson, along with a 50¢ monthly fee for studio space. Students were given instruction in oil, pastel, crayon, and watercolors. Drawing was offered as a separate course.

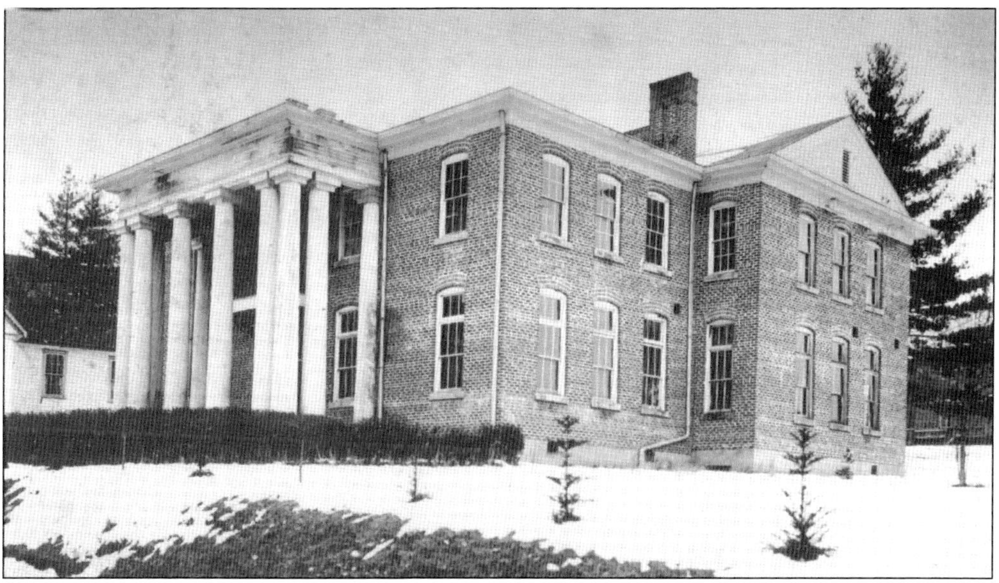

Located on the east side of Watauga Academy, the first science hall was built in 1911. It was renovated in 1939 to become the fine arts building. The first floor contained a lecture room, four recitation rooms, and a laboratory. An alumni hall and four additional recitation rooms were on the second floor. It was destroyed on November 22, 1946, by a fire that also burned the Watauga Academy building.

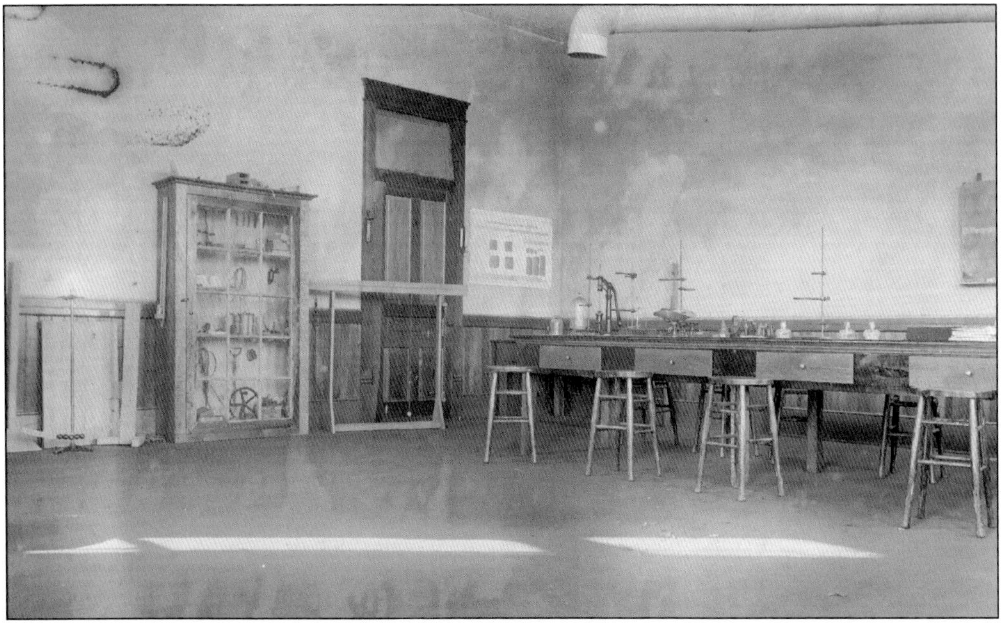

Before the science building was completed, the only laboratory was located in the first administration building. By the time construction of the new building was under way, there were courses in physiology, astronomy, zoology, physics, and botany, and the need for more space was pressing. By 1925, when Appalachian became a normal school, the science curriculum had greatly expanded, offering concentrations in biology, chemistry, and physics. These two photographs show two sides of a divided room. Above is a lab table with a model of the solar system and a telescope. A soil poster can be seen on the left wall next to the door. The photograph below shows a chemistry bench with bottles and beakers at the ready.

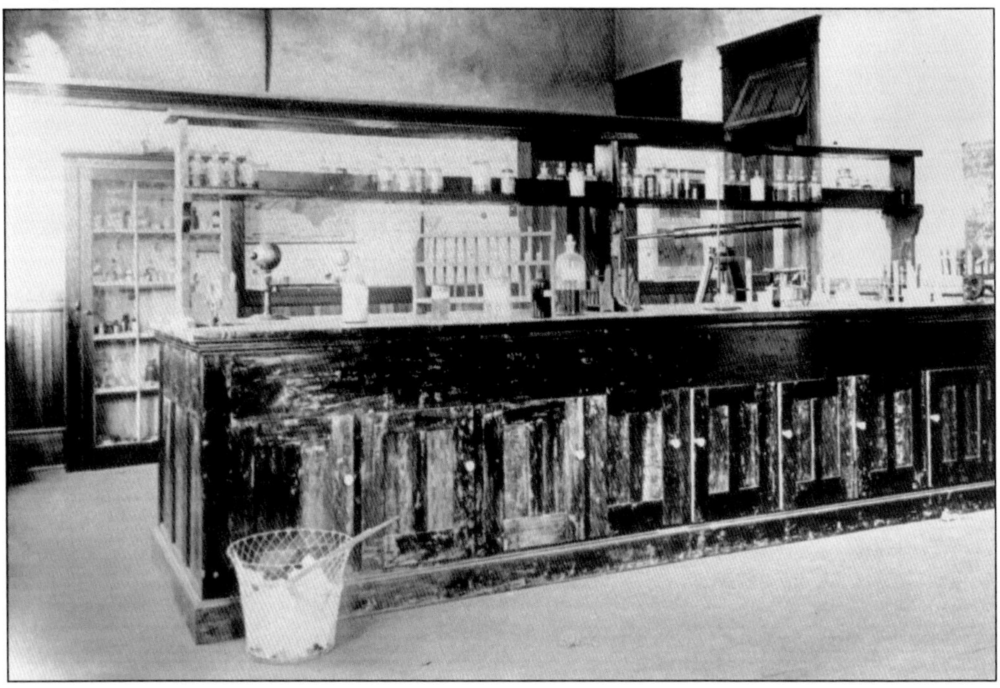

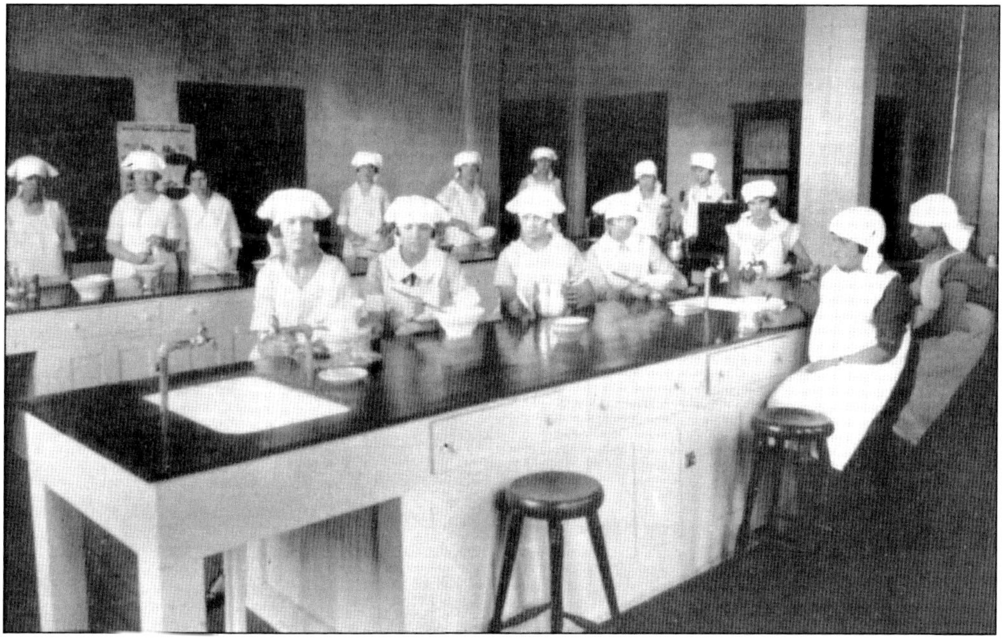

The home economics movement began in the mid-19th century, championed by women such as Harriet Beecher Stowe and Ellen Swallow Richards. By 1910, courses in the subject were offered by most colleges that admitted women. Beginning in 1912, domestic science classes were held in Watauga Academy, and in 1939, the program was moved to the first administration building. The early program included cookery, sewing, and household administration. These two images, from around 1912, show domestic science students (above) and a well-equipped domestic science kitchen (below), located in Watauga Academy. Recipes for drop biscuits and cocoa are written on the blackboard. A stove, a table, and flour tins await the start of class.

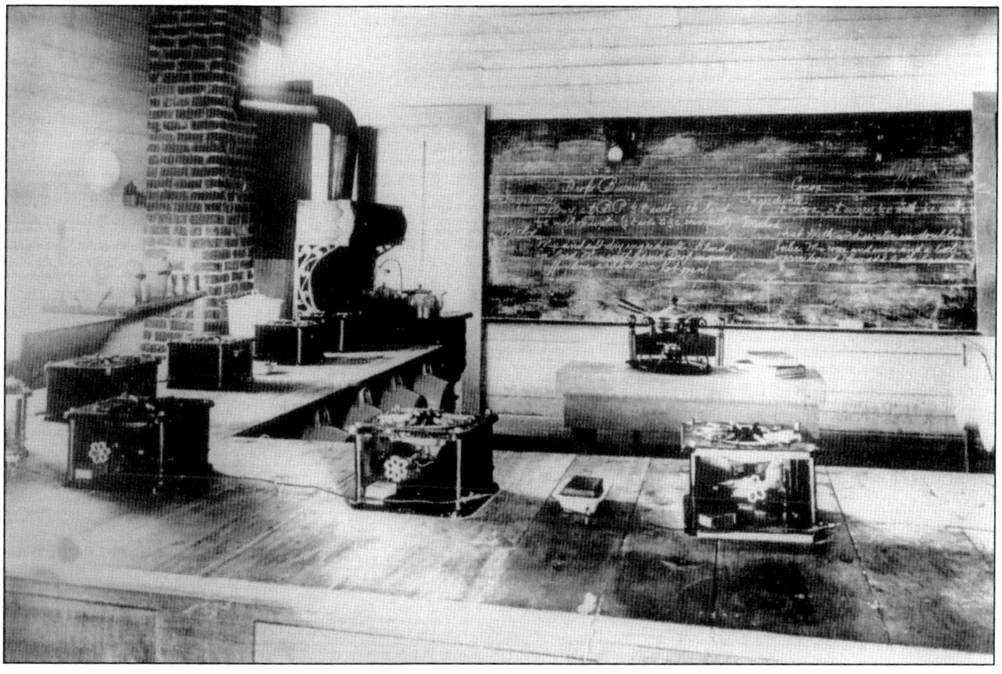

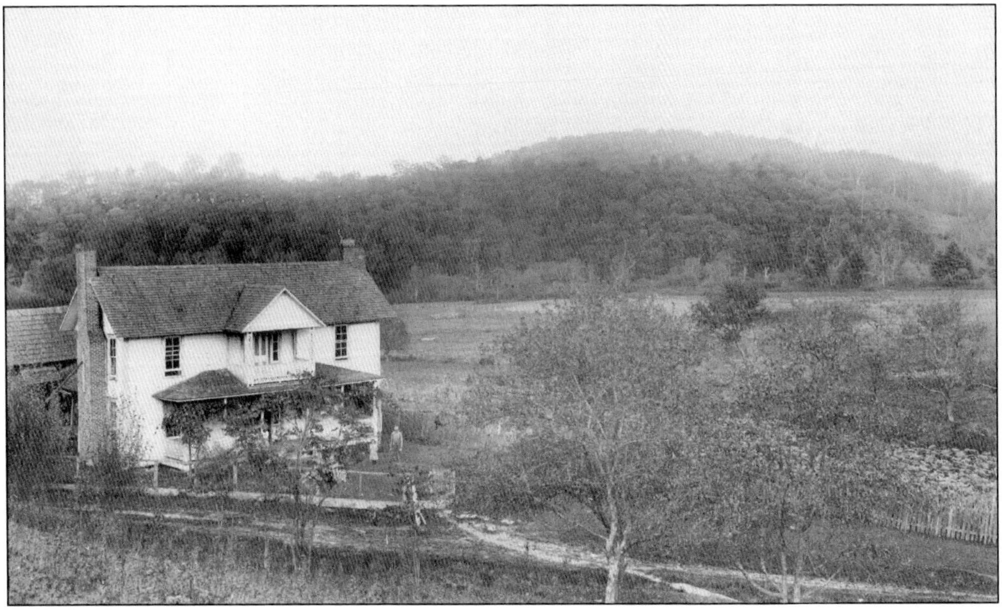

This image shows the Edmisten Farm around 1910. In 1908, Appalachian purchased the farm, located two miles east of the school along the New River, to provide food for the students. The property included 60 acres of meadowland and 140 acres of timberland. In 1915, the school opened the New River Light & Power Company on the property to provide power for the school and local residents.

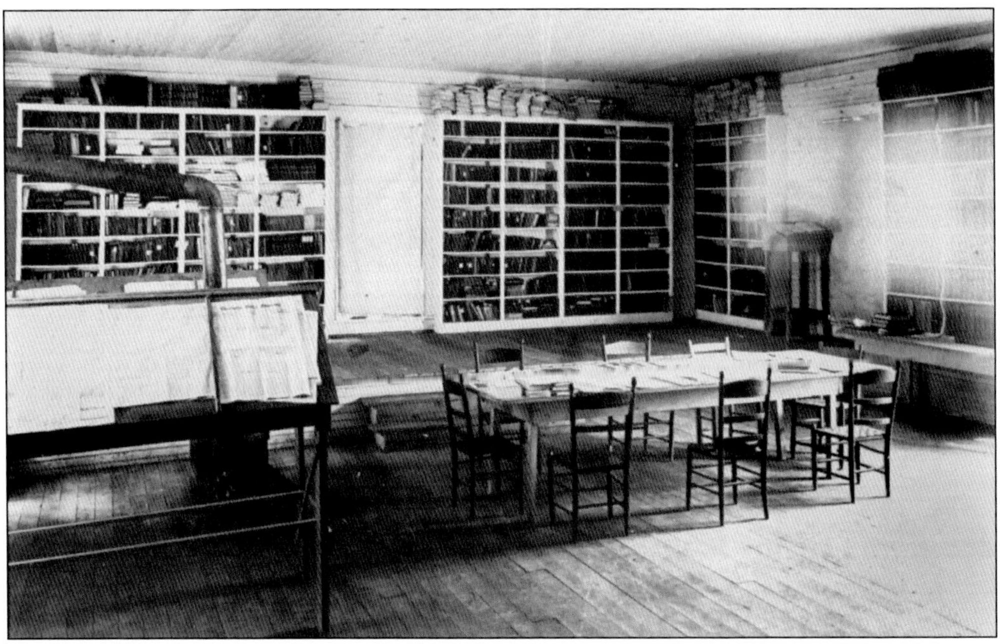

This photograph shows the first library at Appalachian, located on the second floor of Watauga Academy. Outfitted with donations from local churches, the library held roughly 3,000 books in 1907, about three years before this photograph was taken. The school also subscribed to selected newspapers and literary magazines. In 1910, the library was open for only one hour per school day and allowed restricted borrowing.

The town of Boone was named in honor of the legendary Daniel Boone. In 1912, a monument (right) was erected on the Appalachian campus to commemorate Boone's visit to the area in the mid-1760s. The monument sat on Rivers Street (formerly Faculty Street) just north of Justice Hall, where it is believed that Boone laid camp. It was dismantled in 1968 during the widening of Rivers Street; because of its age and construction, it could not be reassembled. A new monument (below) was erected 50 yards east, but it was dismantled in 1994 to make way for the new science building. A sculpture of Boone and his dogs designed by the late Sherry Edwards, a faculty member in Appalachian's art department, now sits on the spot where it is believed Boone camped. A replica of the old monument now stands in Rachel Rivers Coffey Park.

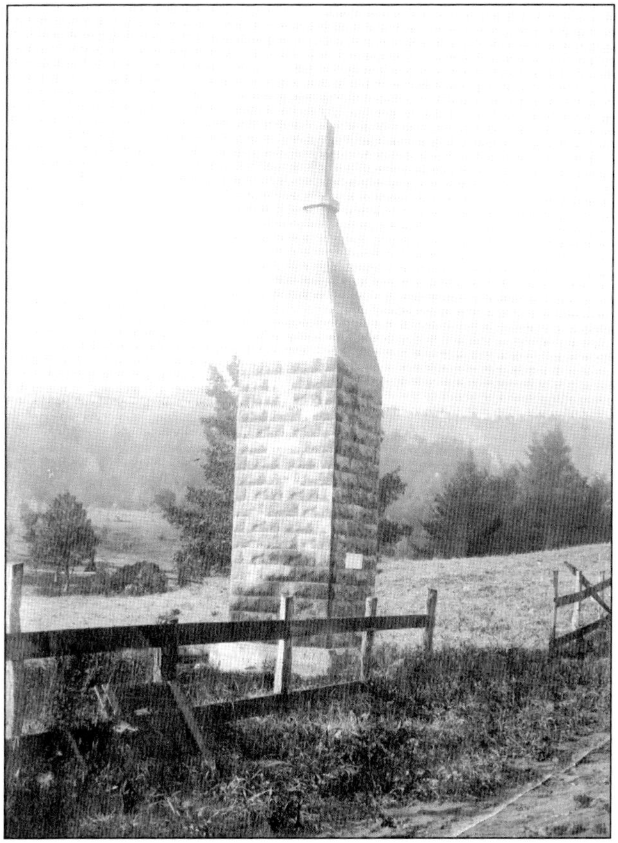

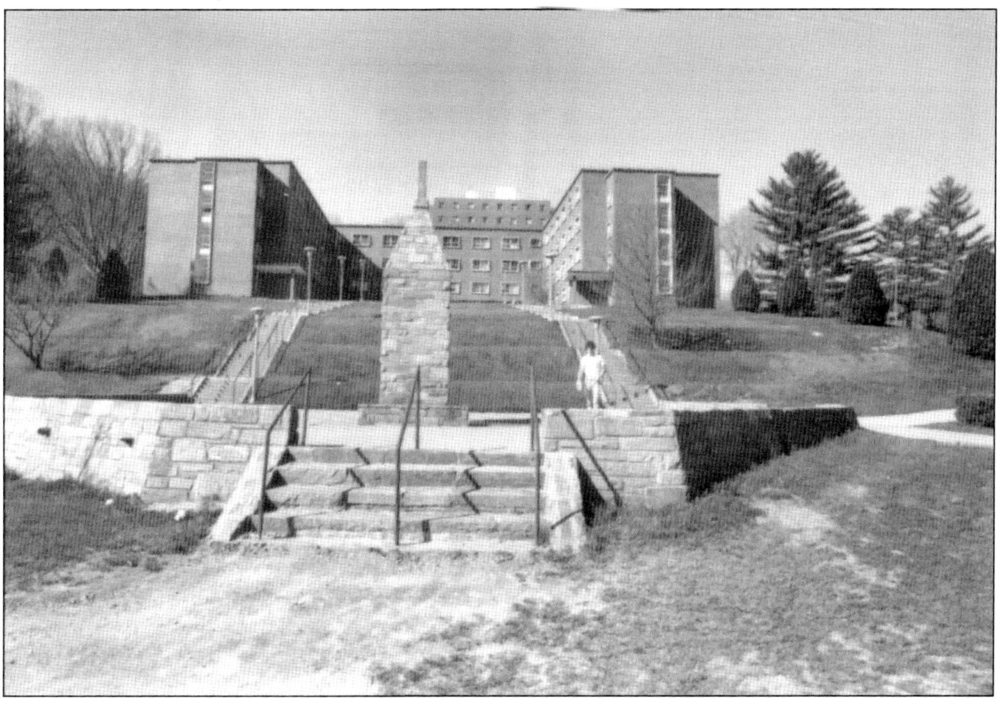

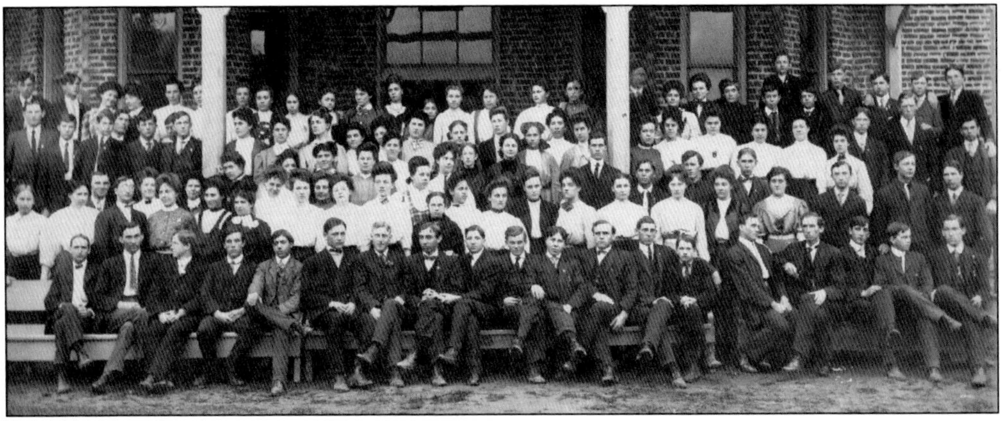

ATS students pose for this photograph around 1910 in front of the first administration building. At the time, room, board, tuition, and fees for the four-and-a-half-month fall or spring term came to $48.50 for men and $44 for women. Textbooks ranged in cost between 15¢ and 50¢. Many students received scholarships and work-study payment to help defray the expense. Summer terms were taught for eight weeks in June and July.

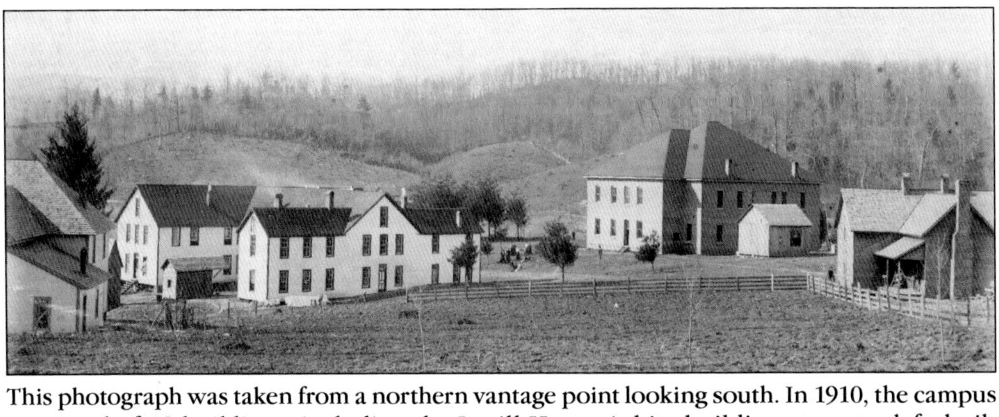

This photograph was taken from a northern vantage point looking south. In 1910, the campus consisted of 12 buildings, including the Lovill Home (white building at center left, built 1906), the administration building (brick, center right, built 1905), two faculty and student boardinghouses, four cottages (far left and far right), Watauga Academy (begun in 1899, finished in 1903), Newland Hall (1908), and the science building (finished in 1911).

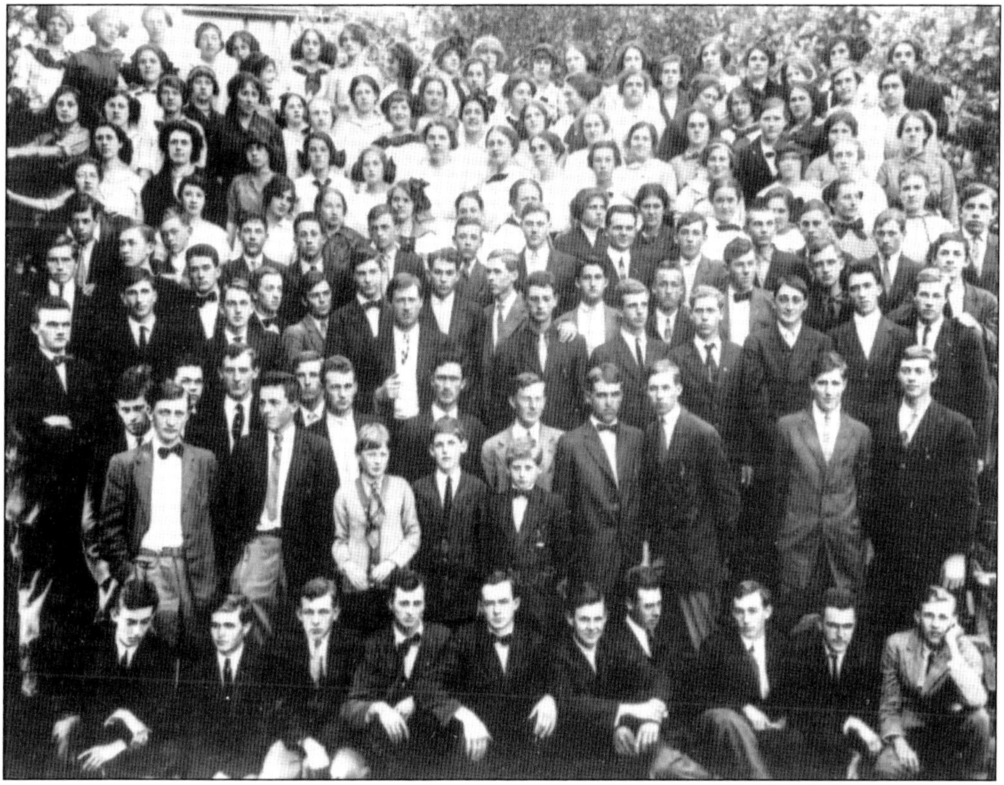

Students pose for a photograph on November 17, 1913. Appalachian still provided high school instruction, and it also gave "special attention to public school teachers and those preparing to teach." No tuition was charged in courses for teachers in training, provided that they spend two years teaching in North Carolina public schools.

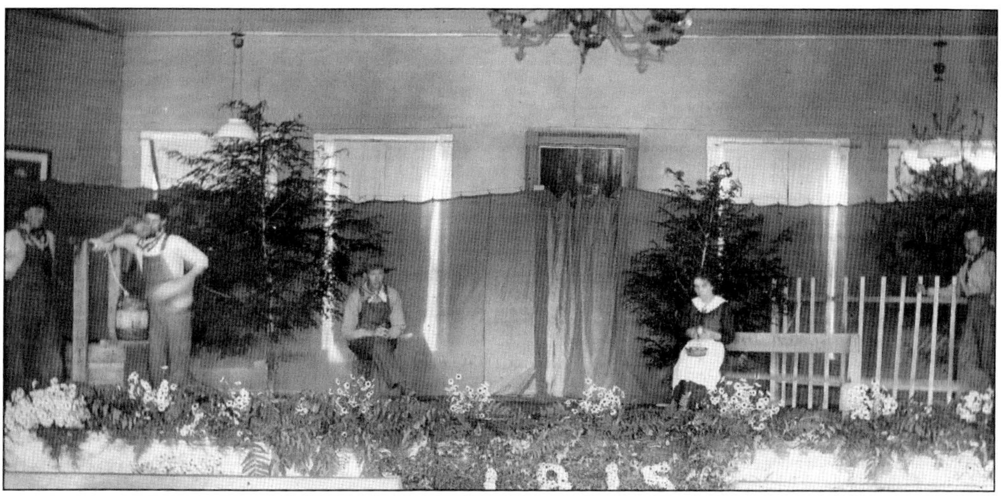

In 1929, Prof. Antonio Antonakos organized the first drama club, which later became the Playcrafters in 1933. Plays, however, were mounted years earlier, as can be seen in this photograph of student actors with "1915" spelled out in flowers on the front of the stage. By the 1950s, theater was taught first in the English department and then in the speech department. The theatre and dance department was created much later, in 1989.

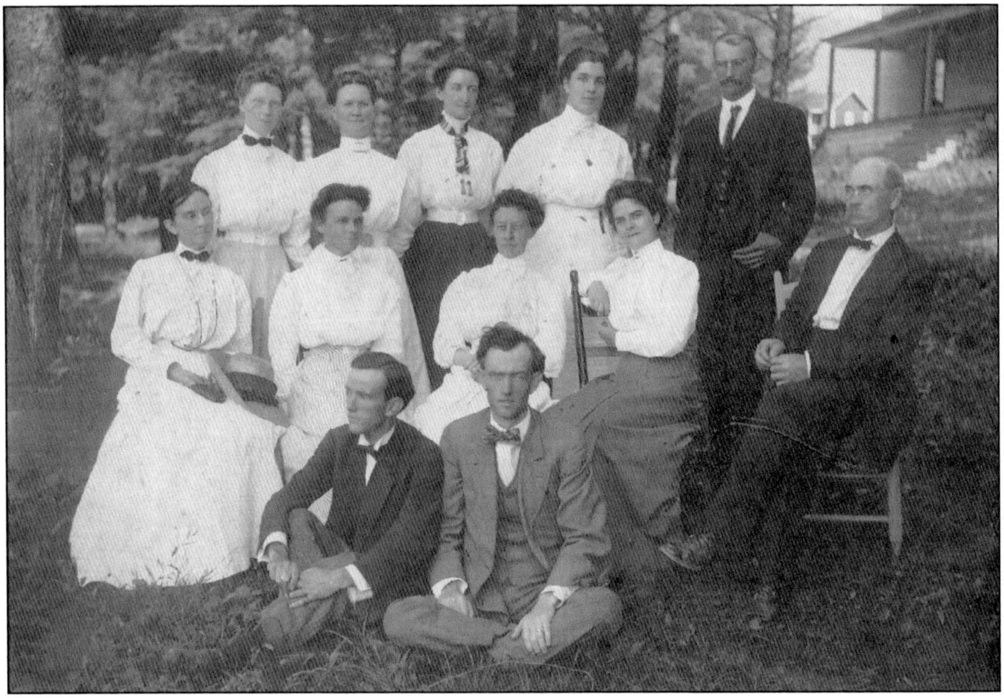

Members of the ATS faculty pose on the lawn of the Watauga Academy building in 1916. James M. Downum, the registrar and a Latin professor, is seated in the chair at right. Emma Moore, the girls' matron from 1907 to 1915 and the librarian from 1921 to 1957, is seated on the far left. Cofounder and president Blan Dougherty stands at far right.

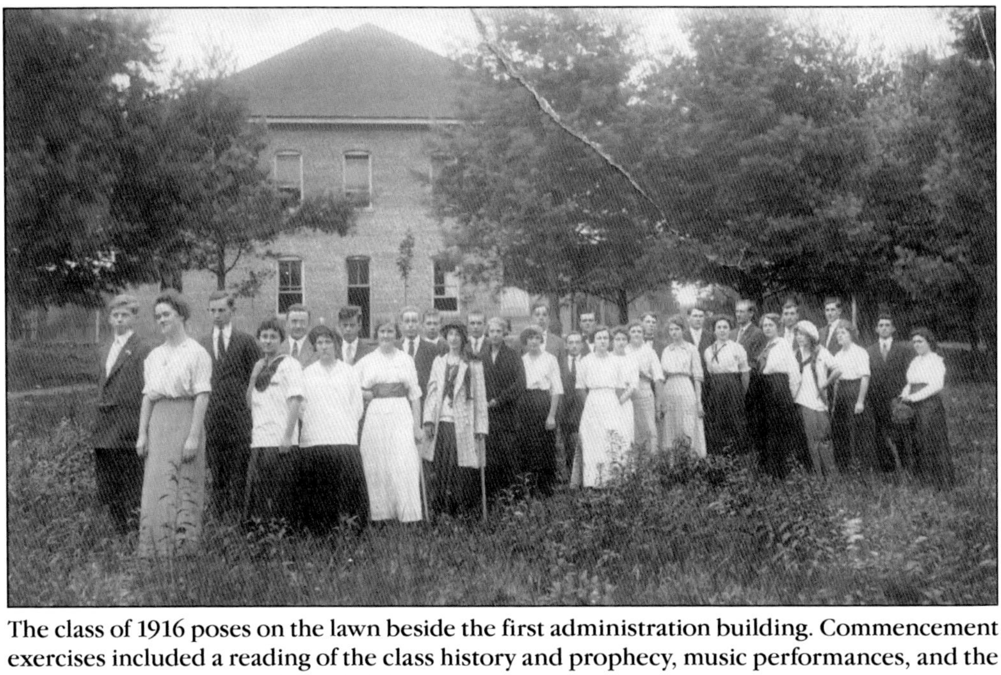

The class of 1916 poses on the lawn beside the first administration building. Commencement exercises included a reading of the class history and prophecy, music performances, and the usual speeches and awarding of diplomas. Commencement was a big event, and many of the local residents attended the ceremony alongside the students' families and friends.

Satie Hunt Broyhill was born on July 13, 1899, the same day Watauga Academy first opened its doors to students. She attended Appalachian Training School to study music, graduating in 1918. She met her husband, James Edgar Broyhill, the founder of Broyhill Furniture, at ATS, and they married in 1921. Satie Hunt Broyhill is the mother of former US senator James T. Broyhill and was a benefactor of Appalachian State University, serving on the board of trustees in the 1950s and 1960s. Her contributions funded the Broyhill Inn and Conference Center, built in 1972, and the Satie Hunt Broyhill Music Center, built in 1983. She passed away in 1998 at the age of 96. Satie Hunt is seen at right in 1918 on the ATS campus. In the photograph below, Satie Broyhill stands with former Appalachian Alumni Association president Jack Neal at homecoming in 1974.

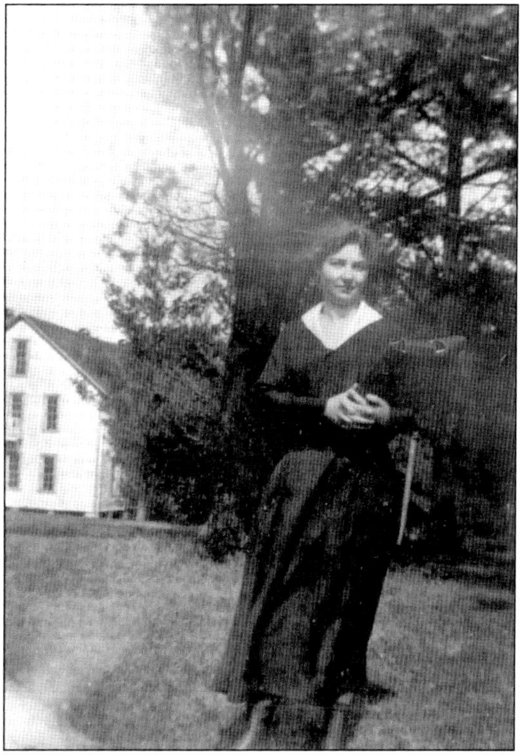

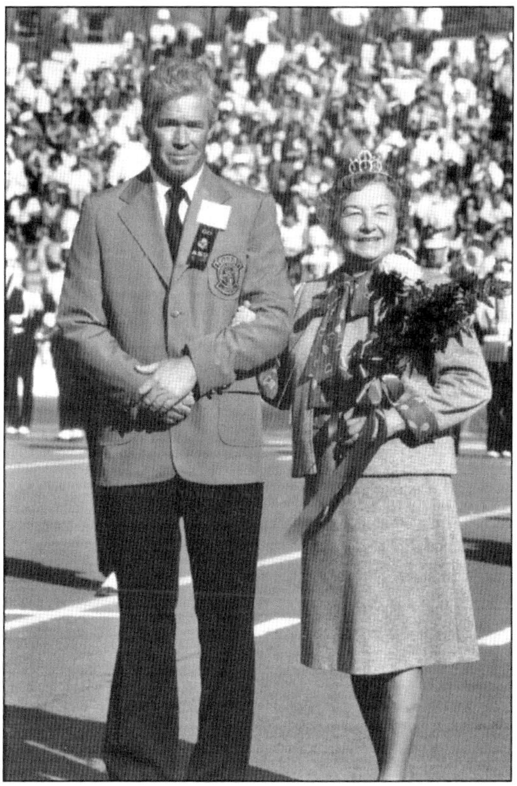

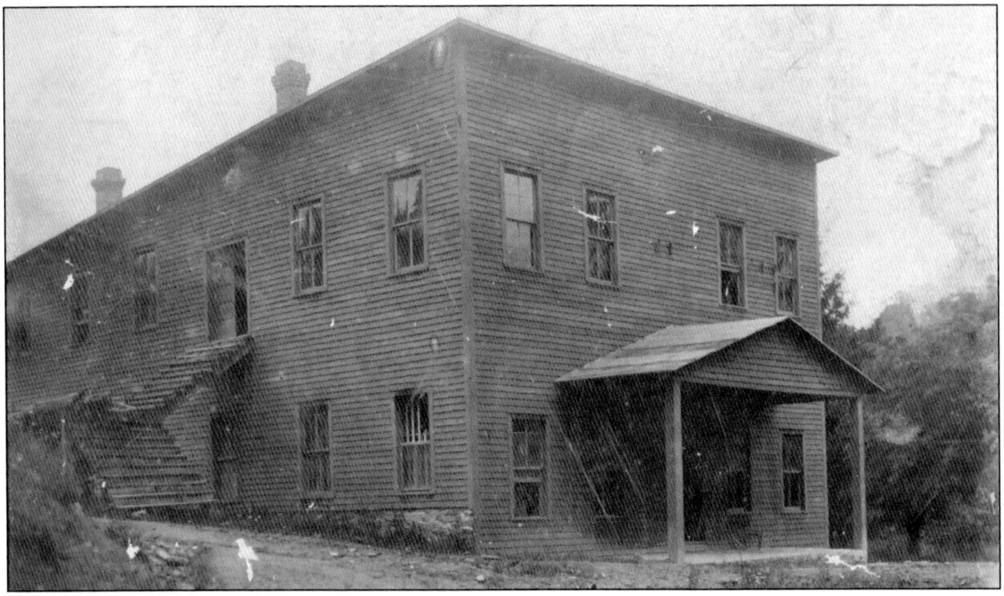

In 1917, the school erected this large wooden building to serve the newly formed manual training program, created and managed by O.L. Brown, the husband of Clara, the first child of Dauph and Lillie Dougherty. The building, located on the southern end of campus, also housed the first gymnasium. It was torn down in the late 1930s.

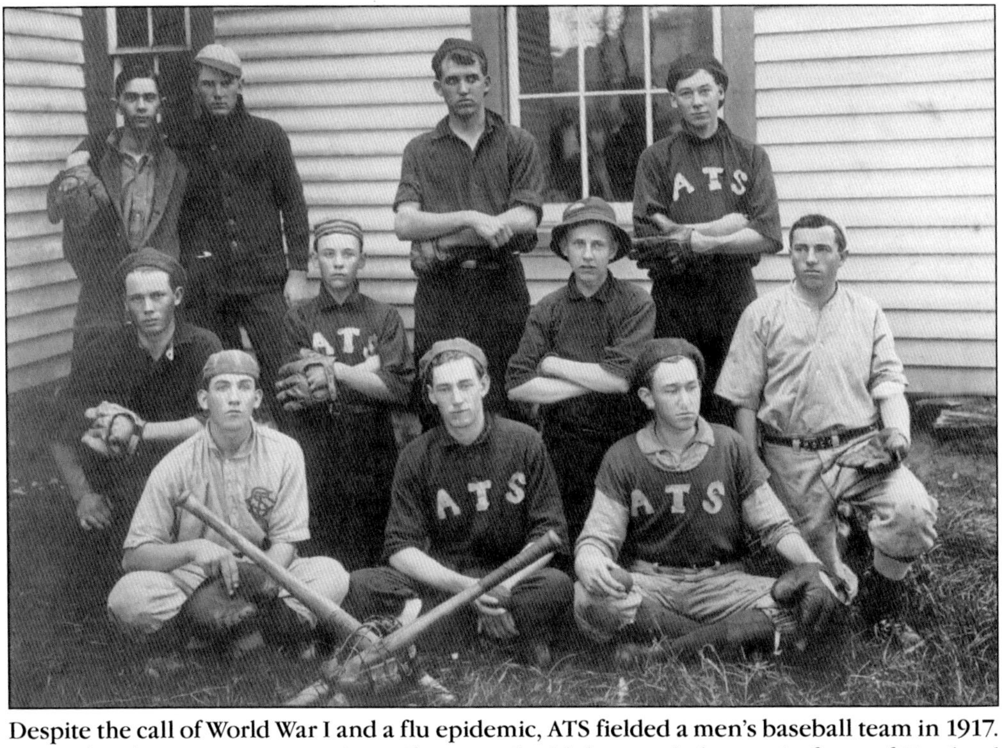

Despite the call of World War I and a flu epidemic, ATS fielded a men's baseball team in 1917. Here, the players pose—some in uniforms and with bats and gloves—in front of Newland Hall, the men's dormitory. According to the 1917 *Dew Drop*, the team could play only home games unless given permission from the faculty to travel outside of Boone.

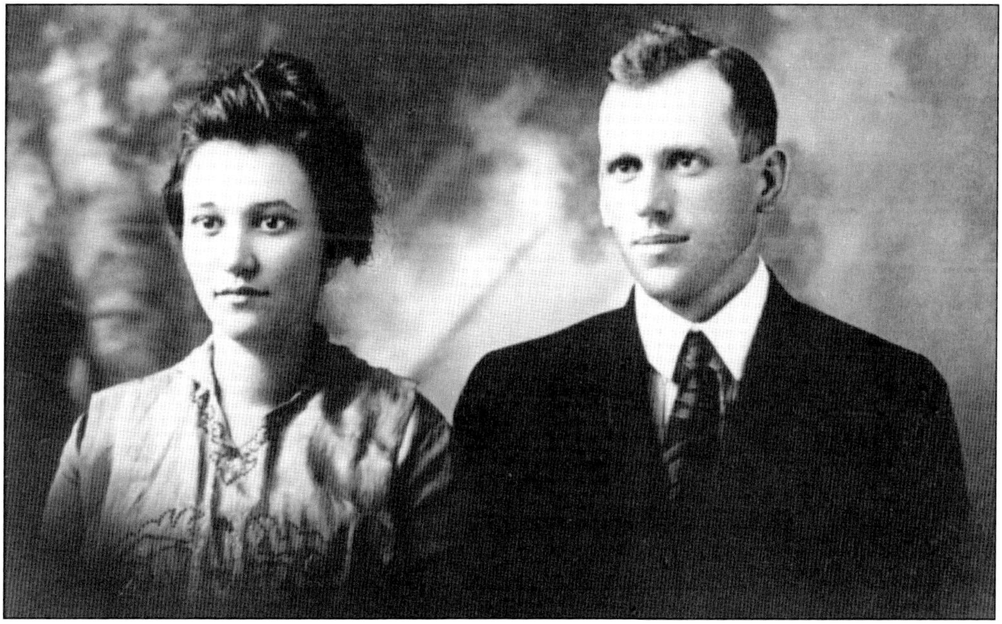

Clara Bartlett Dougherty was the daughter of cofounder Dauphin Disco Dougherty and Lillie Shull Dougherty. She attended Appalachian Training School from 1911 to 1914, meeting and marrying Oscar Lester Brown while still enrolled. Known as "O.L.," Brown was a member of the ATS faculty in the manual training program from 1919 to 1924 and helped found what later became the industrial arts department. Clara Dougherty Brown was matron of Justice Hall, where the family lived, from 1921 to 1925.

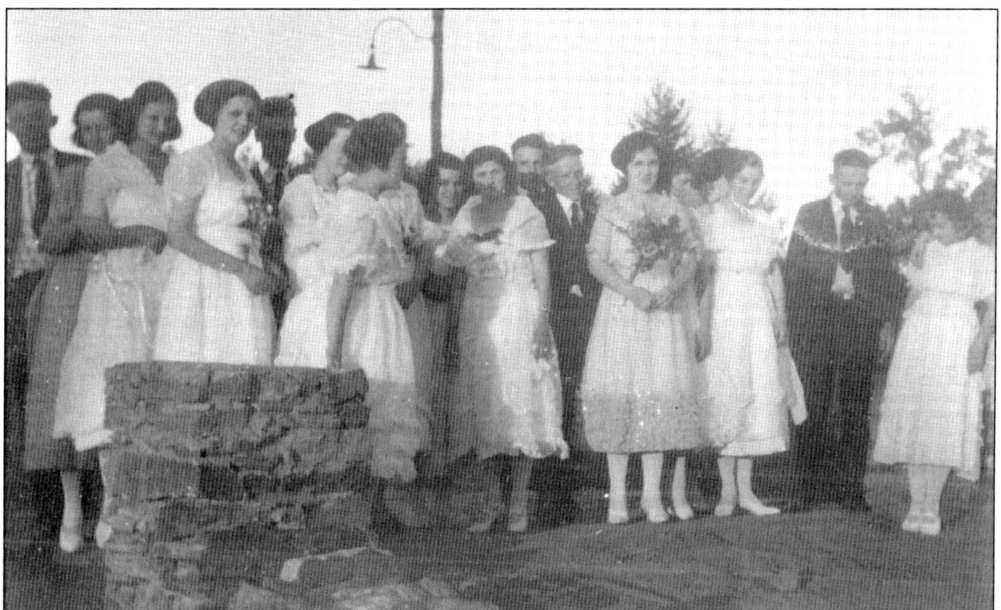

This image shows the Appalachian Training School graduating class on July 4, 1921. The class included Dauph Dougherty's daughter Anne Lewis Dougherty, who later went on to Carson-Newman College. Anne Dougherty married Roy Albert Rufty and taught home economics in multiple counties in North Carolina, including Watauga.

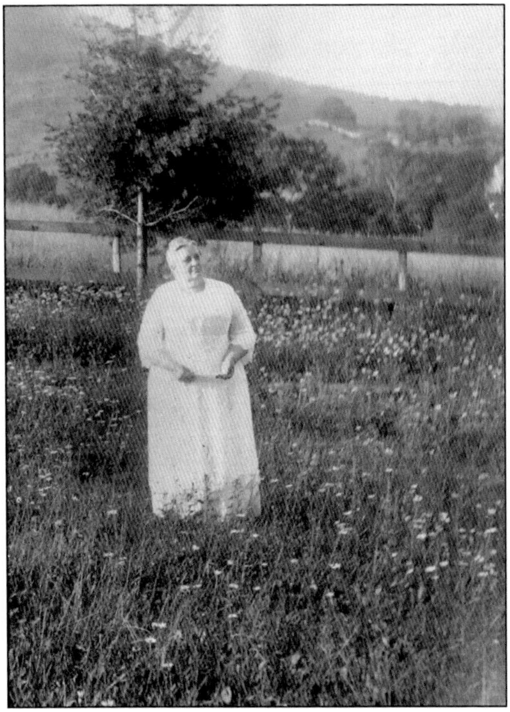

Dr. Blan Dougherty believed firmly that faculty and staff should stand *in loco parentis*. All the dormitories had matrons, who kept a watchful eye on the boarders and enforced school rules. Annie Beatty, shown standing in a meadow in front of Newland Hall, served as the matron for the men's dormitory from 1914 to 1921. Unlike women, who were required to board on campus in Lovill Home, men could choose to board in town.

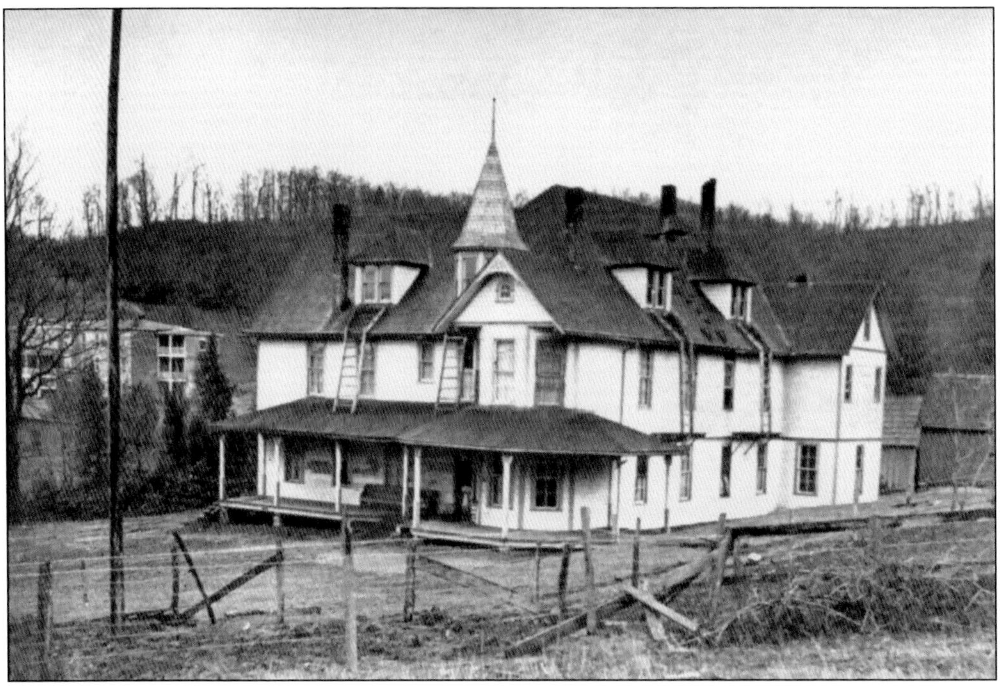

The first Newland Hall, shown in this 1920s photograph, was a two-story wooden structure and the first men's dormitory on campus. Completed in 1908 and named for W.D. Newland, it was located on the southern side of campus near where the first Justice Hall (seen in the background) was built. The old Newland Hall was demolished in the 1930s and replaced by the second Newland Hall, a more modern brick structure, in 1939.

The photograph at right shows two ATS students standing on the Linville River (Tweetsie) Railroad tracks. The narrow-gauge track ran between Boone and Johnson City, Tennessee, from 1918 to 1940. The track between Cranberry, North Carolina, and Boone was destroyed in the 1940 flood, and, because of financial difficulties, the Linville River Railway Company was unable to reconstruct the track. East Tennessee & Western North Carolina Railroad steam locomotive No. 12 is now the main attraction of the Tweetsie Railroad theme park in Blowing Rock, North Carolina. The image below shows the northern view of campus, with a Tweetsie train in the foreground. The first administration building is front and center.

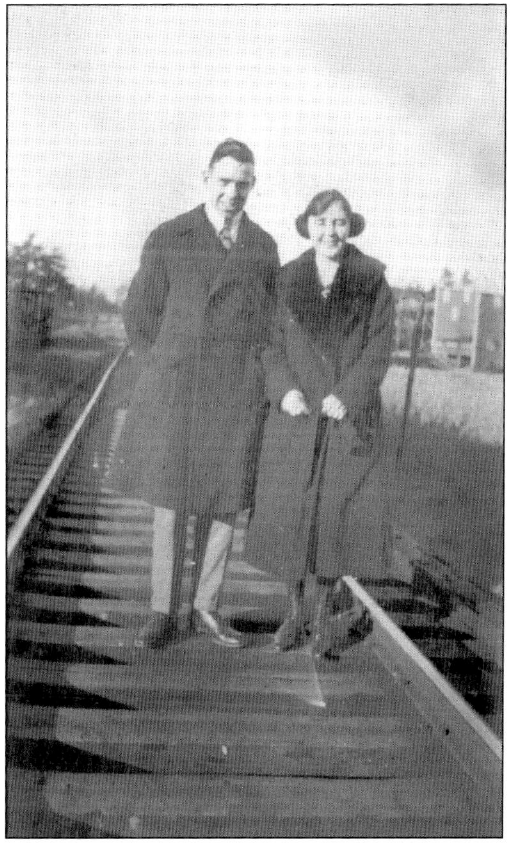

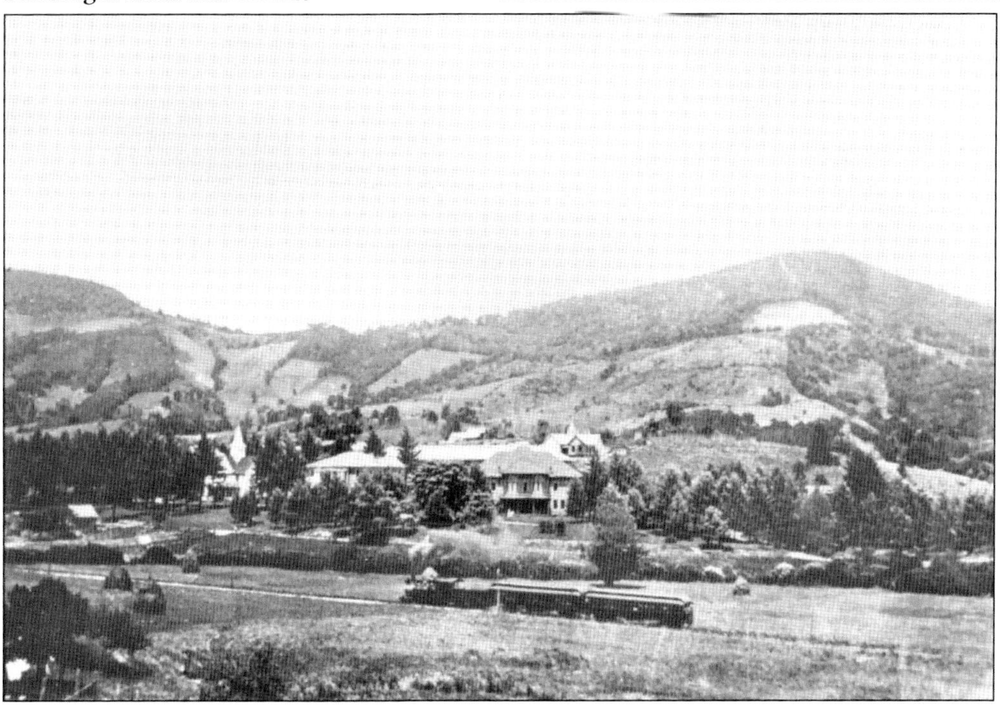

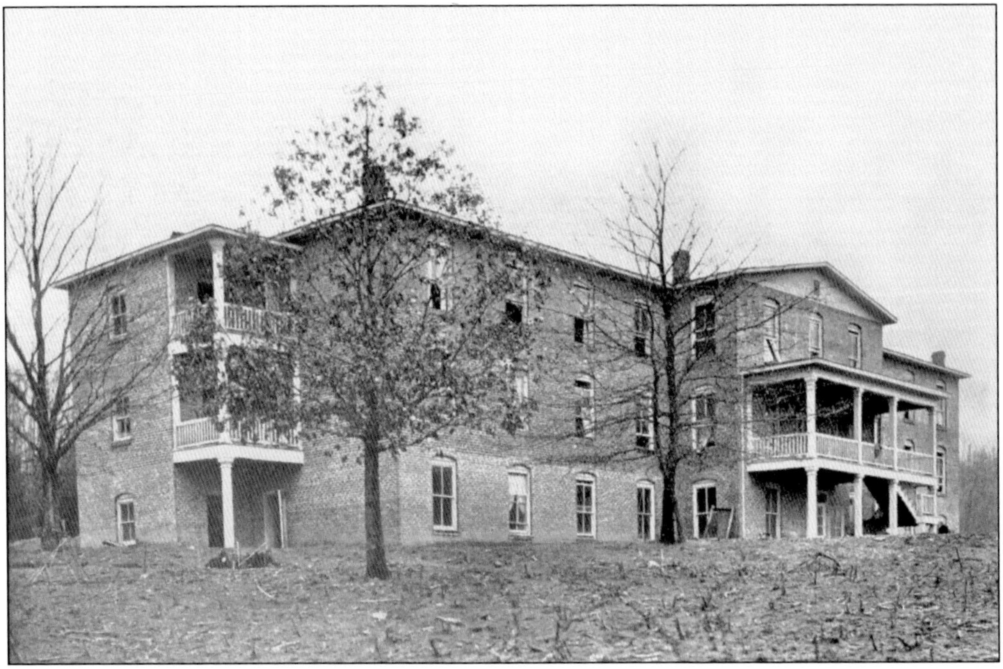

Justice Hall, built in 1920, was a men's dormitory that held up to 100 students. It was located on the southern side of campus near Newland Hall. The Justice Hall annex, constructed behind the main building, accommodated an additional 90 students. The main building was torn down in the 1950s and replaced by the second Justice Hall, completed in 1952.

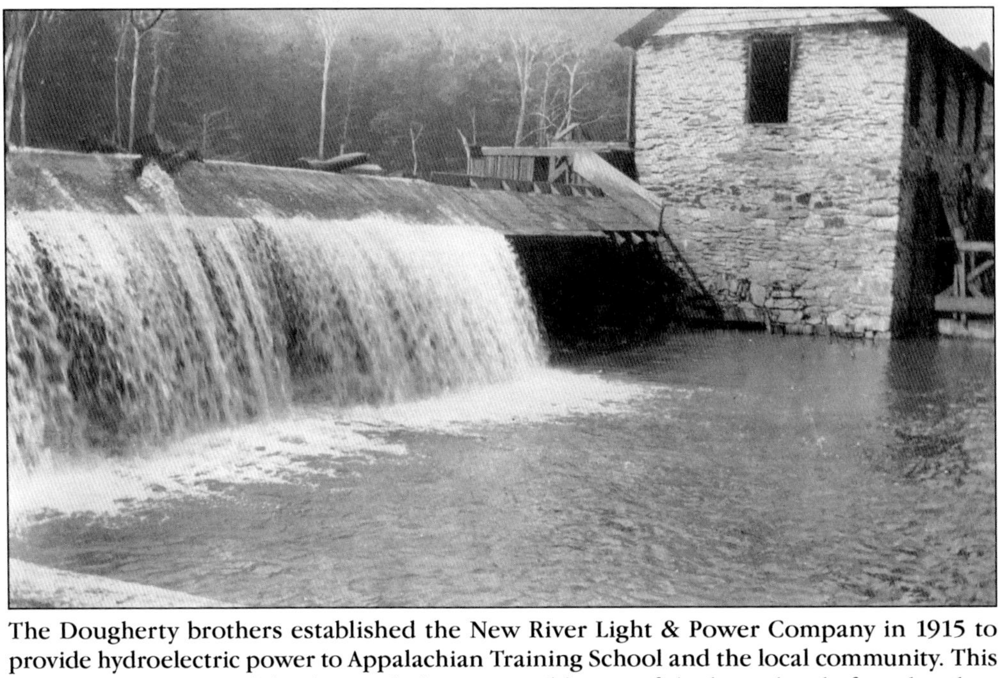

The Dougherty brothers established the New River Light & Power Company in 1915 to provide hydroelectric power to Appalachian Training School and the local community. This July 18, 1923, image of the dam and plant is possibly one of the last taken before the plant burned later that year. A new plant was built on Blowing Rock Road in 1924. New River Light & Power continues to provide power to the Boone area.

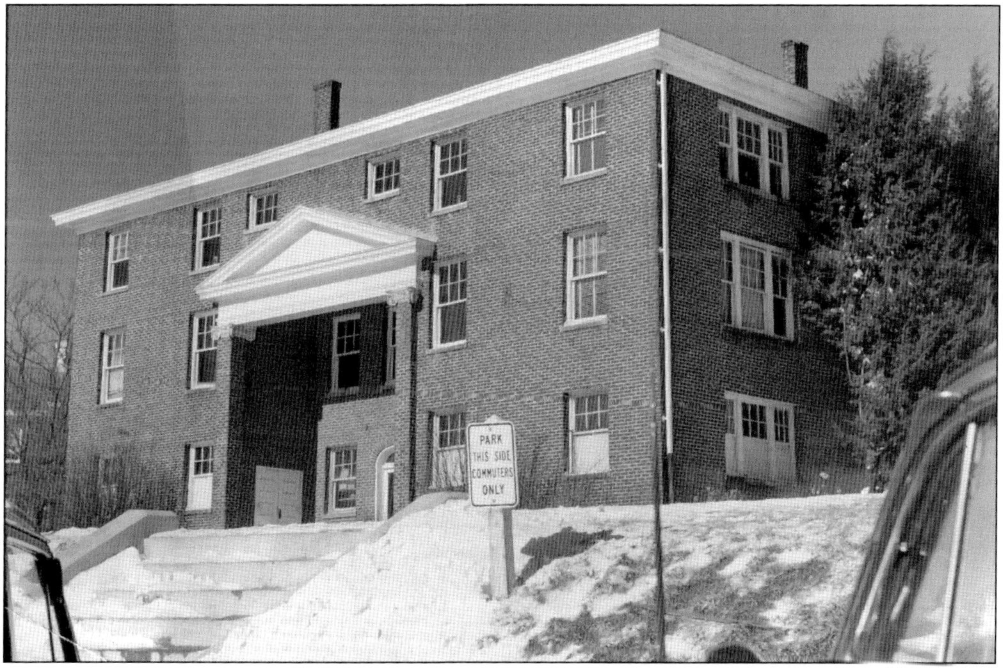

For a time, men and women had separate gymnasiums on campus. The women's gymnasium (above), built in 1924, was located across from the Dauph-Blan and Watauga residence halls on the Promenade. Originally used by both sexes, it became the women's gymnasium when a new facility for men was built in 1934. The building housed offices, classrooms, a basketball court, and a swimming pool in the basement. It was torn down in 1965. The men's gym (below) was located adjacent to College Field, near where Rankin Science Hall is now. It housed offices, classrooms, and the basketball court. It, too, was demolished in the 1960s.

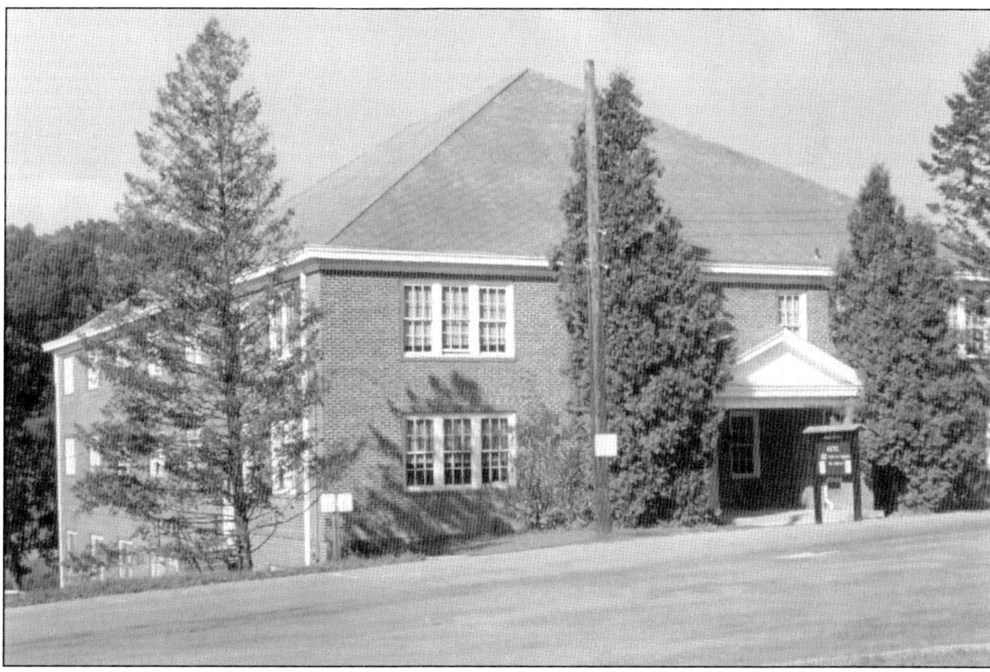

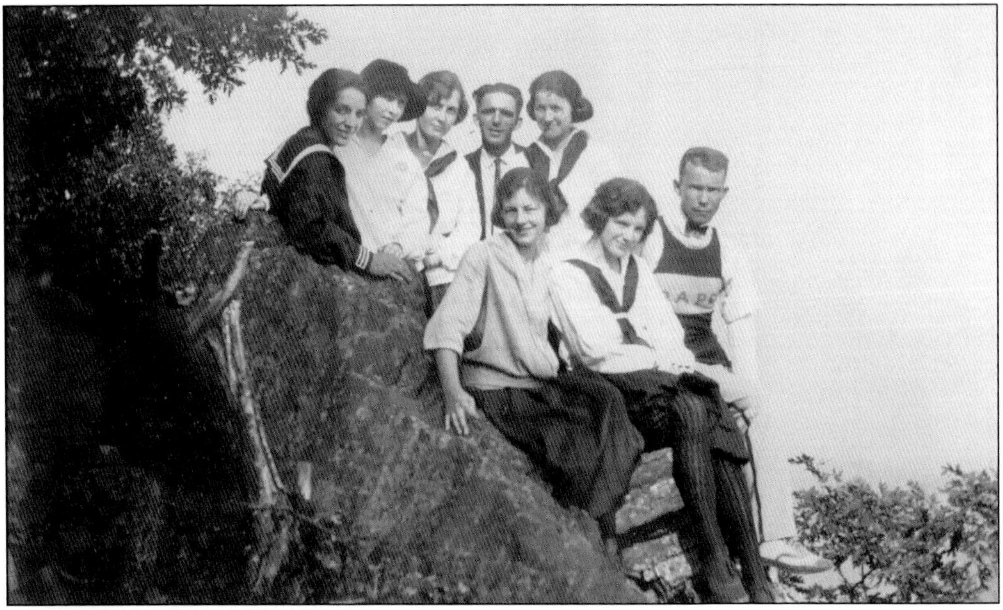

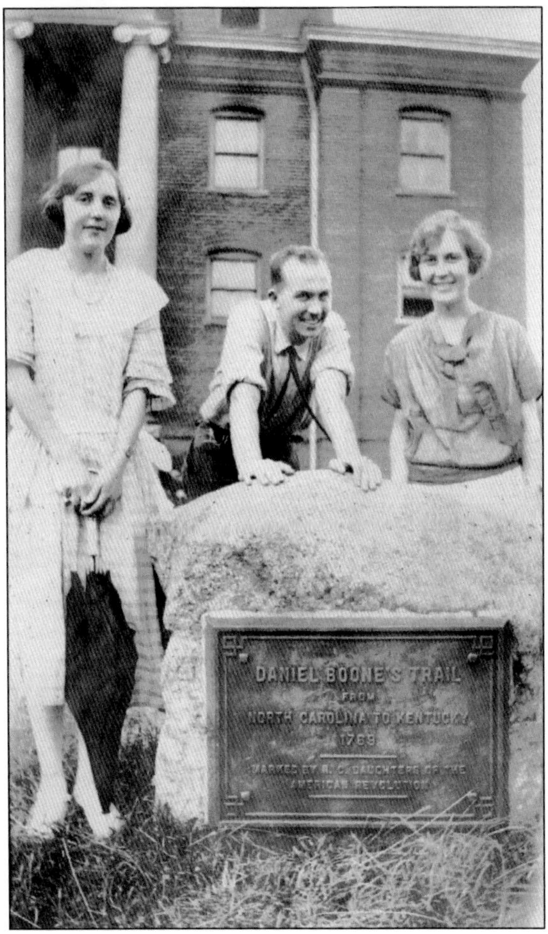

These ATS students are visiting Howard Knob, a popular hiking destination, on July 18, 1923. Named after early settler Benjamin Howard and towering nearly 1,000 feet above Boone, Howard Knob is 4,396 feet above sea level. From 1978 to 1983, the mountain was the site of an experimental wind turbine built by General Electric. The turbine was dismantled in 1983, and the site is now a county park.

From left to right, Lucy Bradshaw, an unidentified student, and Hattie Bradshaw are seen here in 1923 standing outside the Boone courthouse next to the Daniel Boone Trail marker (erected in 1913). From 1913 to 1915, the Daughters of the American Revolution funded the establishment of trail markers that followed Daniel Boone's famous 1769 passage from Boone to the Cumberland Gap. Six markers were established in Watauga County, including the one at the courthouse.

The Physical Plant and Steam Generator Plant complex is a well-known landmark on campus. The Steam Generator Plant was built in 1924 and housed a steam-powered generator maintained by the New River Light & Power Company. The Services Annex building was constructed in 1949 and housed the physical plant. Later, in 1975, the campus added a physical services building. The plant stopped using coal in 1973 and removed the smokestack. A new tower was built in the early 1990s, and steam is now generated for heat and hot water on campus using natural gas. New River Light & Power Company was established in 1915 and continues to provide electricity for Appalachian State University and the Boone area. These two photographs show the plant in 1960 (right) and in 2014 (below).

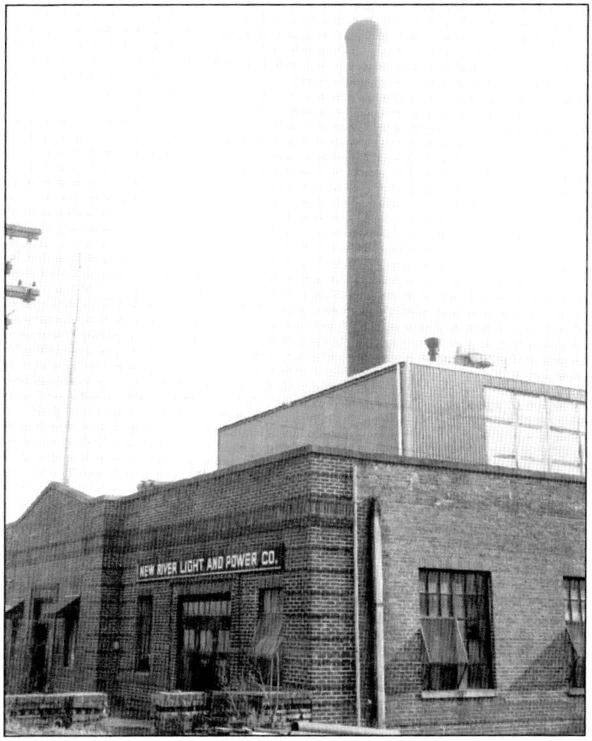

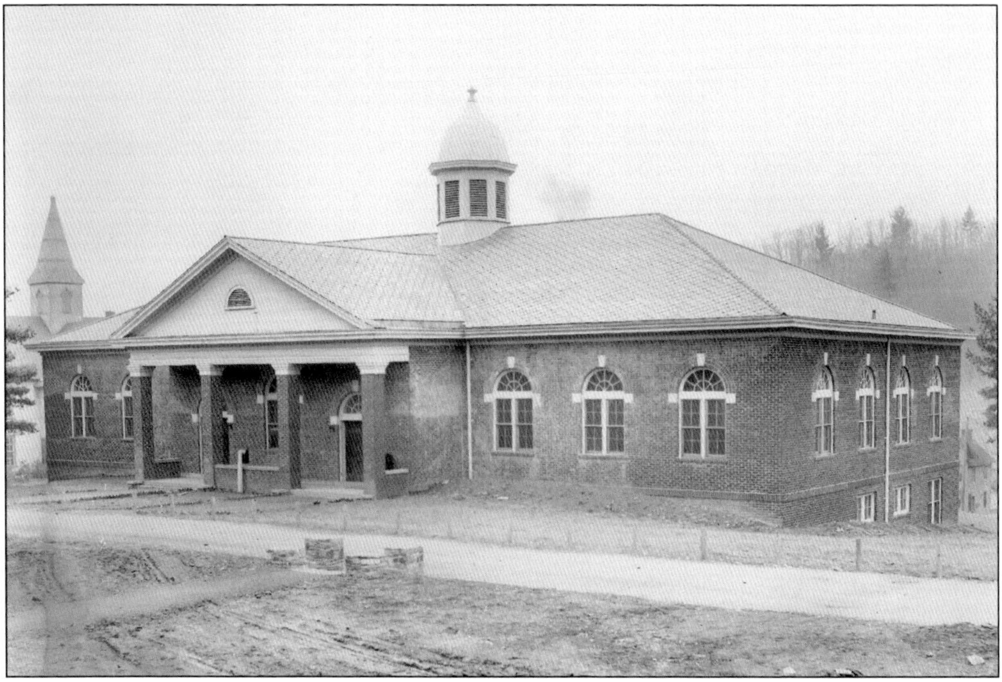

The Central Dining Hall (above) was built in 1925 and served as the main dining hall until it was torn down in 2009 to complete the courtyard of the new dining hall. In 1981, the building was dedicated to John and Vivian Welborn, pictured left and center, respectively, in the image below. John Welborn was the cafeteria manager from 1939 to 1973, and his wife, Vivian, taught in the home economics department from 1944 until her retirement in 1974. Vivian was also the campus dietitian from 1948 to 1963.

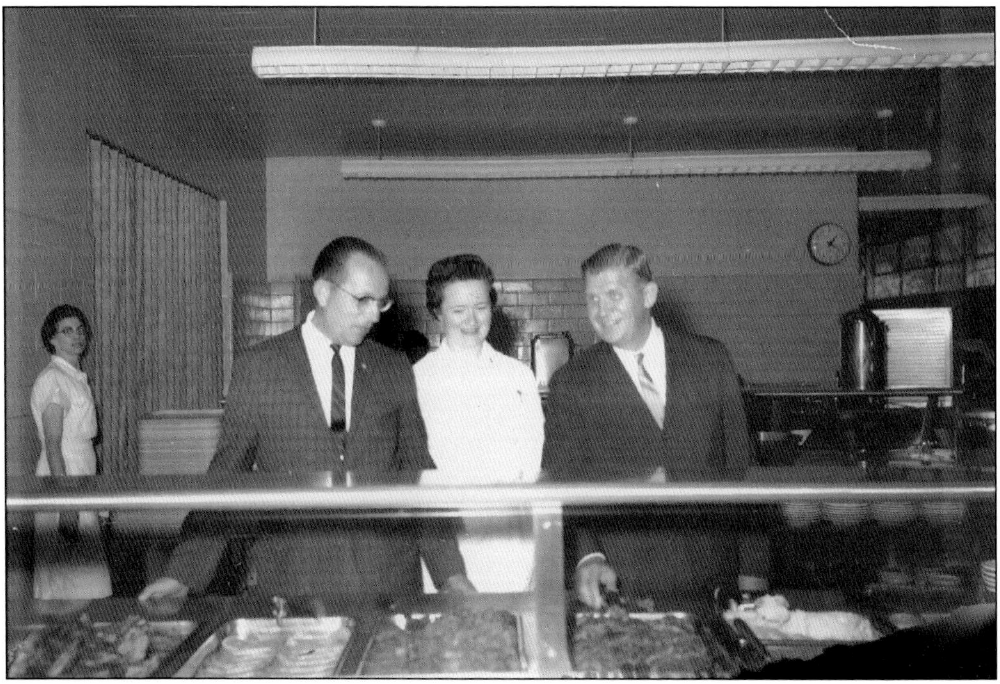

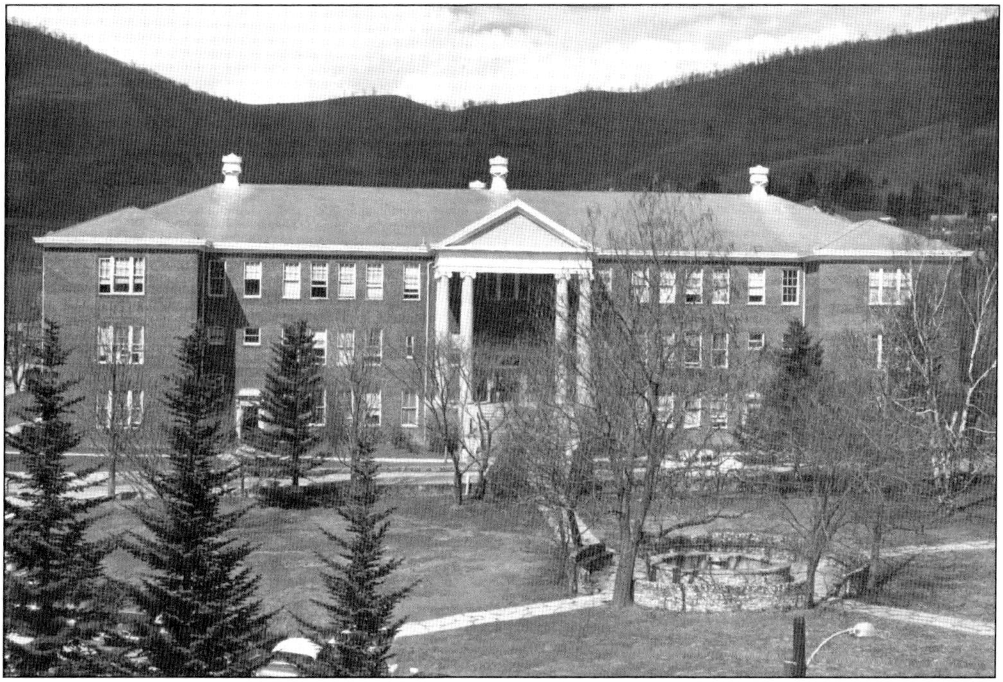

The second administration building, seen here, was a three-story brick structure completed in 1924 on what was then Appalachian Street, where Anne Belk Hall is currently located. It housed recitation rooms, offices, an auditorium, a study hall, and a library. The basement floor had laboratories and scientific equipment. This image shows the front of the building, which had a portico that overlooked the Promenade. This building was destroyed by fire in December 1966.

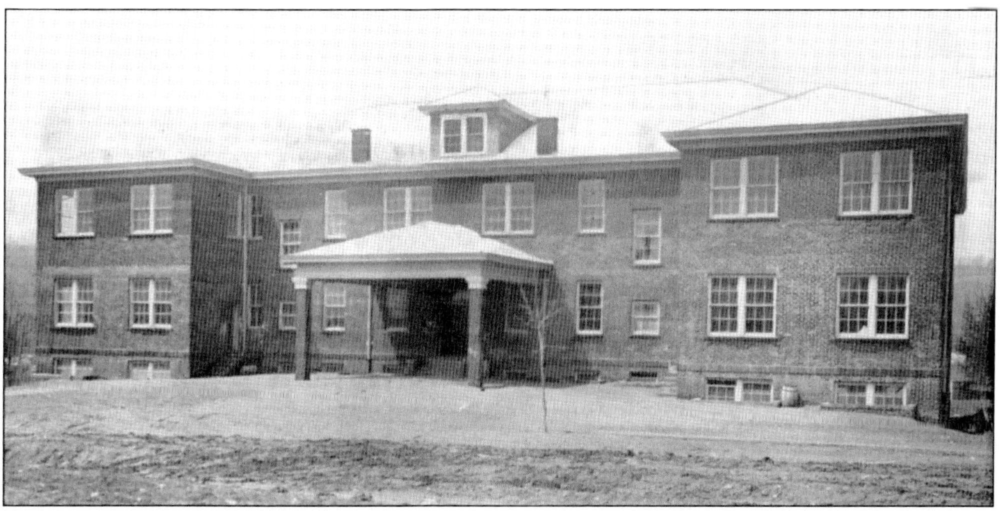

The education building, first constructed as Boone Grade School, housed Appalachian Elementary School, also known as the demonstration elementary school, from 1925 to 1954, when it was moved to Whitener Hall. The education building, which stood where the second Belk Library is now located, was torn down in the late 1960s. The demonstration school was a cooperative program between Watauga County Schools and Appalachian State that provided a grade school taught by Appalachian State teachers and students.

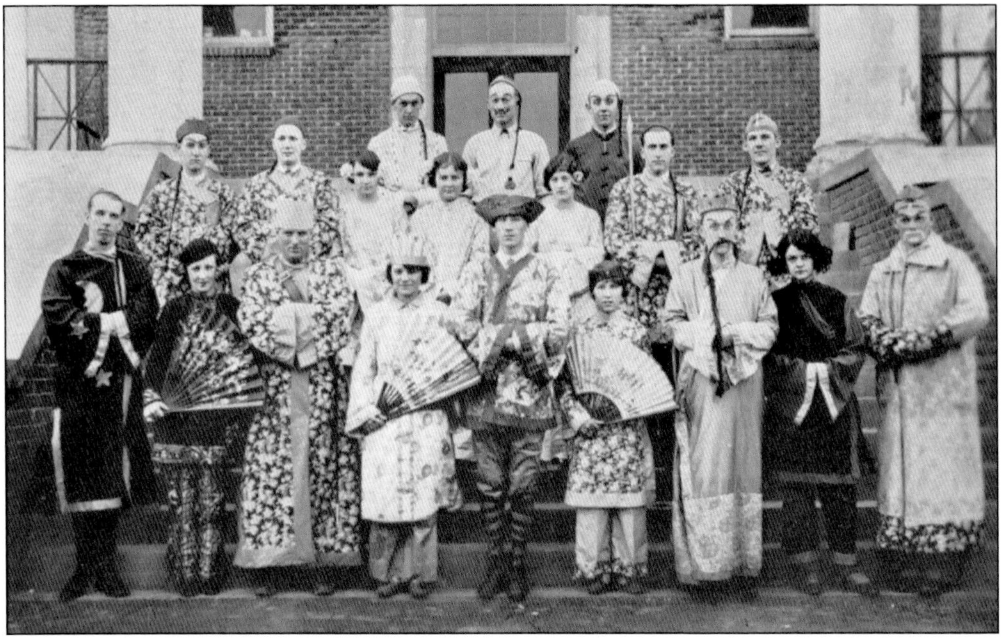

Student actors pose in costume for *The Crimson Eyebrows*, a 1922 musical written by May Hewes Dodge and John Wilson Dodge. The play is based on a historical event in China at the beginning of the Common Era and was apparently a popular performance piece for high schools. It was performed at Appalachian State Normal School (ASNS) in 1926.

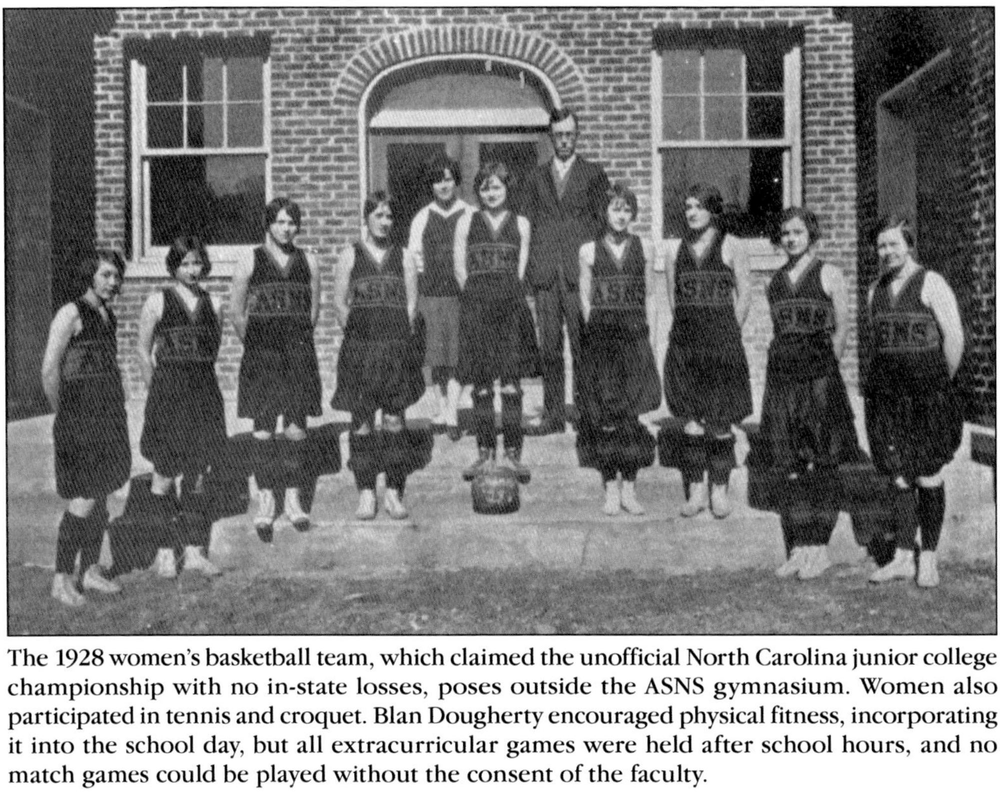

The 1928 women's basketball team, which claimed the unofficial North Carolina junior college championship with no in-state losses, poses outside the ASNS gymnasium. Women also participated in tennis and croquet. Blan Dougherty encouraged physical fitness, incorporating it into the school day, but all extracurricular games were held after school hours, and no match games could be played without the consent of the faculty.

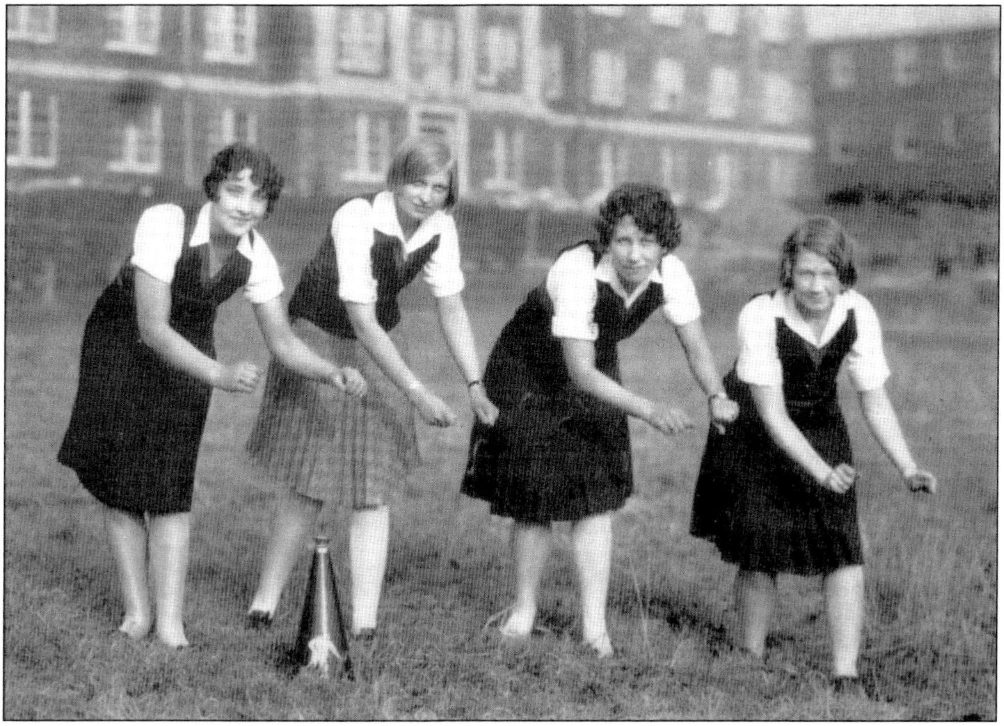

From left to right, 1929 ASNS cheerleaders Ruth Hollifield, Margaret Clay, Gladys Sweat, and Kathleen Regan demonstrate a cheer in front of the new girls' dormitory, completed in 1929 and later known as Dauph-Blan Hall. The dormitory was located between the second administration building and White Hall on the Promenade, facing south, and was torn down in 1980.

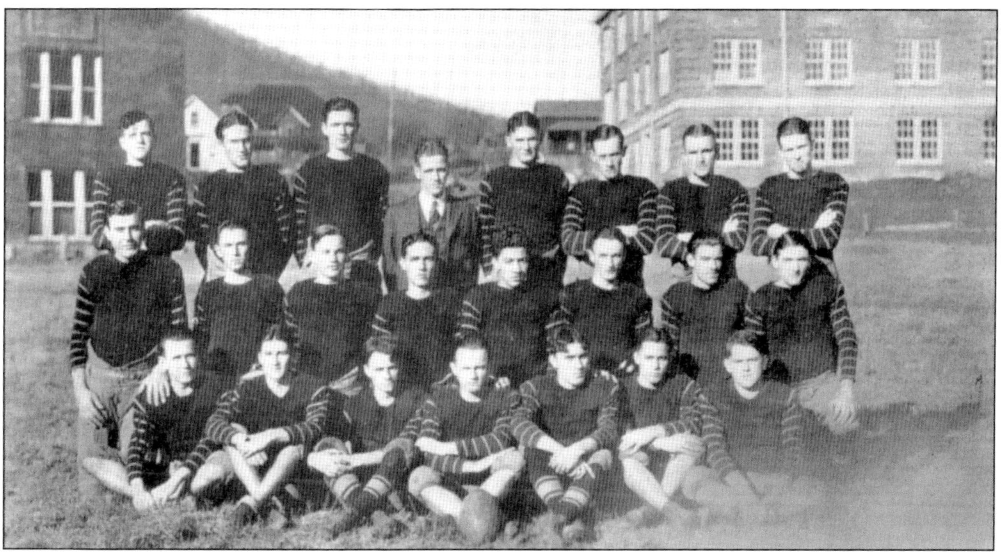

The 1929 ASNS football team poses for this photograph. Graydon Eggers, an English professor at Appalachian from 1927 to 1969, was the coach. He is fourth from the left in the third row. The team won only three out of nine games that year, but they beat local rival Lees-McRae Institute (now College) 51-0.

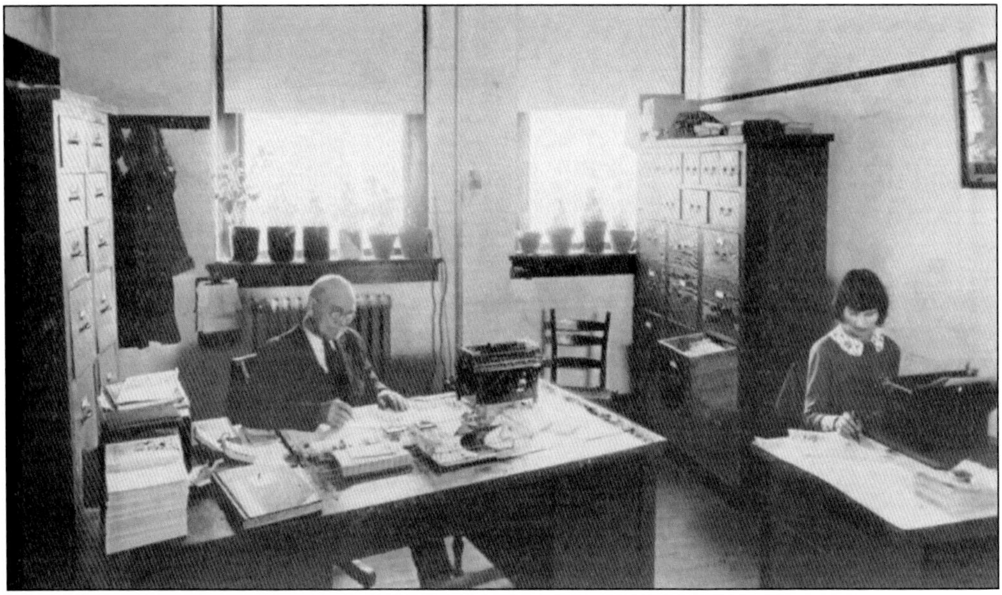

This 1929 photograph of the registrar's office, located in the second administration building, shows registrar James M. Downum sitting on the left. Downum was the first registrar at Appalachian, serving from 1925 to 1933. He began his career at the school in 1911 when he was hired as a Latin professor.

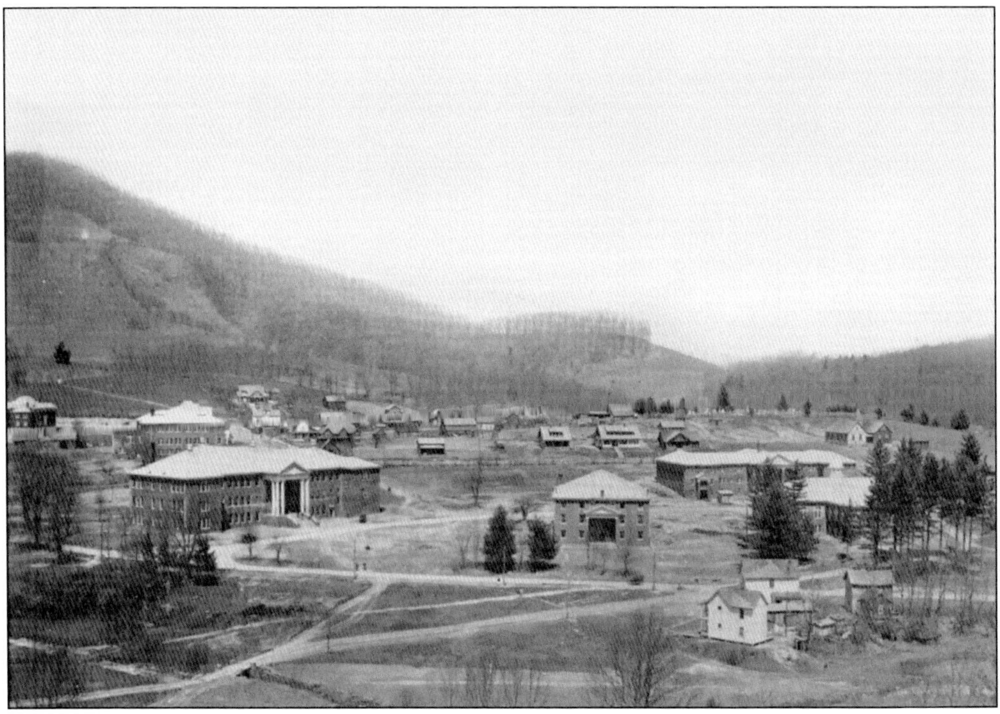

The Appalachian State Normal School campus in 1928 is seen above. The large structure to the left is the administration building, and the old women's gymnasium stands at center, just to the right of two freestanding trees. The cafeteria is behind the stand of trees at the far right, and the first White Residence Hall can be seen behind and slightly to the left of the cafeteria.

Two

APPALACHIAN STATE TEACHERS COLLEGE

This chapter covers the school's years as Appalachian State Teachers College (1929–1967). Dr. Blan Dougherty served as president for 25 years after the school became Appalachian State Teachers College (ASTC), but he faced student protests in the 1930s and 1940s over the strict rules for campus life that he endorsed. The times had changed, so in 1943, at the age of 73, he did as well, deciding to allow smoking and dancing on campus for the first time. Dougherty, in fact, even insisted on offering dance lessons for the faculty.

Beginning in 1955, new president Dr. William Plemmons instituted further changes to the campus infrastructure, the curriculum, and campus life. Nearly 20 buildings were completed during the ASTC years, and many others were renovated and expanded. The graduate curriculum was revised. Students became more outspoken sometimes demonstrating for further privileges. In 1961, student protests led to a loosening of restrictions on the dress code, the elimination of the women's curfew, and the extension of library hours. In the late 1960s, rallies both for and against the Vietnam War were held on campus. Plemmons retired two years after Appalachian received full university status from the state legislature and became Appalachian State University in 1967.

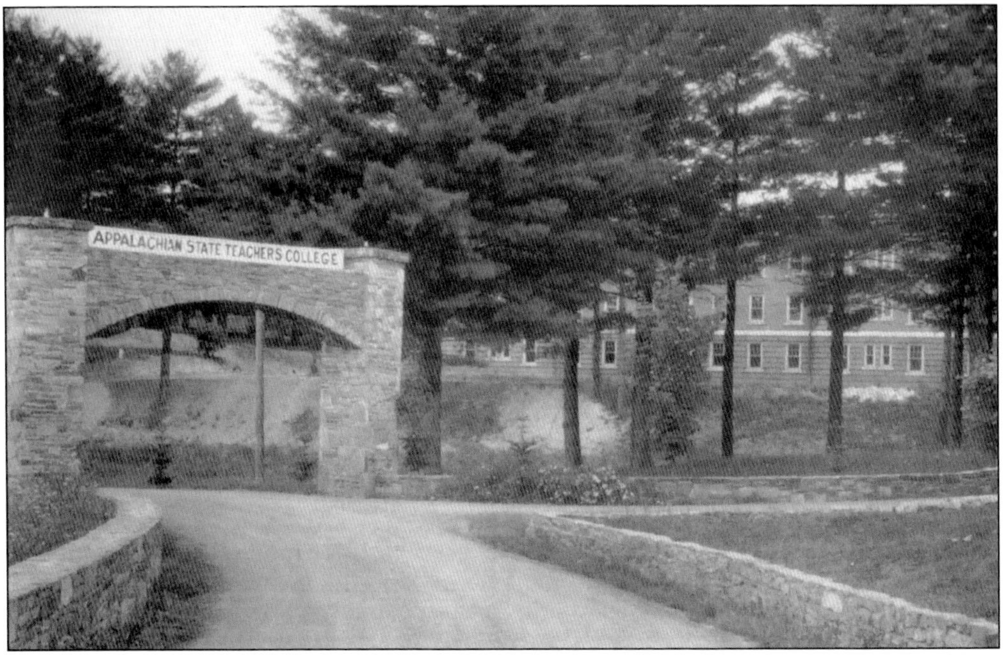

Seen here is the main ASTC entrance. In 1929, Appalachian State Normal School was approved for bachelor's programs, and the name changed to Appalachian State Teachers College. Instruction was now offered in eight departments: applied arts, biology and chemistry, education, language, health and physical education, history and government, mathematics and physics, and social science.

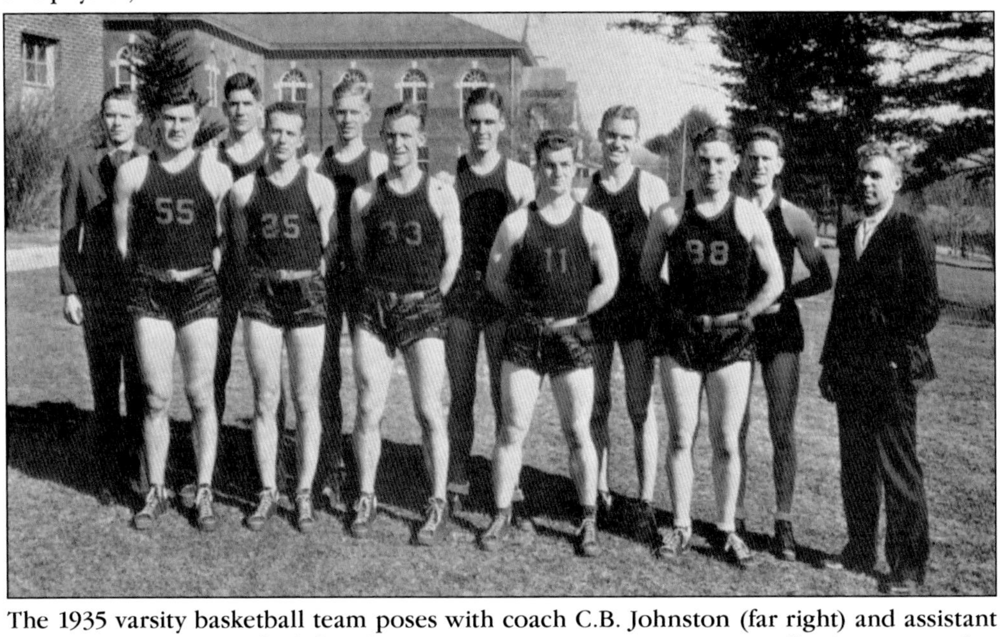

The 1935 varsity basketball team poses with coach C.B. Johnston (far right) and assistant coach Van G. Hinson (far left). The Mountaineers went 15-5 in intercollegiate games that season. They went 6-4 against North State Intercollegiate Athletic Conference (also known as the "Little Six") teams, which, in addition to ASTC, included Catawba, Lenoir-Rhyne, Atlantic Christian, Guilford, Elon, and High Point.

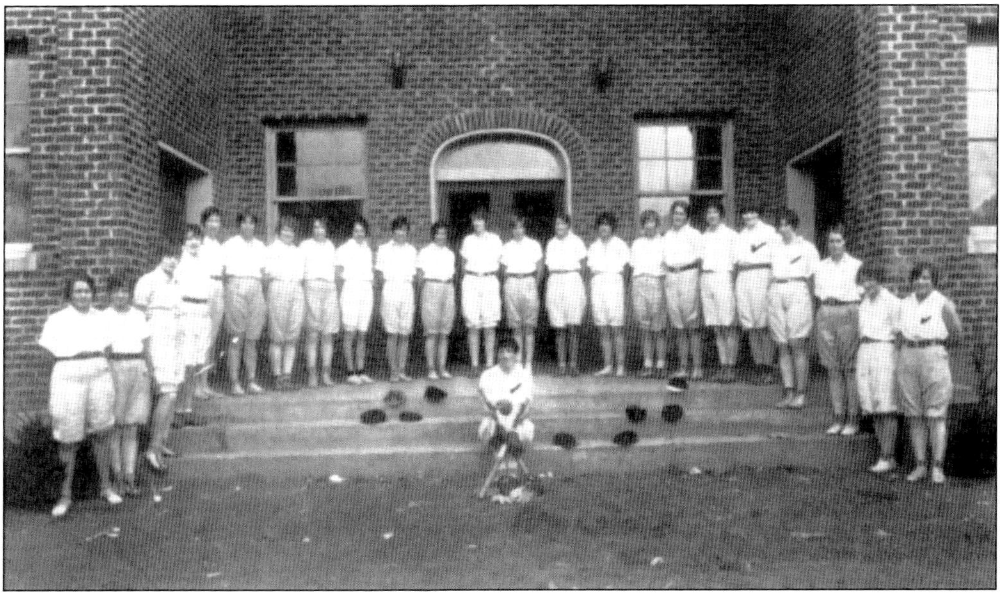

According to the 1930 *Dew Drop*, athletics were intended to promote "interest in every student for clean sports, true sportsmanship, and fair and honest competition," and a physical education course was required for all students. The school encouraged both men and women to take part in competitive sports and offered a variety of options. Listed as the women's baseball team in the 1930s *Rhododendron*, the group of athletes above poses in their uniforms outside of White Hall. Below, the 1937 women's field hockey team poses with their hockey sticks.

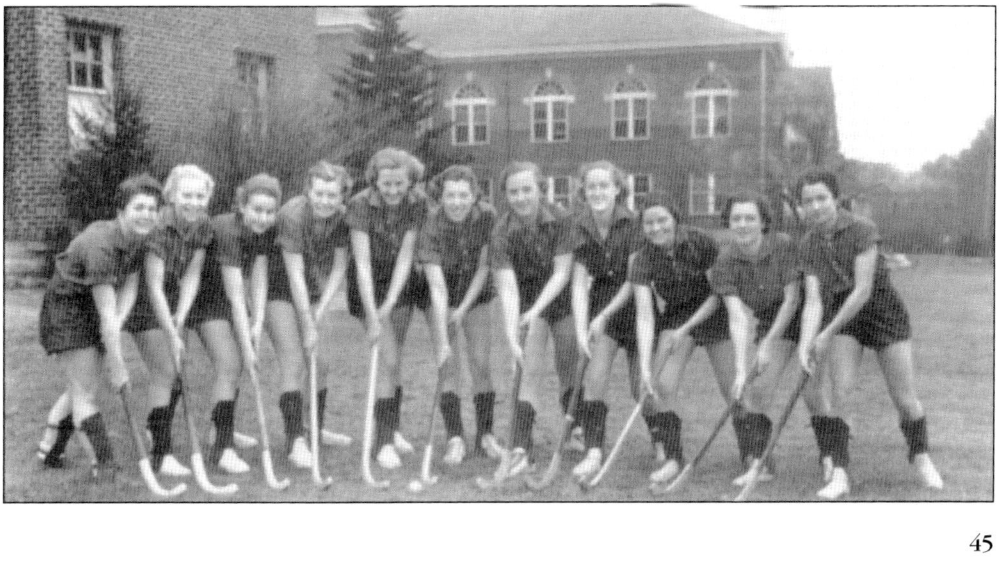

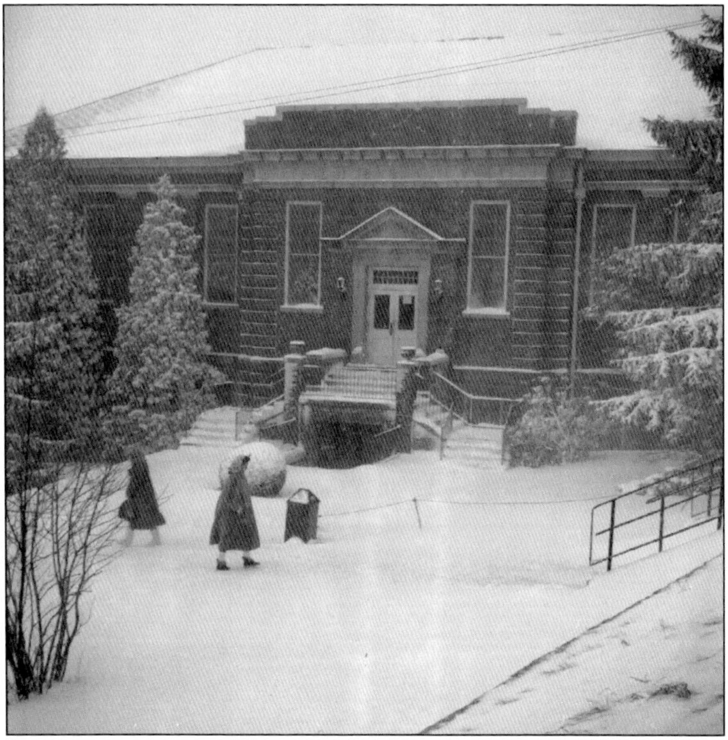

In 1960, an addition (below) to the front of the old D.D. Dougherty Library was completed, changing the look of the 1935 building (left). The library housed 140,000 volumes and included a curriculum library, a juvenile library, and the Department of Library Science. Nine years later, the Carol Grotnes Belk Library opened and the Dougherty Library was converted to offices and classroom space.

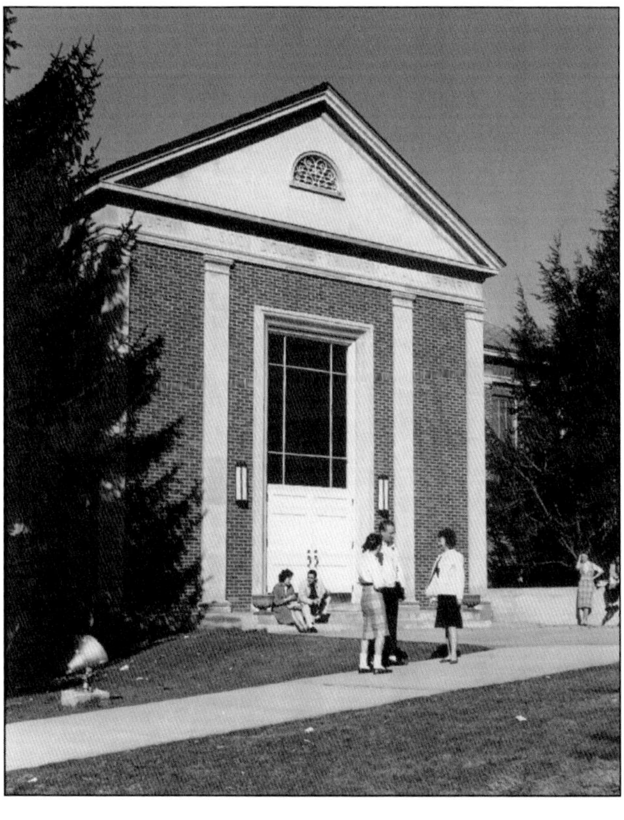

Lillie B. Harden, seen here, was the matron of Dauph-Blan Residence Hall, built in 1929 and later called Watauga Hall. Harden enforced strict rules for her female boarders, who according to the 1926 *Dew Drop* had to have "permission to leave their homes. Lady teachers must accompany women when they are away from their boarding places." Harden was the sister of O.L. Brown, the son-in-law of Dauph and Lillie Dougherty.

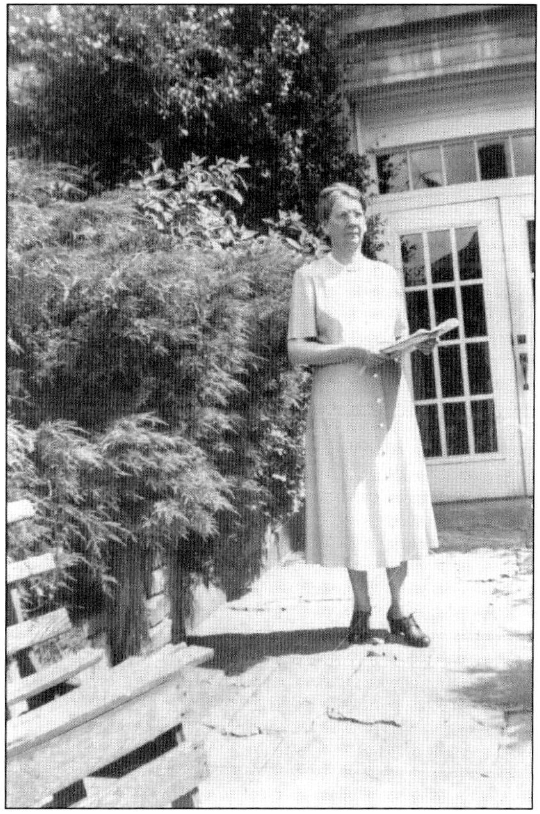

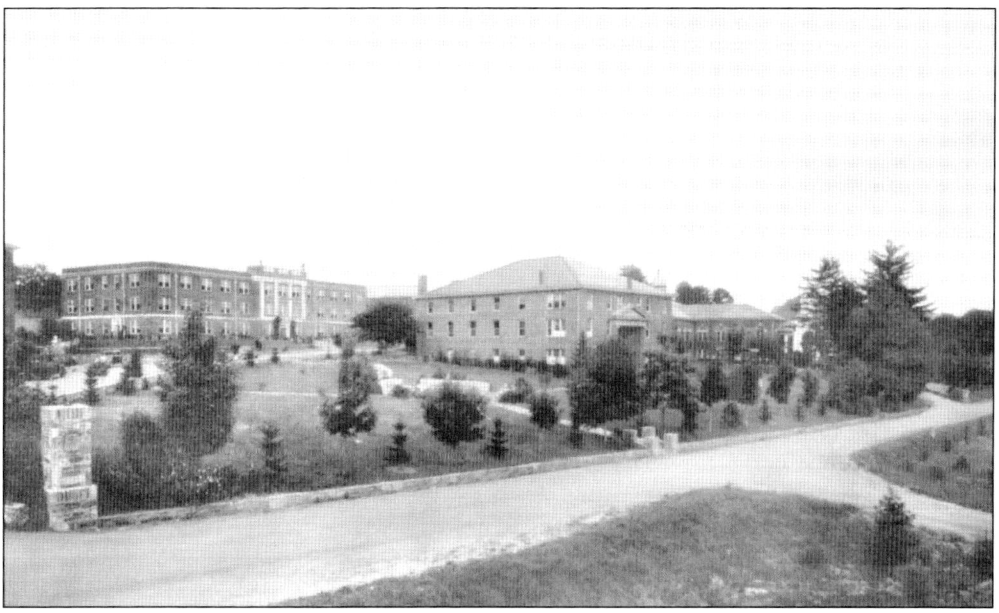

The west side of campus is seen here in 1937. Dauph-Blan (Watauga) Hall is on the left, and the women's gymnasium is in the foreground. Part of the Central Dining Hall can be seen behind the gymnasium. In 1937, ASTC owned 550 acres, including a main campus of 35 acres and 17 buildings.

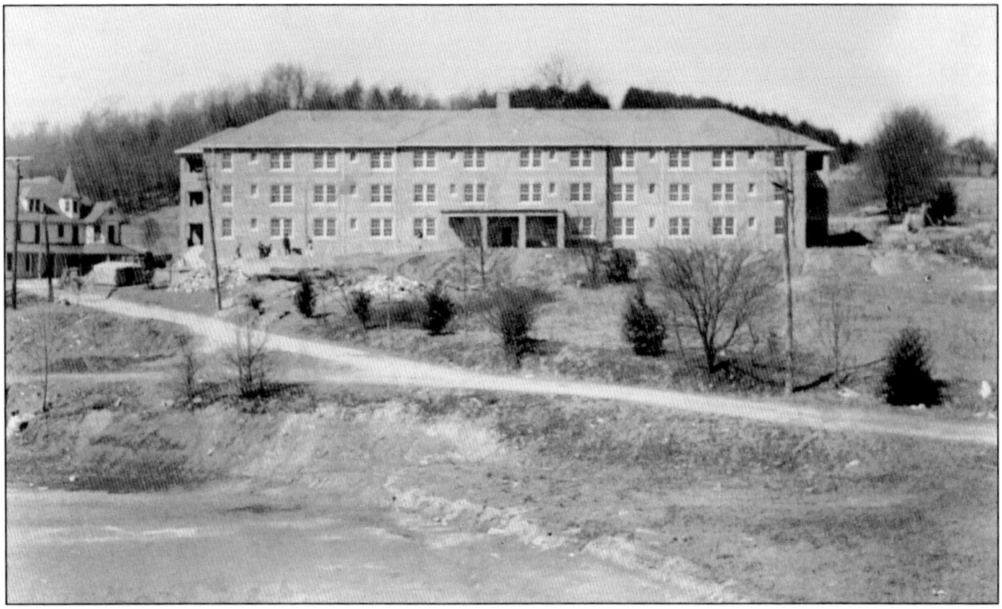

In 1938, the campus had 17 buildings, not counting housing for faculty and married students or farm structures. This image shows the construction of the second Newland Hall, a men's dormitory. The building was completed in 1939 and demolished in the mid-1990s. The first Newland Hall, built in 1908, is at left in the background. A third Newland Hall was built on approximately the same site in 1996.

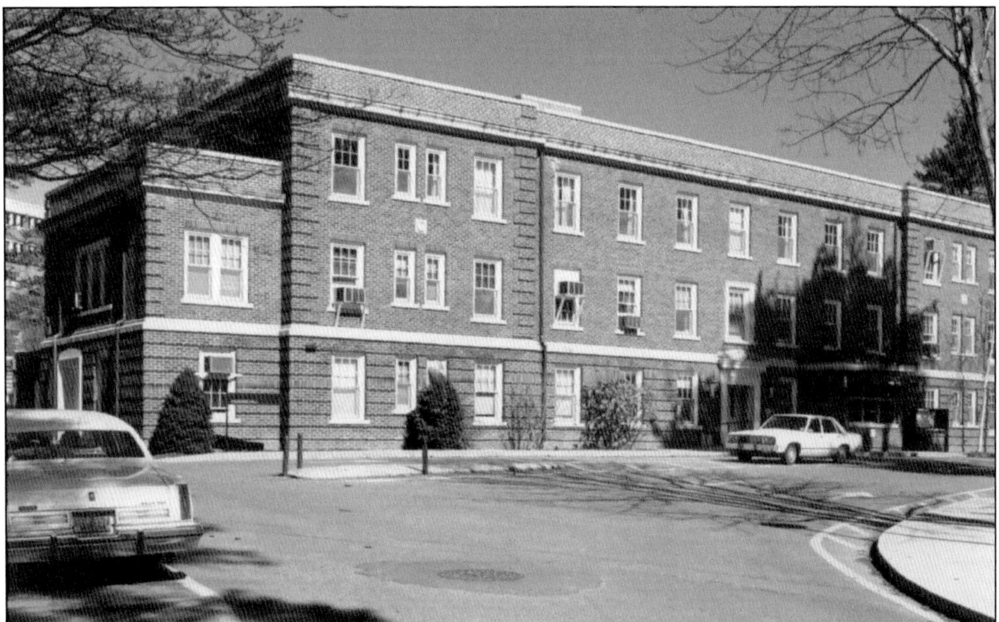

The building that is currently Founders Hall was constructed in 1932 as the college infirmary and became Watauga County Hospital in 1938. Many Watauga County residents were born in the old hospital between 1938 and 1968, when it was renovated to become the administration building annex. The building continues to house administrative offices, but it was renamed Founders Hall in the early 1980s.

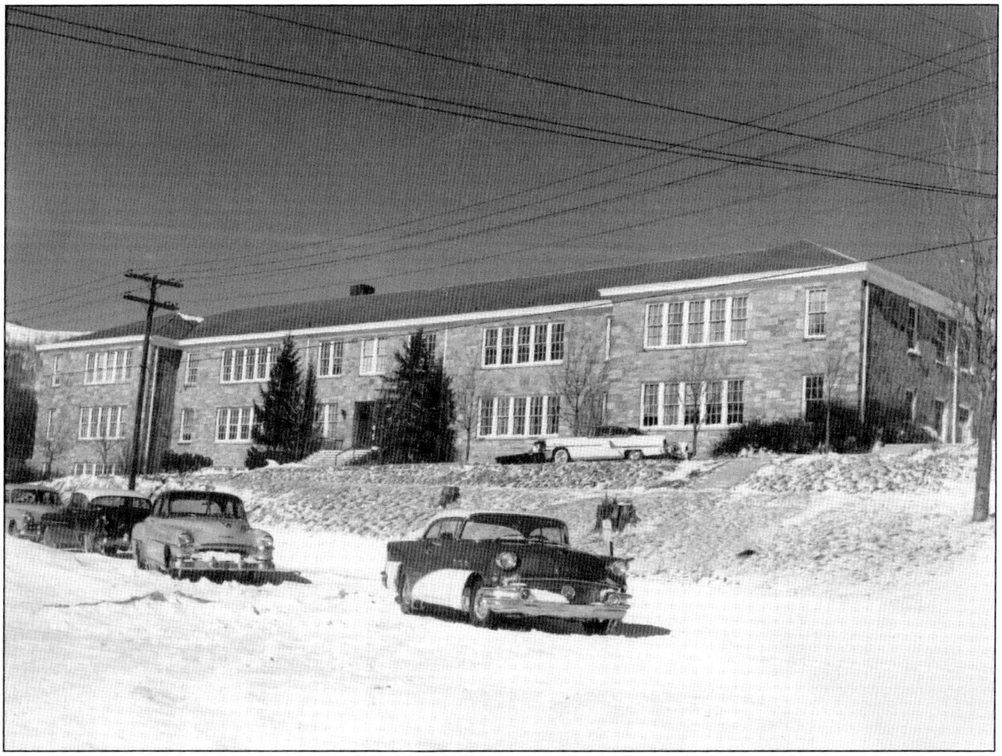

Chapell Wilson Hall (above) was built in 1938 and housed Appalachian High School until 1965, when the new Watauga High School opened its doors. The building was then renovated and named for Chapell Wilson (right), who taught education and psychology at Appalachian Training School from 1922 to 1925. He served as director of the demonstration schools at ASNS and ASTC and served as the first dean of graduate studies until his death in 1957. Chapell Wilson Hall still stands on campus today, housing the Department of Theatre and Dance.

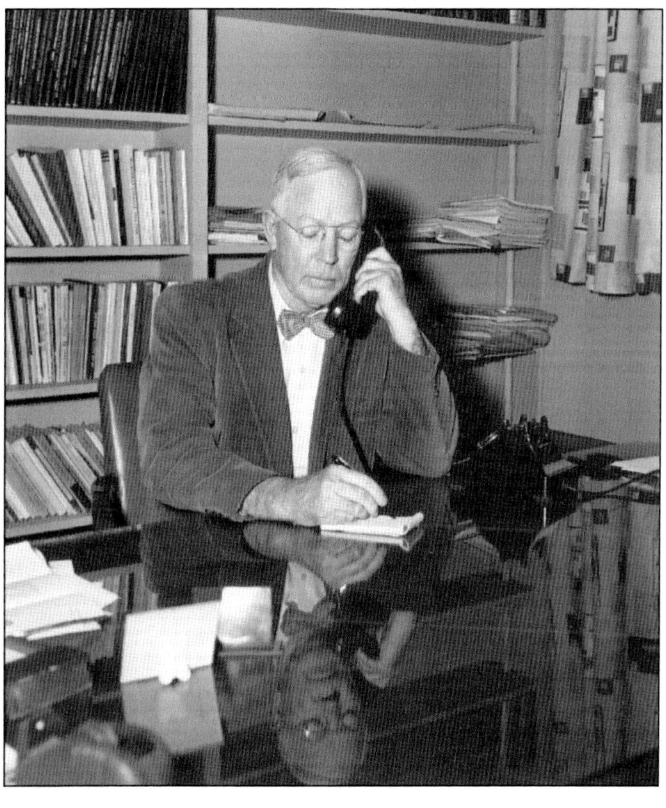

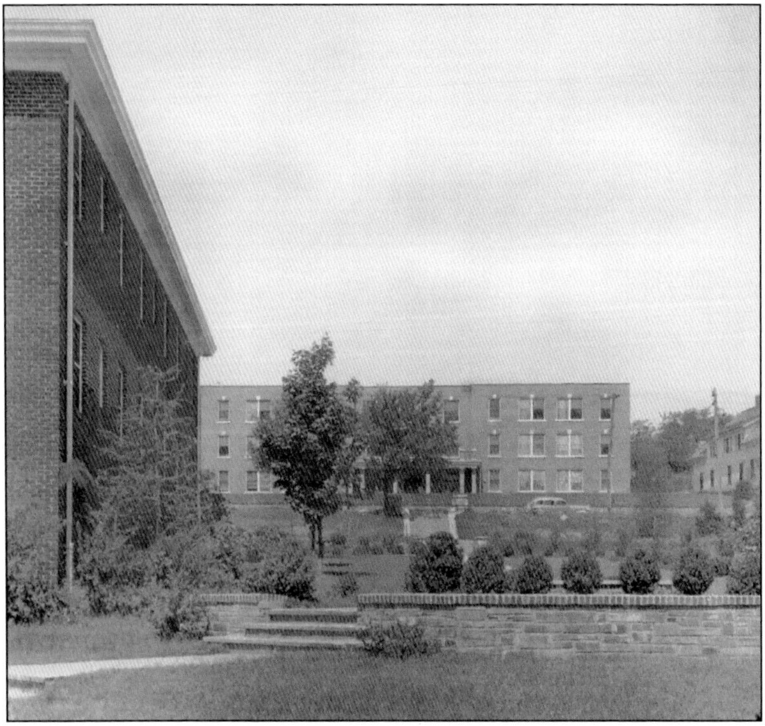

In 1938, on Locust Street west of Coffey Hall, the college constructed a building with 8 apartments and 30 rooms for faculty and staff housing. The structure was converted into a women's dormitory in 1953 and named North Hall. It was demolished in 1993 to make way for an addition to the Plemmons Student Union.

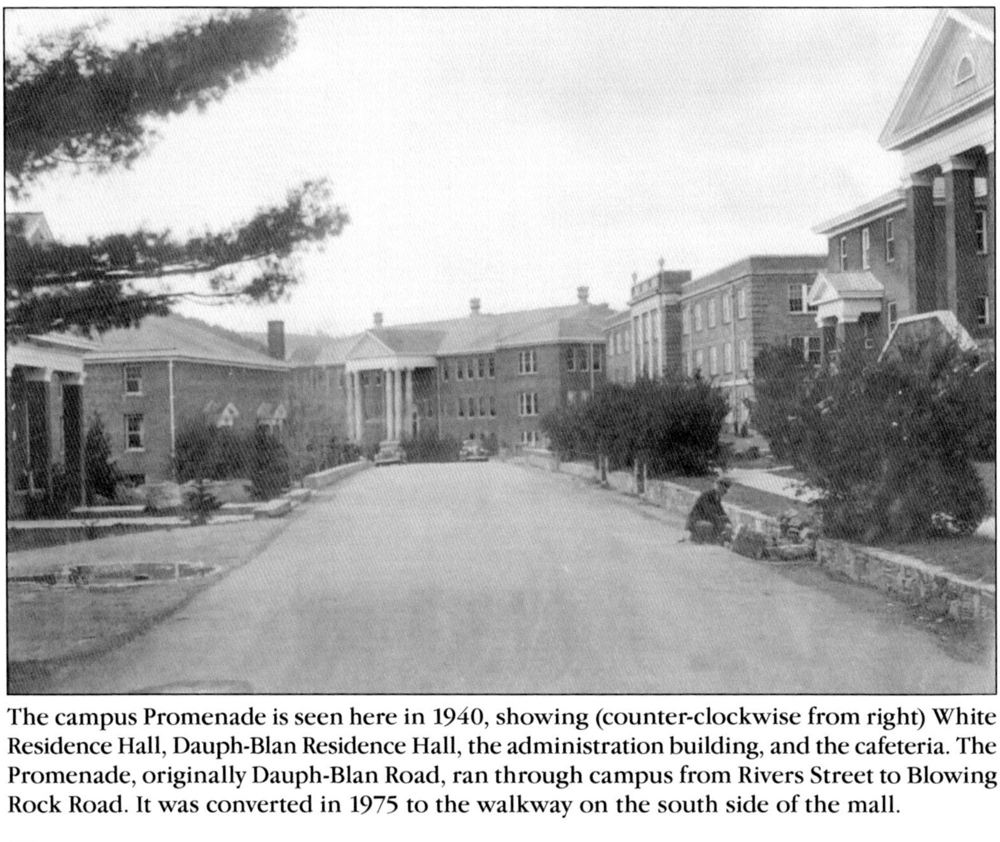

The campus Promenade is seen here in 1940, showing (counter-clockwise from right) White Residence Hall, Dauph-Blan Residence Hall, the administration building, and the cafeteria. The Promenade, originally Dauph-Blan Road, ran through campus from Rivers Street to Blowing Rock Road. It was converted in 1975 to the walkway on the south side of the mall.

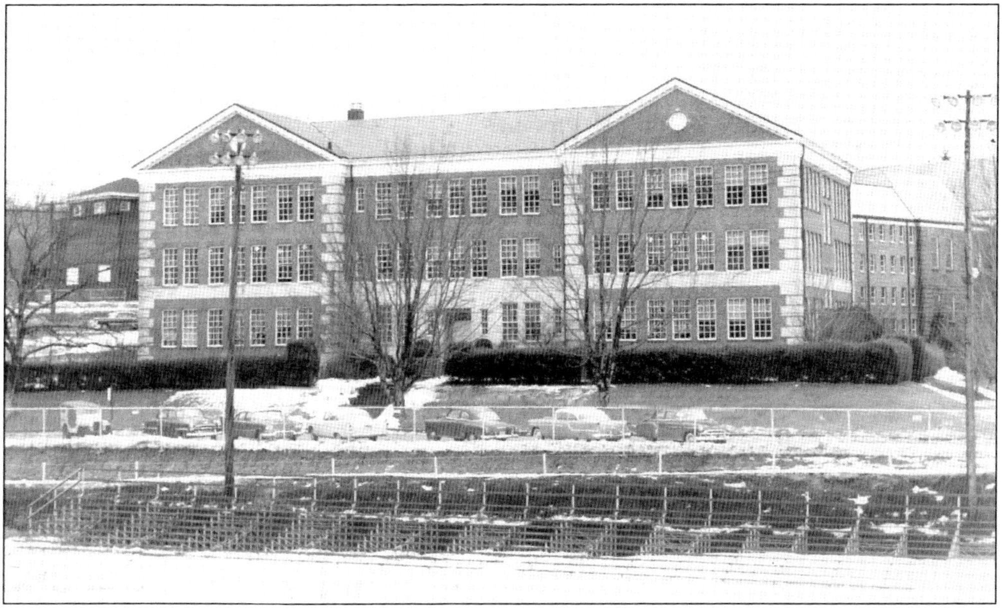

Located on Appalachian Street behind the then-standing second administration building, Smith-Wright Hall was constructed in 1940. It housed the science department until the Rankin Science Building was completed in 1963. It is now home to the Department of Psychology and various laboratories. The building was named for Arlie Raymond Smith, a chemistry professor from 1921 to 1958, and James Thomas Carr Wright, a professor of mathematics at Appalachian from 1920 to 1961.

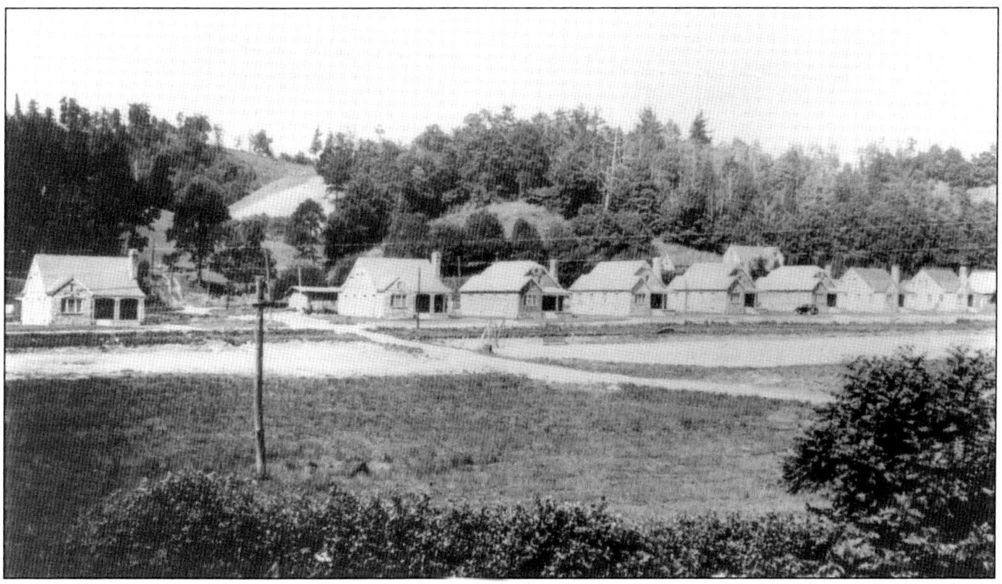

Faculty houses ran along the south side of Rivers Street on the eastern end of campus, approximately where John E. Thomas Hall and the parking lot to the east of it are now found. Originally, there were 16 faculty homes constructed on what was then known as Faculty Street. They were completed around 1940 and torn down in the early 1990s. This image shows the northern sides of the faculty houses, with the field across Faculty Street in the foreground.

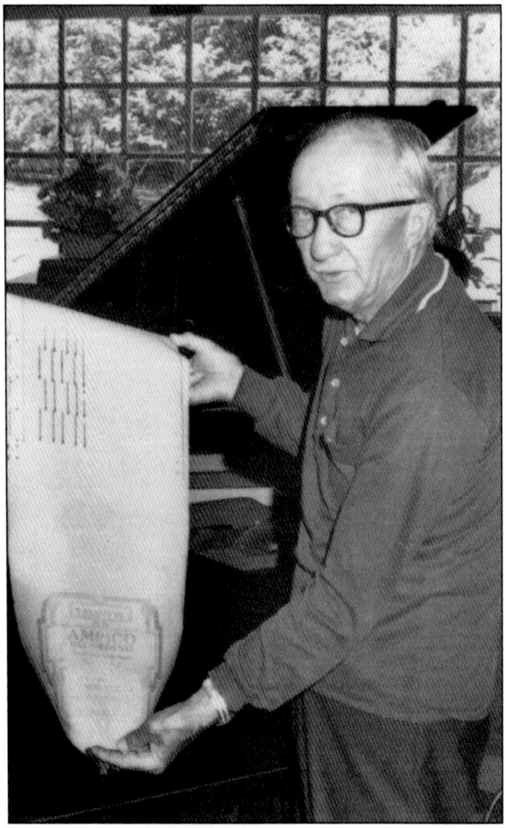

William Amos "Doc" Abrams is seen here displaying a sheet of music. A folklore scholar, Abrams collected hundreds of folksong variants from performers throughout western North Carolina. He chaired the English department at Appalachian from 1932 to 1946. His collection of folksongs is currently housed in the William Leonard Eury Appalachian Collection at Appalachian State University.

Whitener Hall, constructed in 1954, replaced the old education building that had housed Appalachian Elementary School (the demonstration school) until the early 1970s. The building was named for Daniel J. Whitener, a former history professor at Appalachian, in 1975. Located on College Street next to the First Baptist Church, the building housed the history and social sciences departments until it was demolished to make way for the new library parking deck in 2006.

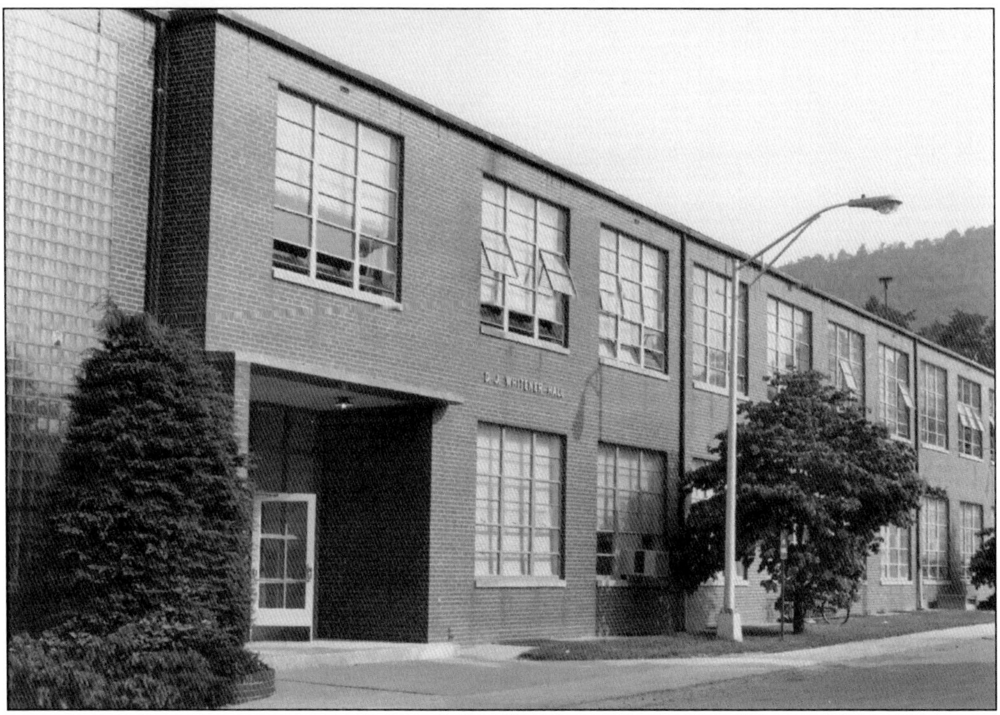

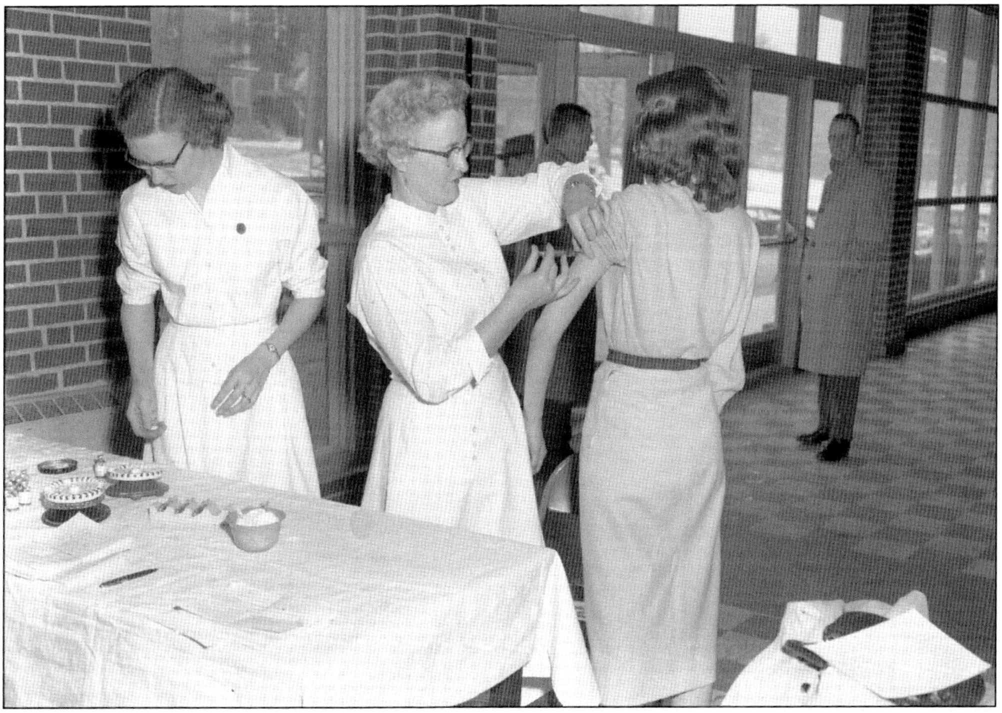

Nurse Mary S. Shook (center) delivers a polio vaccination to an ASTC student in this 1957 photograph. Appalachian provided a series of clinics to administer the vaccine, reportedly vaccinating 90–95 percent of the student body. The clinics were held in Broome-Kirk Gym and were free to all under the age of 20.

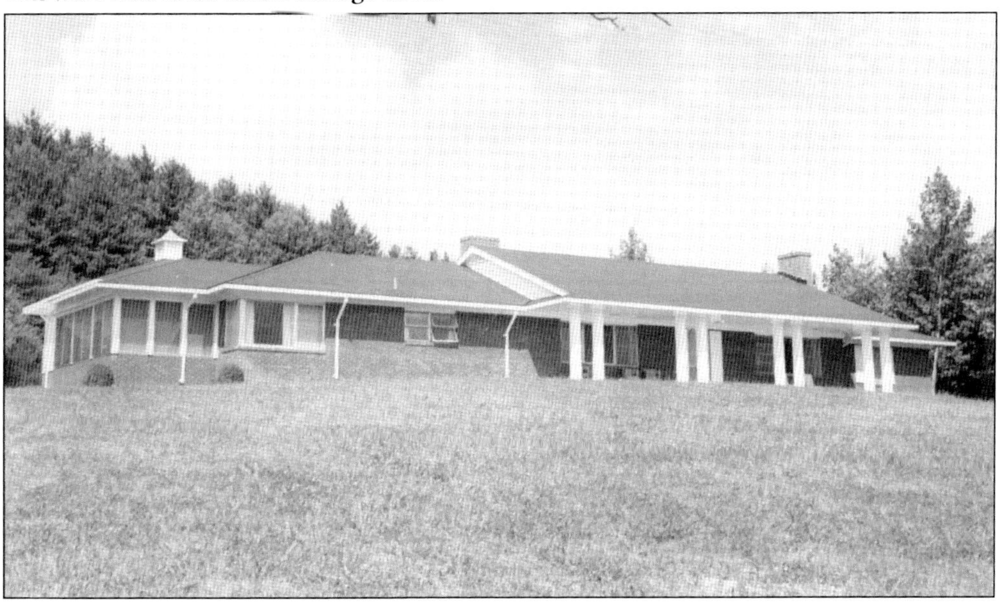

The first president's home was built in 1957. Dr. William Plemmons was the first president or chancellor to live in the home, which was located at the southern end of campus on Bodenheimer Drive. It served as the home for chancellors Wey, Thomas, and Borkowski before it was demolished in 2000 to allow construction of the Living Learning Center.

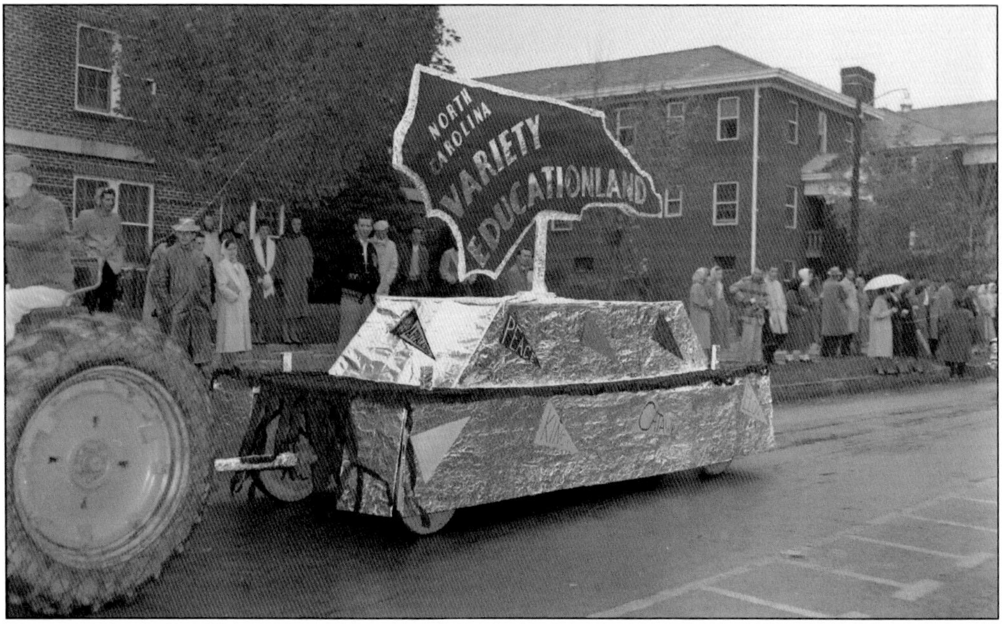

The 1957 homecoming parade makes its way around the Promenade, passing by Dauph-Blan and White Halls. This student-made float pays homage to a popular slogan for North Carolina: "Variety Educationland." *The Appalachian* reported that there were approximately 20 floats in the 1957 parade.

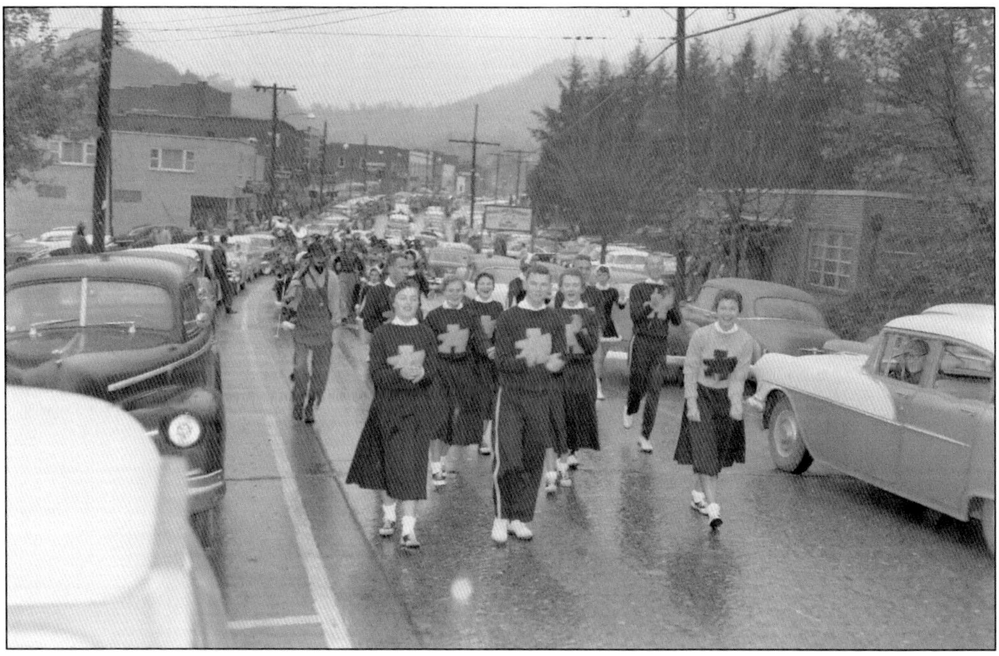

The 1957 homecoming parade is seen again here, with ASTC cheerleaders and Appalachian's mascot Yosef (at left, in overalls) marching down King Street toward the college. Downtown Boone can be seen in the background. The Mountaineers won the homecoming football game 19-7 over the Emory & Henry Wasps, and the year's first snow is reported to have fallen while the game was under way.

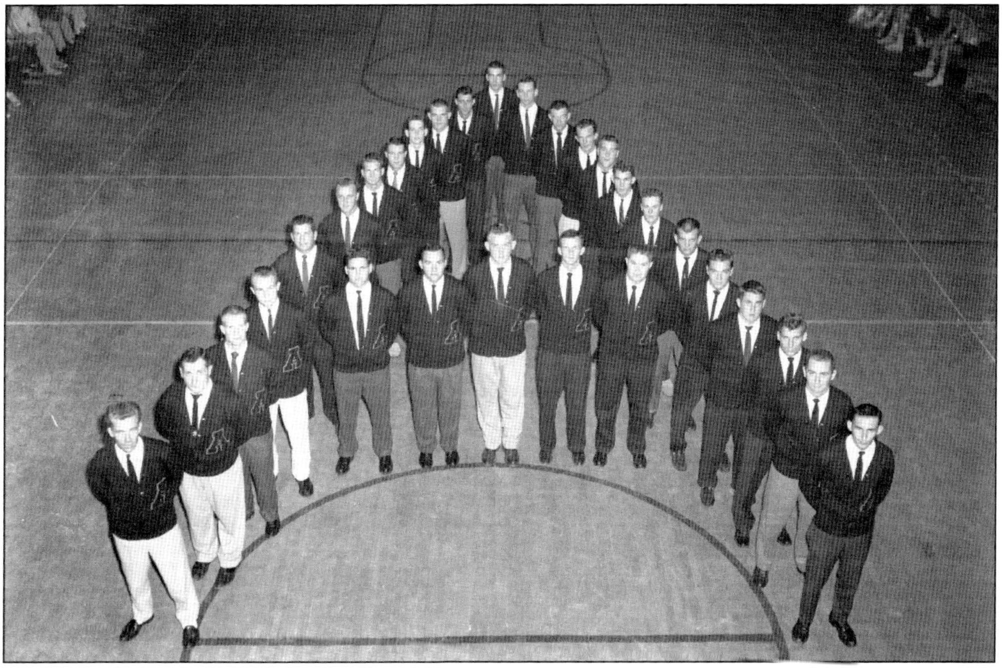

The Men's "A" Club was a student athletic organization formed by elected members of the college's varsity athletic teams. In this 1958 photograph, the club members form an "A" on the basketball court of Broome-Kirk Gym. The club sponsored various programs for the school's athletes and held a yearly spring picnic.

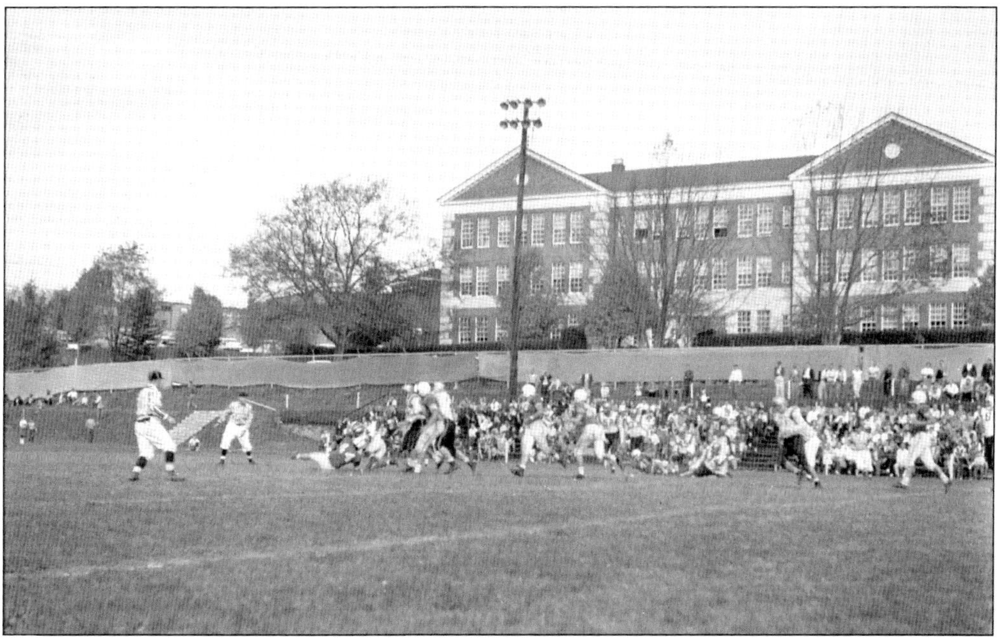

This photograph shows the homecoming game between the Mountaineers and the Catawba College Indians on October 18, 1958. ASTC won 6-0. College Field was located south of Smith-Wright Hall (seen in the background), approximately where Rankin Science Hall currently stands. Conrad Stadium, built in 1962, replaced the field.

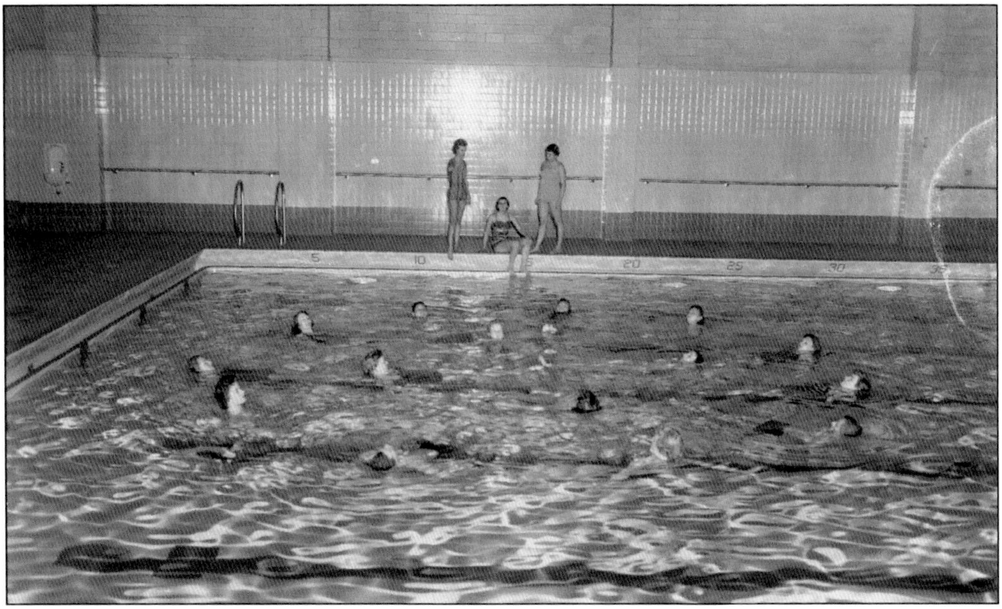

The Flying Fish were an ASTC student club of swimmers, all of whom held senior lifesaving certificates. In this 1958 photograph, club members swim in circle formation at the pool in Broome-Kirk Gym. The club frequently sponsored swimming education programs and intramural swimming. They also participated in aquatic water shows and swimming competitions.

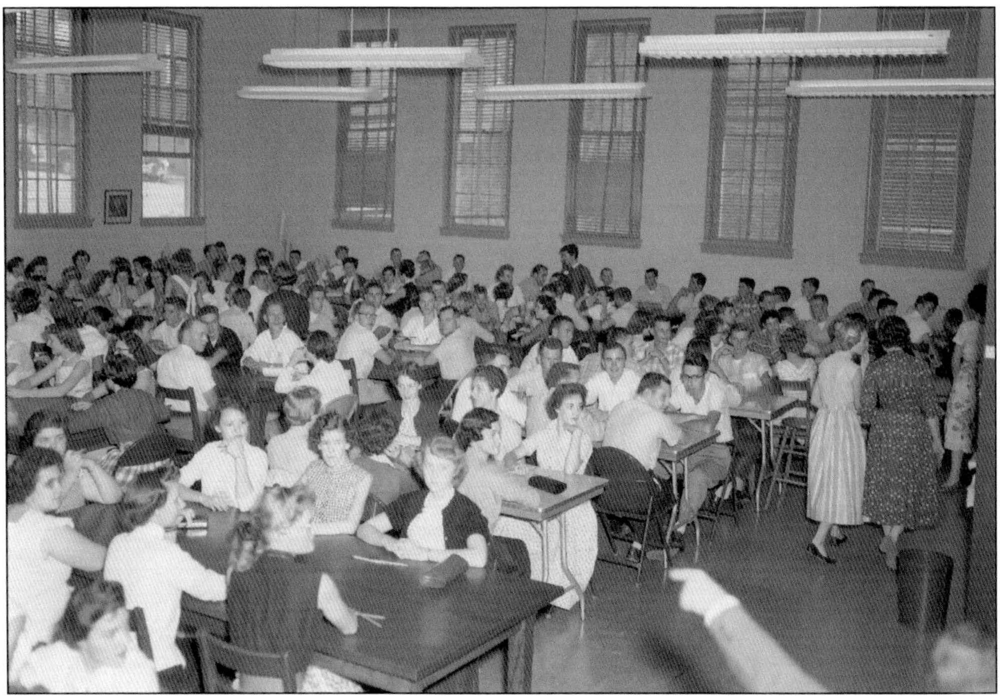

Freshman take their placement tests in the D.D. Dougherty Library in 1958 as a part of orientation. In addition to testing, freshman orientation included campus tours, advising, and registration, as well as social events such as dances, games, and club meetings, many of which are still held.

Dr. Blan Dougherty, seen in this image shaking hands with an elementary school student, served as president of Appalachian until he retired on June 30, 1955. During his 55 years with the school, he taught classes and served as the Watauga County Schools superintendent, and he was at different times a member of the state board of education, the state board of equalization, and the state textbook commission.

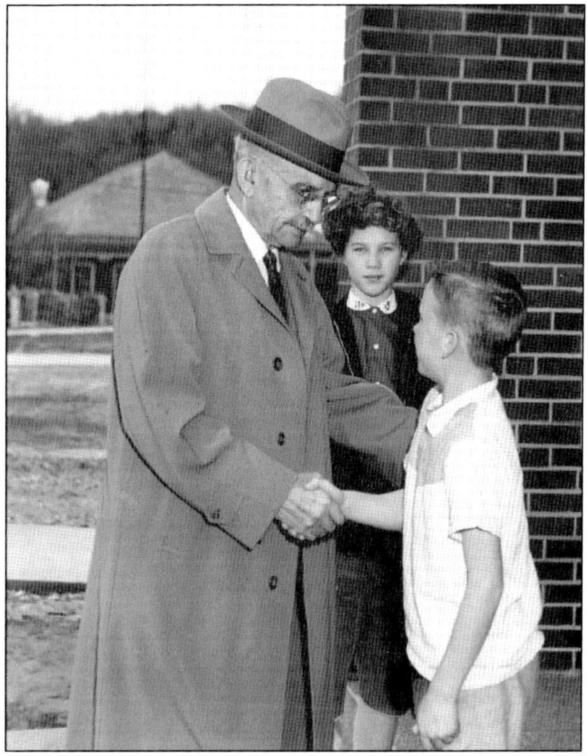

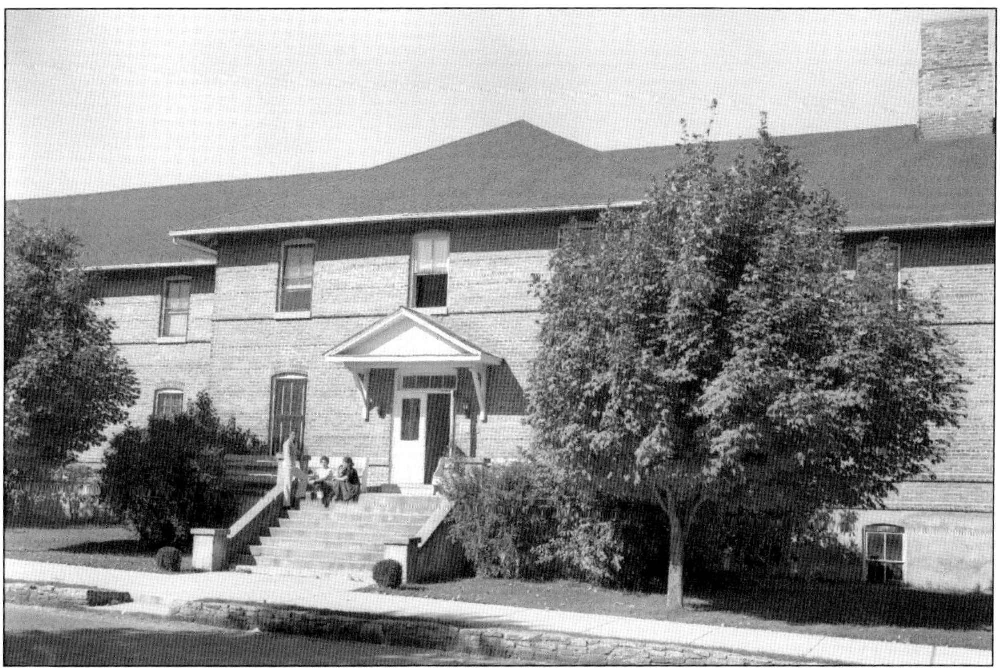

The second Lovill Home was built in 1915 as a women's dormitory. Sandwiched between White Hall and East Hall, it fronted the Promenade. This 1958 image shows the front entrance, which faced south. The building was demolished in 1967 after the more modern third Lovill Home was completed.

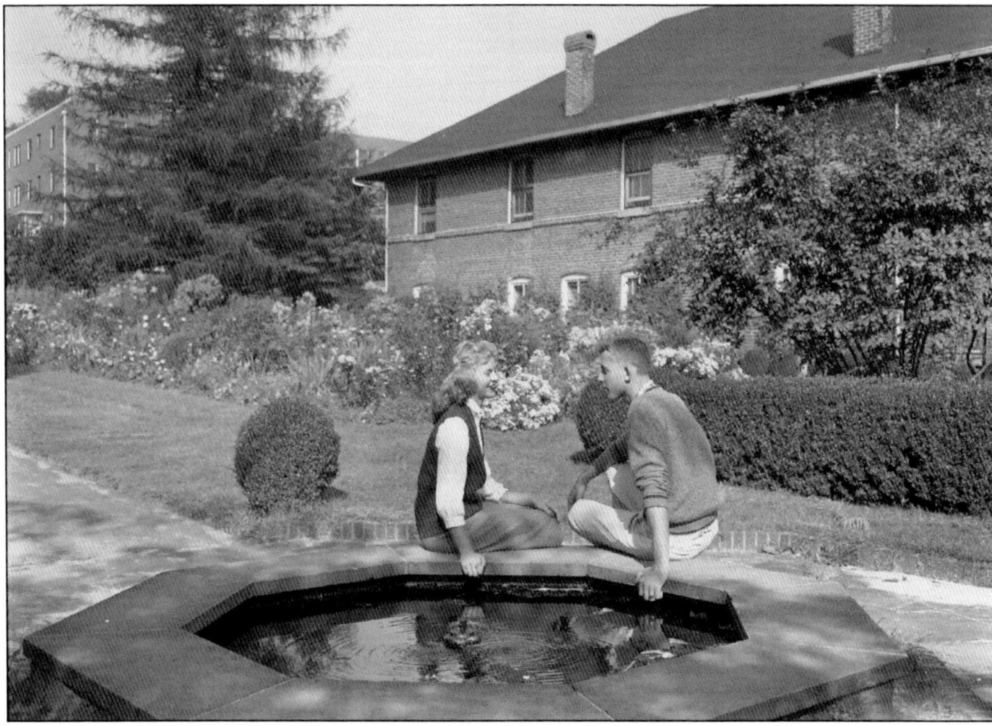

Students spend a little downtime chatting by the ASTC fountain in 1958. Located behind the second Lovill Home, the fountain was on the Promenade between White Hall and the current East Hall, where Sanford Hall now stands. East Hall is visible in the background. The fountain, which eventually became the target of vandals, was replaced by three sculptures of students with a teacher, all created by artist Myra Weisgold for the university's centennial celebration in 1999.

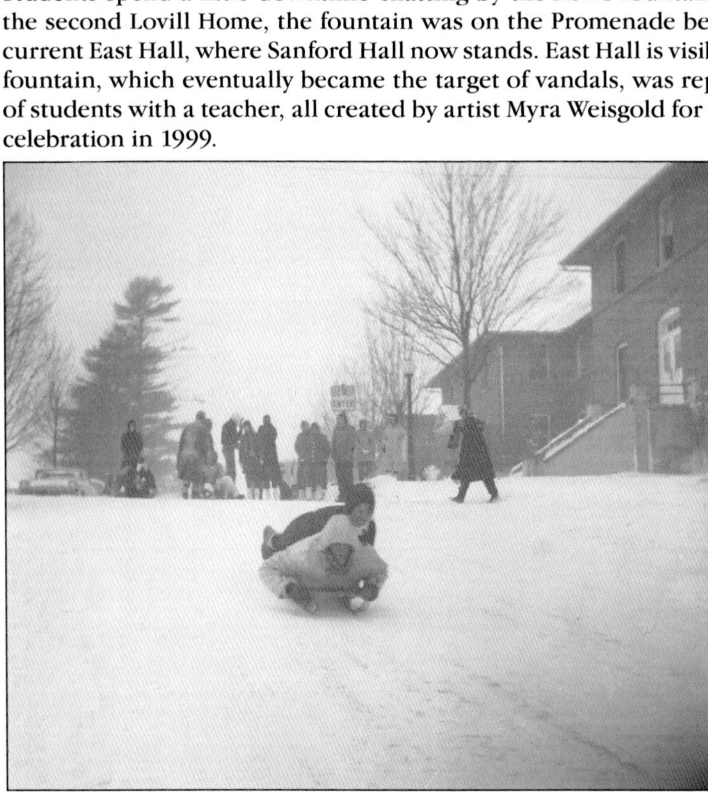

Students take advantage of this January 10, 1959, snowfall by sledding down a section of the Promenade in front of the Lovill Home. Then, as now, snow was common throughout the winter months, and students had frequent opportunities to sled and ski. Winter weather was never an excuse for canceling classes at ASTC, however, and all sledding was done after hours.

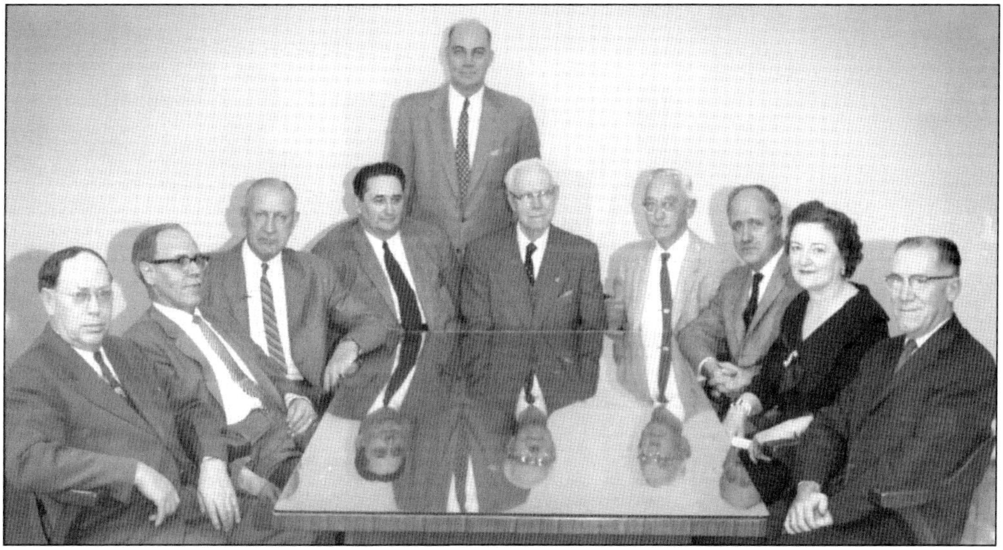

A group of ASTC faculty and administrators are seen here in 1960. From left to right are V.C. Howell, history department; Herman Eggers, registrar; G.L. Sawyer, social studies department; David Barnard Dougherty, vice president; William Howard Plemmons, president; James D. Rankin, professor emeritus of English and former interim president; J.T.C. Wright, mathematics and physics department; Graydon Eggers, English department; Virginia Linney, music department; and William Leonard Eury, librarian.

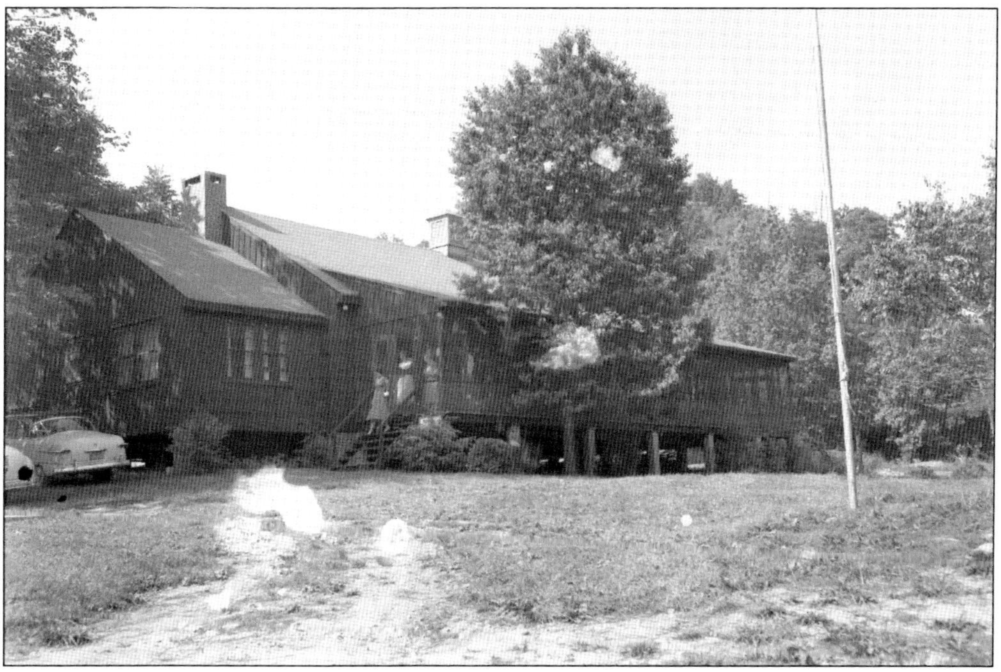

Camp Broadstone, seen here in 1961, is located in Valle Crucis and began as an athletic camp for boys. Founded and managed by Bob Breitenstein, the camp opened in 1956. Breitenstein was dean of men at Appalachian, and he served as both an assistant coach (1960–1963) and head coach (1969) of the football team. Purchased by the university in 1961, the camp continues to offer summer camps and year-round programs for elementary and high school students.

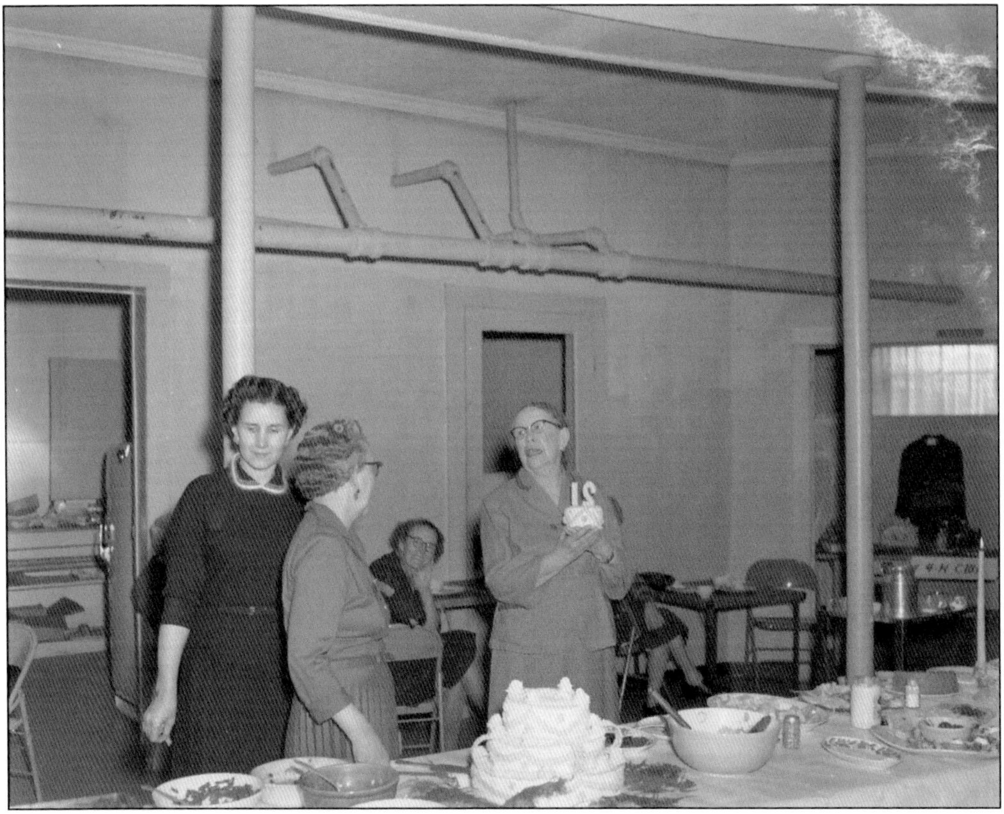

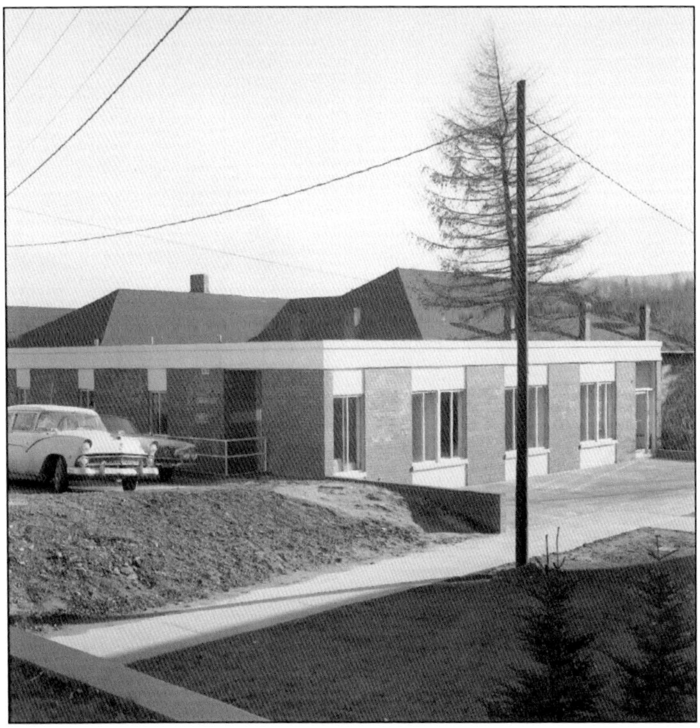

Above, former chairman of the home economics department Lucy Brock (right) is seen with friends at her retirement party in 1961. Brock began teaching at Appalachian State in 1938 and taught home economics for 21 years. The Lucy Brock Child Development Laboratory is named in her honor. It provides care for children up to five years old and serves as a model program to train individuals in pre-kindergarten child care. It is now managed by the Reich College of Education. The old Lucy Brock Nursery School building (left) was constructed in 1965.

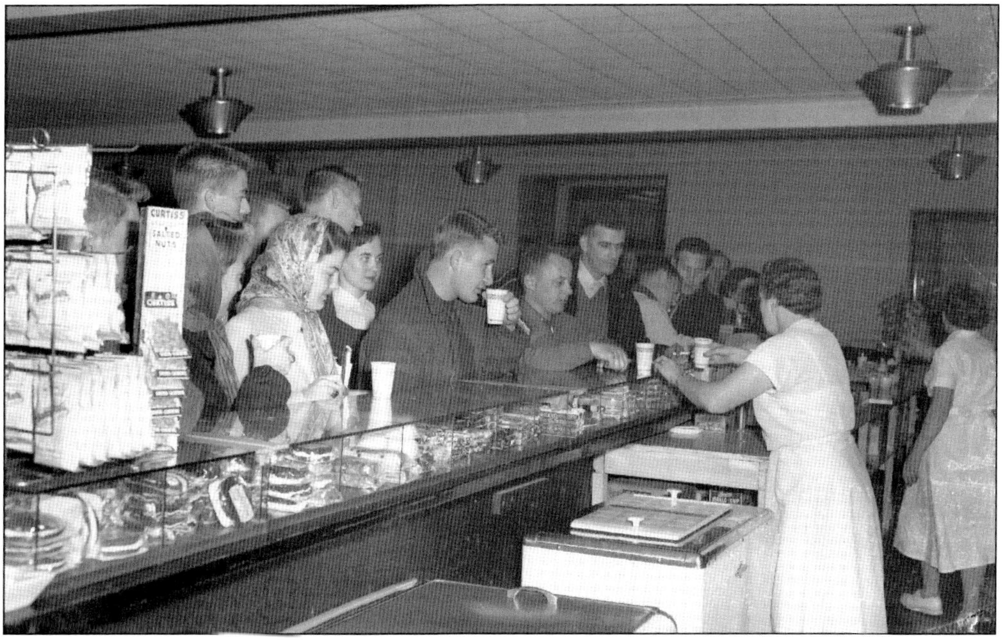

The first soda fountain and snack bar, located in the bookstore beginning in 1955, was a popular hangout spot. The first campus bookstore was located in the second administration building. A new bookstore was built in 1934 at the corner of Locust Street and College Avenue, approximately where the current bookstore is located. Torn down in 1967, the building gave way to a third bookstore, which opened in 1969 and has undergone a number of renovations, with the most recent in 2004. In the photograph above, students line up at the counter of the snack bar in 1958. Below, students are served at a table.

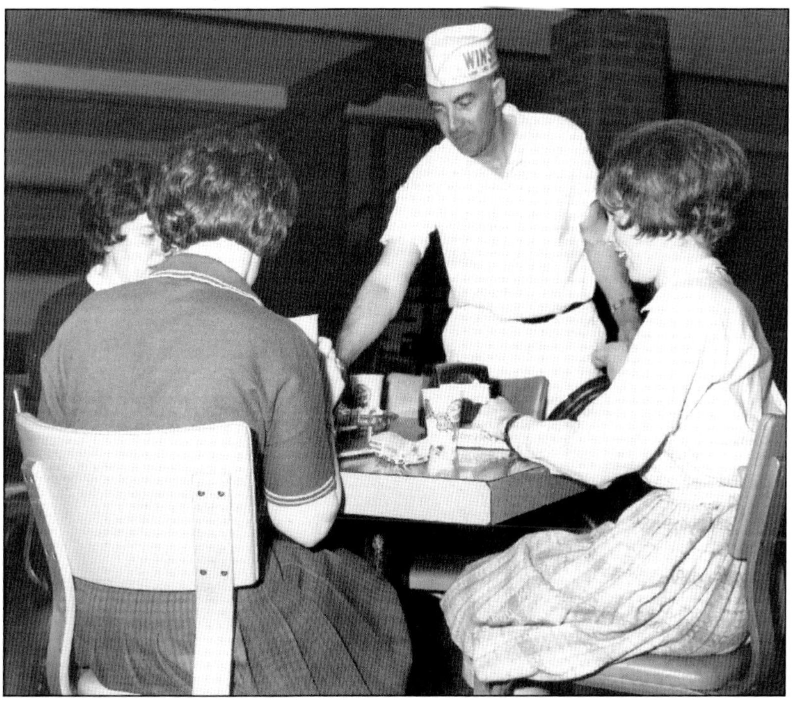

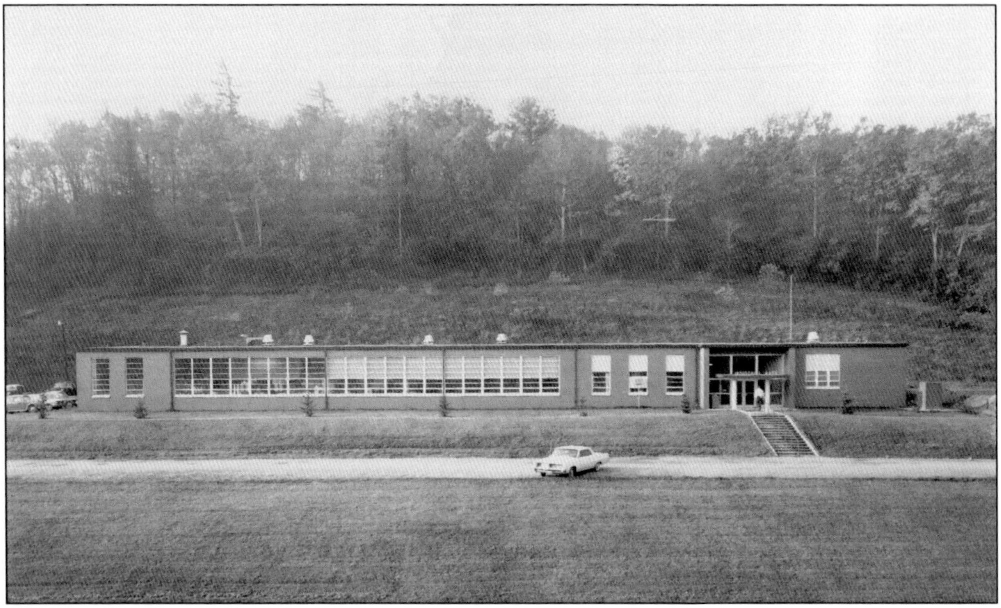

The Kerr Scott Building was completed in 1961 to house the Department of Industrial Arts and Technical Education. Kerr Scott was the governor of North Carolina from 1948 to 1953 and a US senator from 1954 to 1958. A portion of the building was rededicated as Katherine Harper Hall in 2007 in honor of Katherine Harper, the cofounder of Harper Corporation of America.

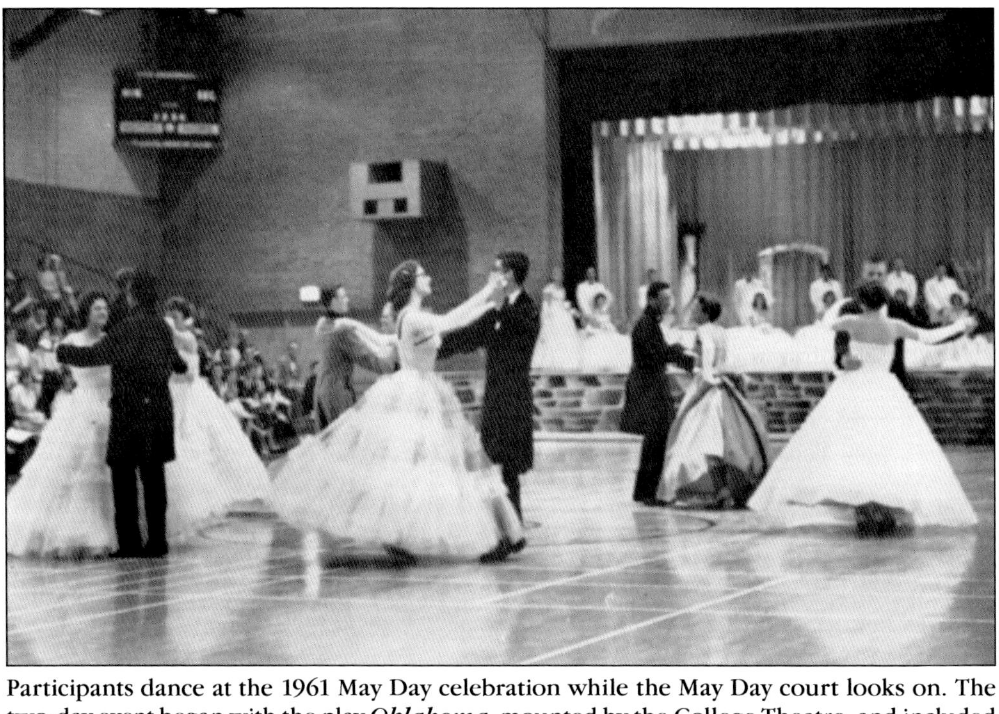

Participants dance at the 1961 May Day celebration while the May Day court looks on. The two-day event began with the play *Oklahoma*, mounted by the College Theatre, and included movies, a mixer, a concert, and a tea for the May Day court and their families. The First May Day Festival was sponsored by the YWCA in 1930.

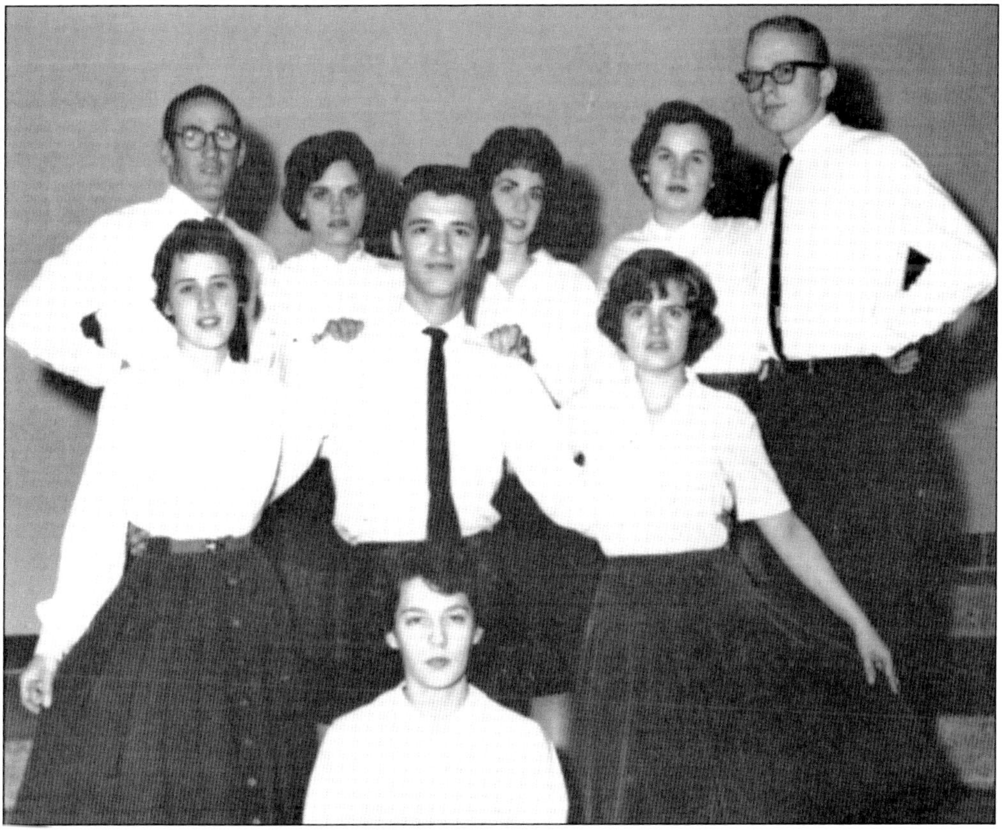

Members of the Varsouvianna Club pose for a photograph in 1962. Varsouvianna was a folk-dance group sponsored by the Department of Health, Physical Education, and Recreation, which offered both modern and folk dancing courses. The group performed dances all over western North Carolina and promoted dance education.

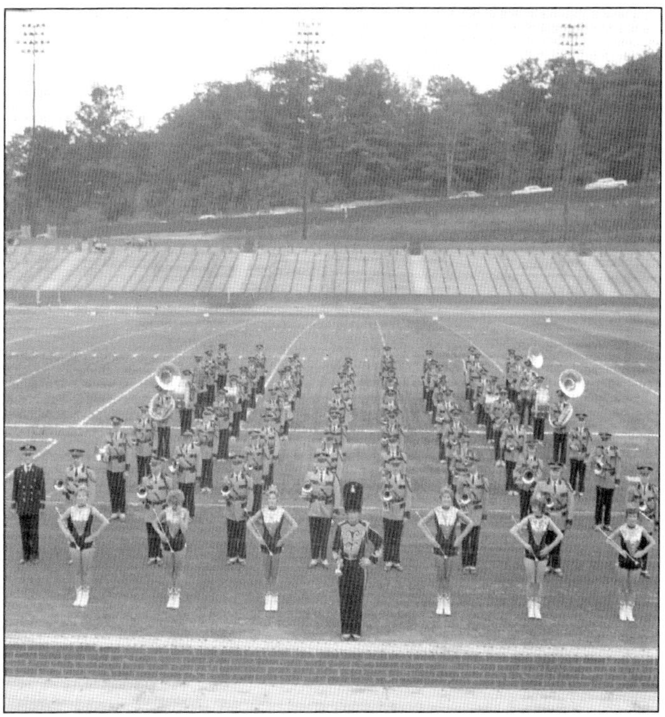

The ASTC marching band performs at Conrad Stadium in September 1962. Formed in 1939 by music professor Gordon Nash, the band was managed by the music department and performed for sporting and other events.

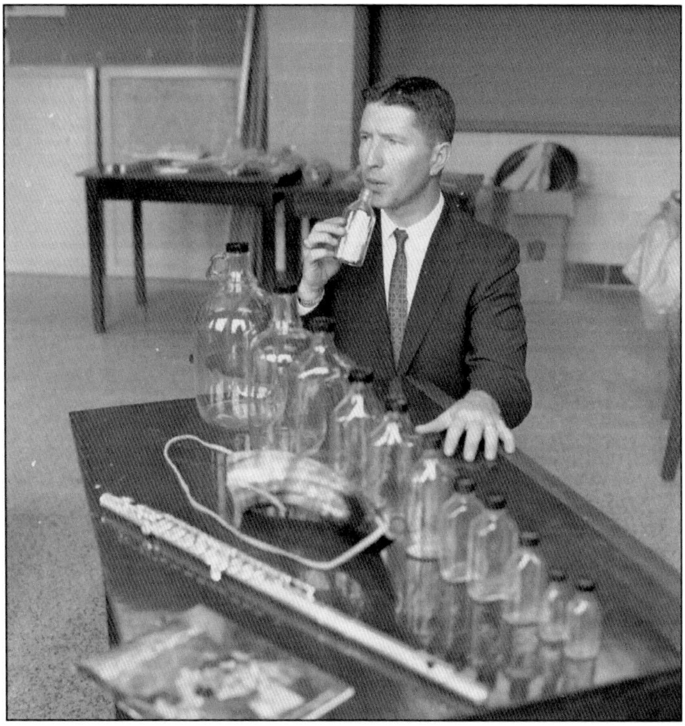

William Spencer, a professor and the chairman of the Department of Music Education, demonstrates to his music class the variety of sounds that can be produced from glass bottles. Spencer began teaching at Appalachian State in 1951, served as department chairman from 1958 to 1971, and retired in 1986.

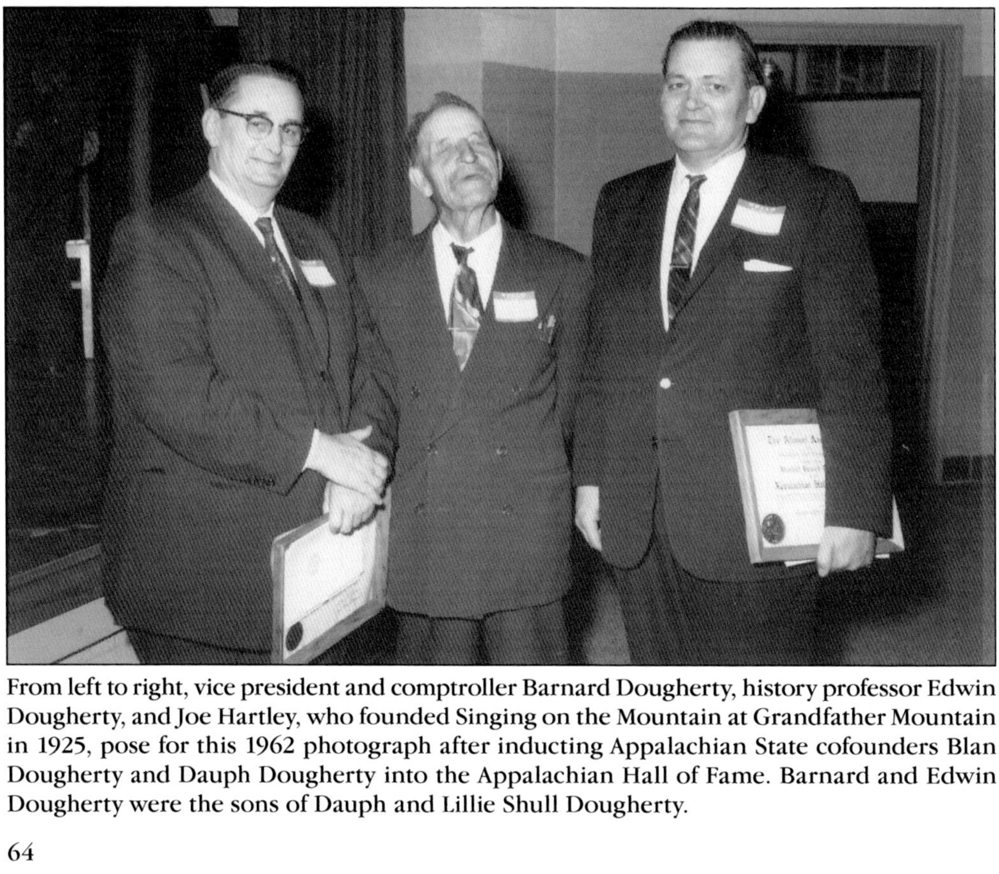

From left to right, vice president and comptroller Barnard Dougherty, history professor Edwin Dougherty, and Joe Hartley, who founded Singing on the Mountain at Grandfather Mountain in 1925, pose for this 1962 photograph after inducting Appalachian State cofounders Blan Dougherty and Dauph Dougherty into the Appalachian Hall of Fame. Barnard and Edwin Dougherty were the sons of Dauph and Lillie Shull Dougherty.

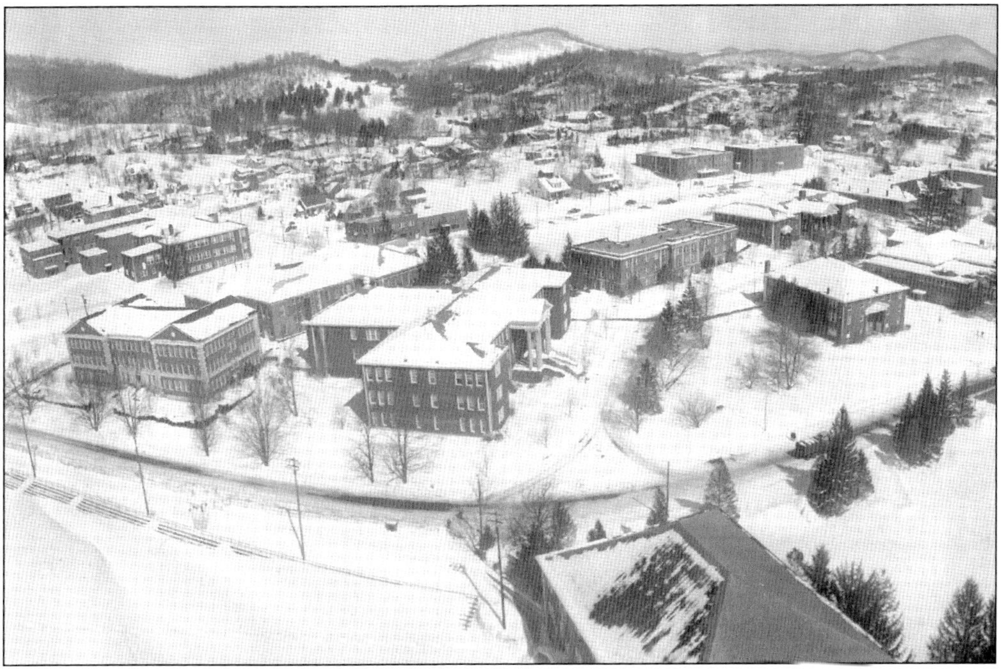

This winter image shows the roof of the men's gymnasium in the center foreground. Across Rivers Street, from left to right, are Smith-Wright Hall, the administration building, the women's gymnasium, and Welborn Hall. In the background, also from left to right, are Whitener Hall, the education building, D.D. Dougherty Library, Watauga (Dauph-Blan) Hall, White Hall, the Lovill Home, North (Workman) Hall, and Coffey Hall.

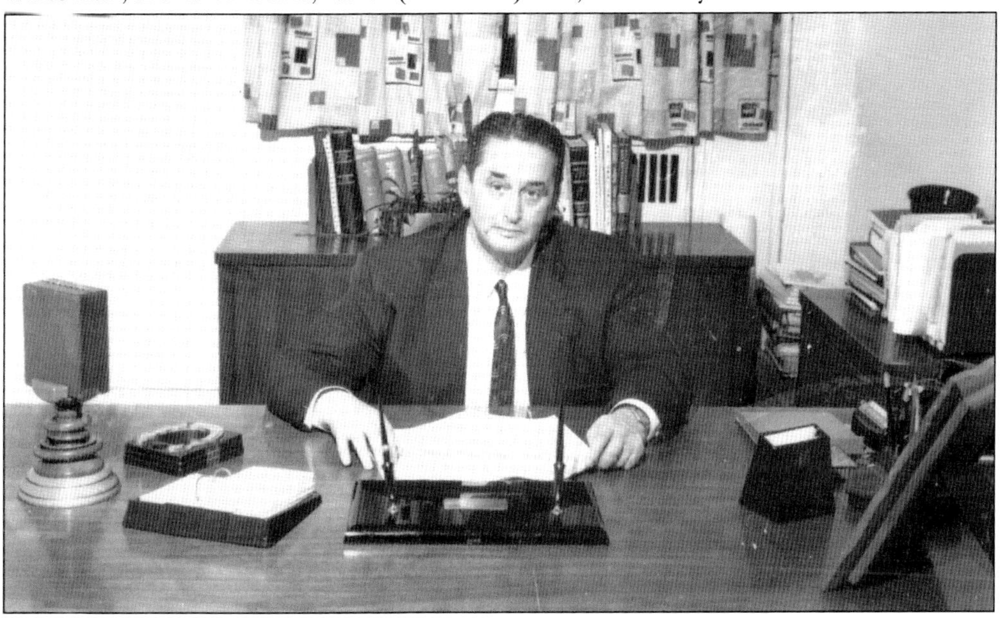

Barnard Dougherty was the oldest son of D.D. Dougherty and Lillie Shull Dougherty. He graduated from ASTC in 1932 but had already joined the staff in 1929, serving as assistant business manager. He rose to become business manager in 1938, taking over from his mother at her retirement, and then to vice president and comptroller in 1955.

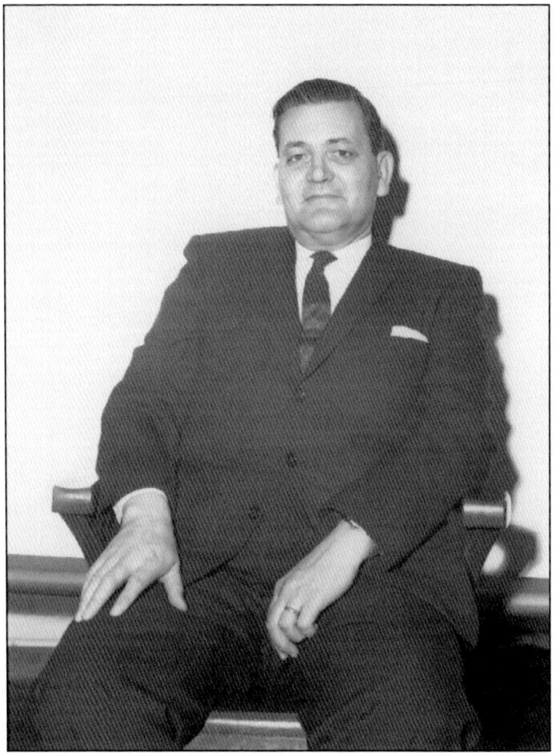

Like his brother Barnard, Edwin Shull Dougherty (left) was an ASTC undergraduate, earning a bachelor's of science in social studies in 1934 before moving on to Peabody College for his master's degree. He began teaching history at Appalachian in 1939 and retired in 1974.

Librarian Allie A. Hodgin serves patrons in the D.D. Dougherty Memorial Library, built in 1935. Hodgin served as reference librarian from 1934 to 1974. The library was previously located in Watauga Academy and then in the first and second administration buildings. It moved to the first Belk Library in 1968 and to the new Belk Library in 2005.

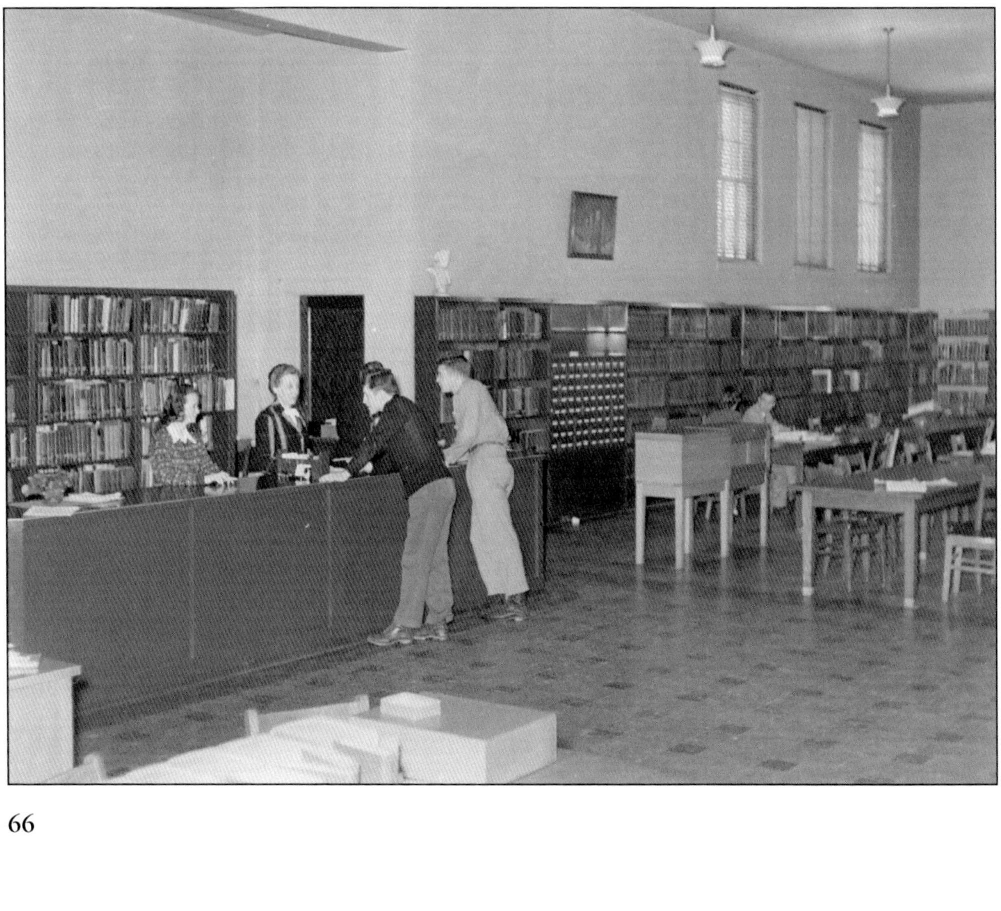

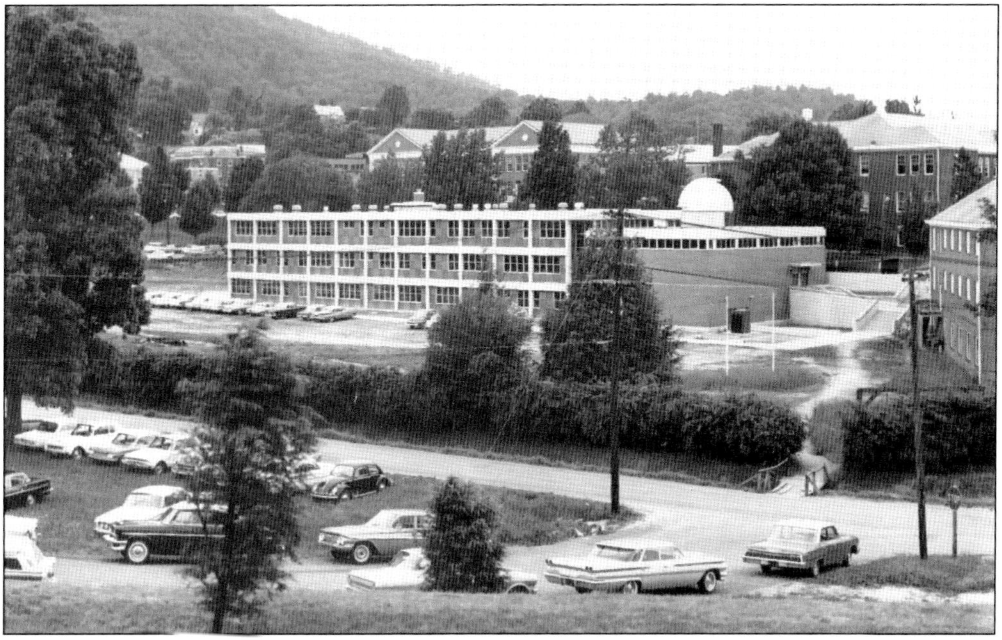

Rankin Hall (above) was built in 1963 as a state-of-the-art education facility for science studies. It housed the school's first Dark Sky Observatory. The building fronts Rivers Street and is between Edwin Duncan Hall and Varsity Gymnasium. It was named after James Daniel "J.D." Rankin (below), an English professor at Appalachian from 1921 to 1929 and the dean of the school from 1929 until 1955. After B.B. Dougherty's retirement in June 1955, Rankin served as interim president until a permanent replacement was named that September. He retired in 1955, becoming the dean emeritus.

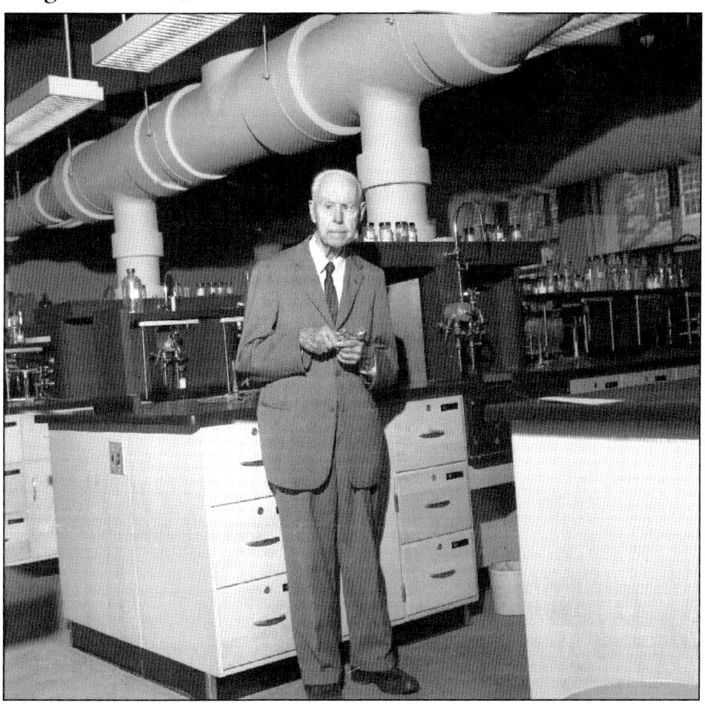

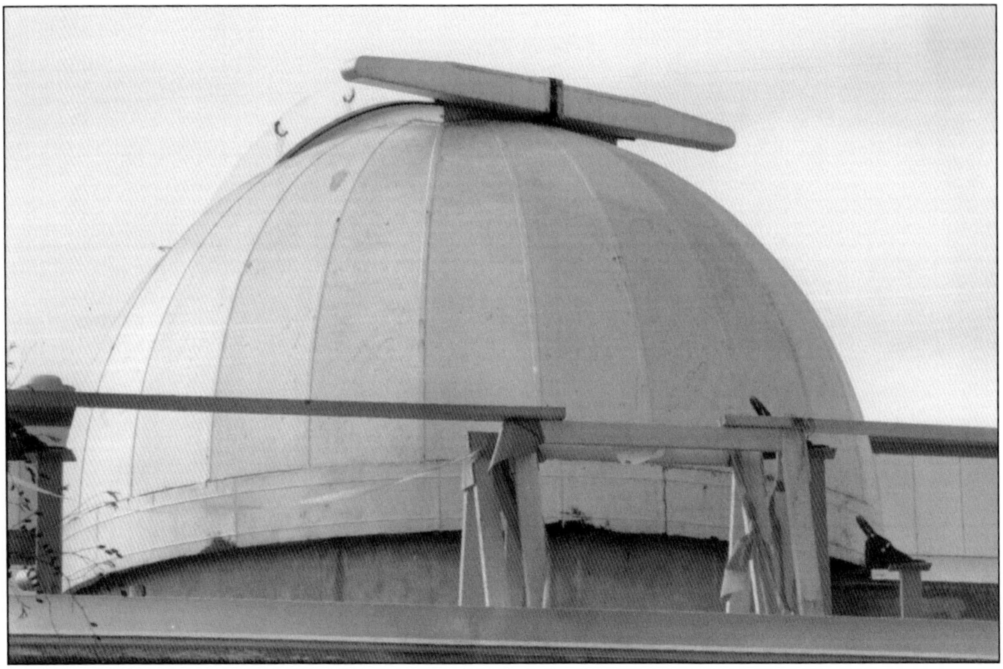

The original Dark Sky Observatory (above) was located on top of Rankin Science Hall, which was built in 1963. In 1981, a new observatory was built roughly 20 miles northeast of campus. It is managed by the Department of Physics and Astronomy and serves as a research facility for faculty and students. The observatory currently has four telescopes used for digital imaging and spectroscopy.

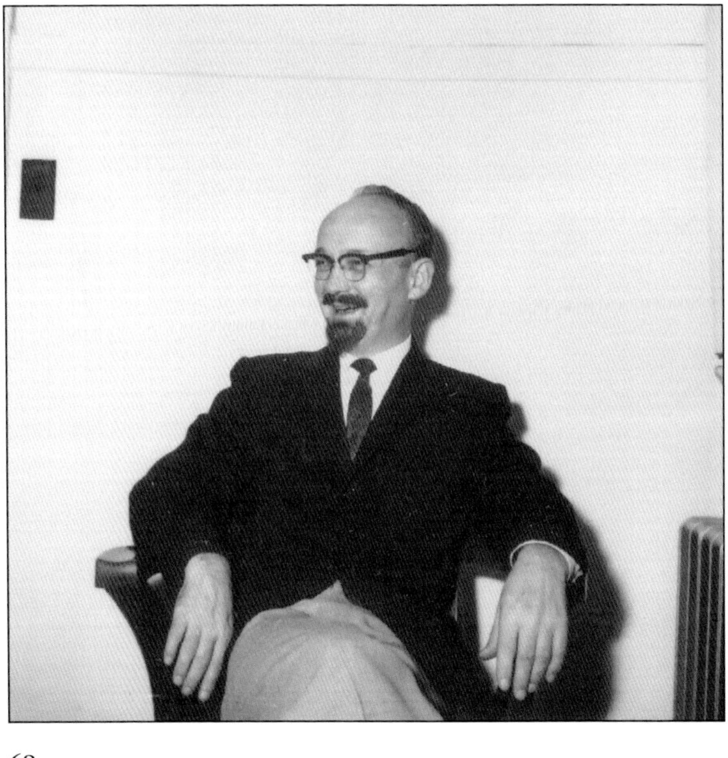

Cratis Williams sits in his office in October 1962. Williams, who began teaching English at Appalachian in 1942, served as dean of the graduate school from 1956 to 1975, acting chancellor for academic affairs in 1974, assistant chancellor from 1976 to 1979, and interim chancellor after Herbert Wey's retirement in 1979. He was a renowned ballad collector and performer and was instrumental in the development of the field of Appalachian studies.

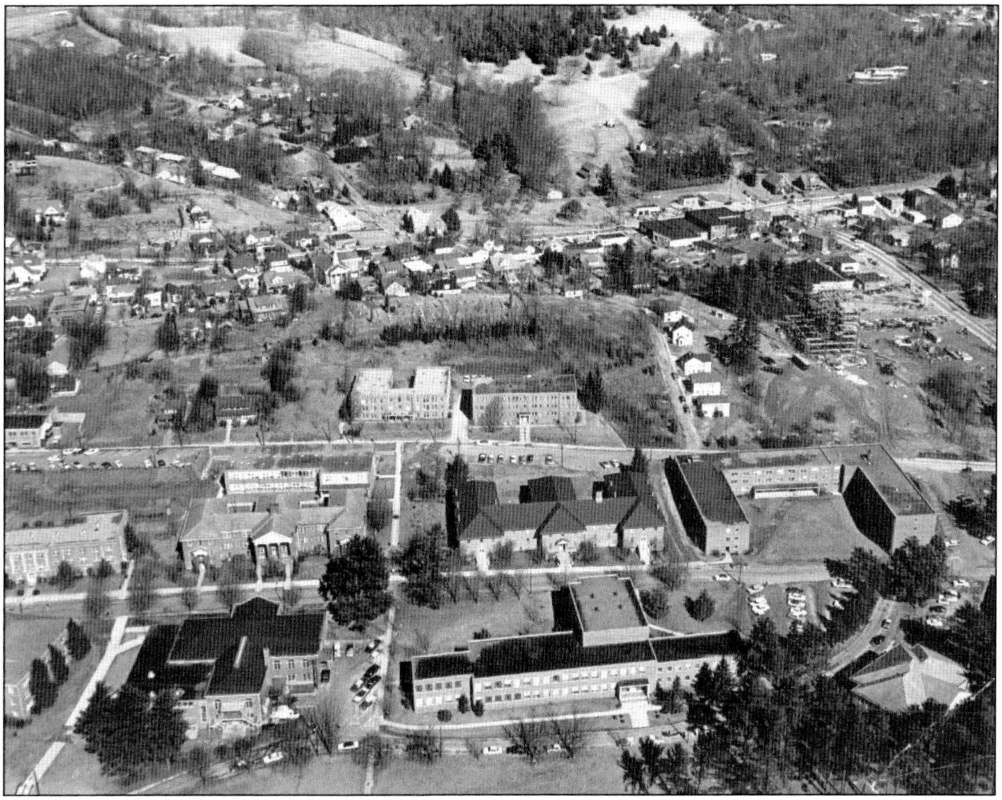

Visible in the foreground of this 1960s aerial view of campus are, from left to right, a section of the women's gymnasium, Welborn Cafeteria, and I.G. Greer Hall. The Promenade runs between these buildings and (in the middle distance, from left to right) Dauph-Blan Hall, White Hall, the Lovill Home, and East Hall, with Locust Street running behind. Beyond Locust Street stands North Hall (the U-shaped building at center) and the faculty apartments building, with the row of white faculty houses farther to the right. King Street can be seen in the background.

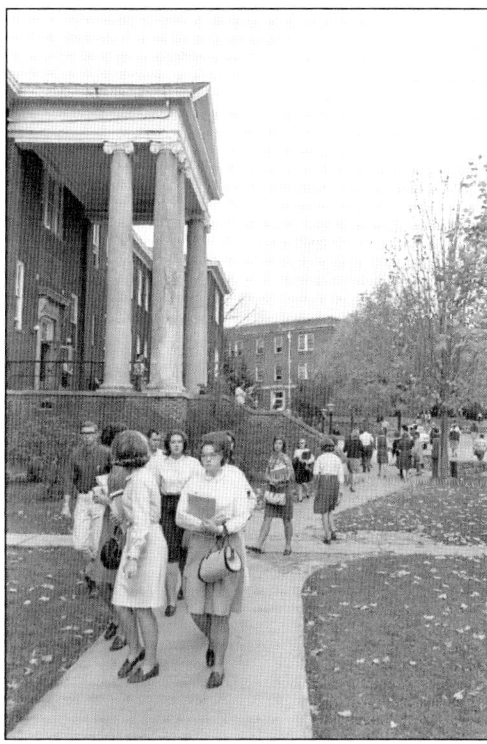

Coeds go to class in this early-1960s photograph. The second administration building is on the left, with Dauph-Blan Hall in the background. The Promenade is to the right. In 1963, a new demerit system, primarily for disciplining freshman, was adopted for female students. According to the administration, the system would foster self-discipline and make the work of house councils easier.

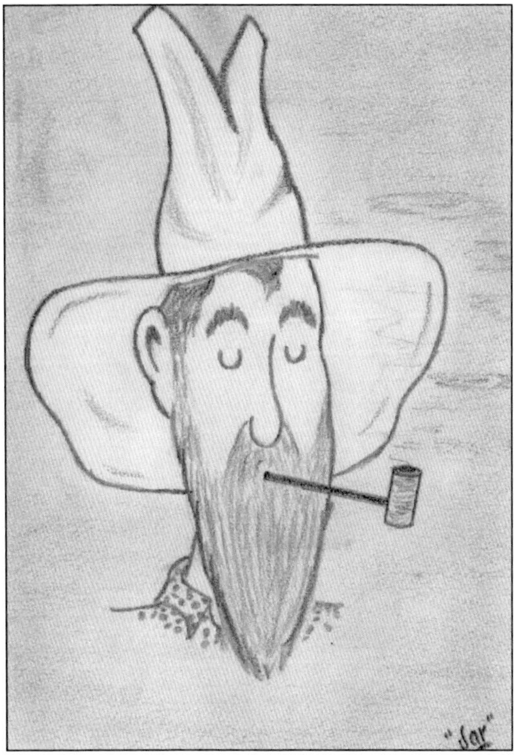

The Mountaineer has long been Appalachian's mascot. Legend has it that the name Yosef was created in 1942, when the yearbook was short one photograph for the freshman class. To even things out, yearbook staff members obtained a mountaineer caricature for the empty spot and named him Yosef, which is a shortened form of "your self." A similar sketch (left) was also on the cover of the 1942 *Rhododendron*. Yosef's appearance has undergone several changes through the years. In the photograph below, a mid-century Yosef poses at the 1965 homecoming game.

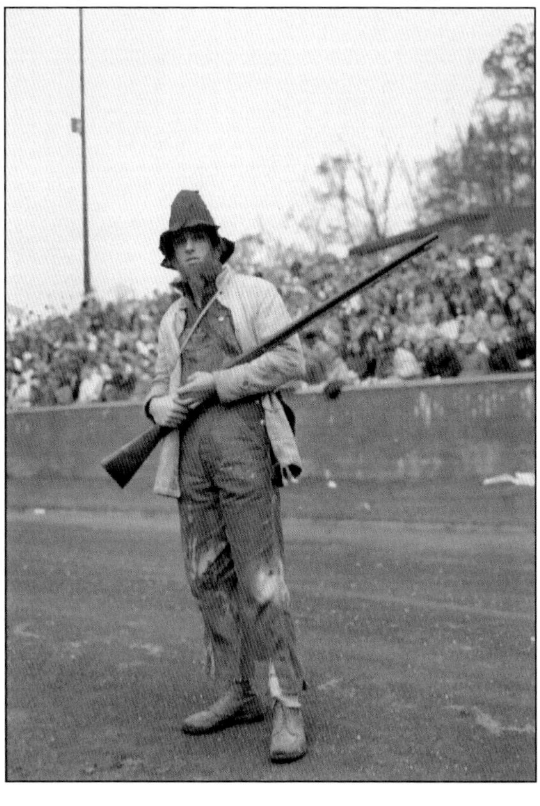

Edwin Duncan Hall, completed in 1965, housed the Department of Education, as well as other departments, at different times. The building was named for Edwin Duncan, a business and financial leader and president of Northwestern Bank. In 2011, the Reich College of Education moved from Edwin Duncan Hall to the newly constructed education building on King Street.

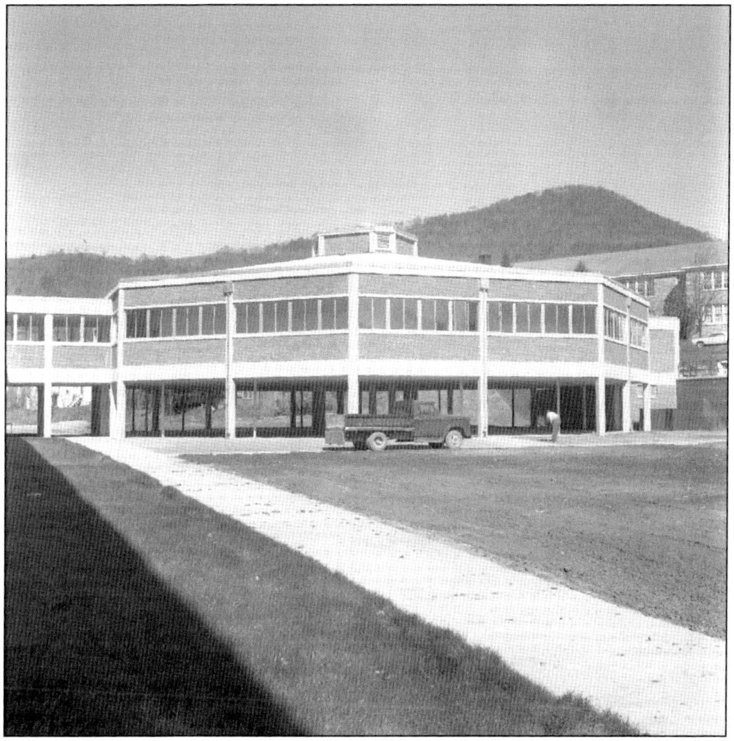

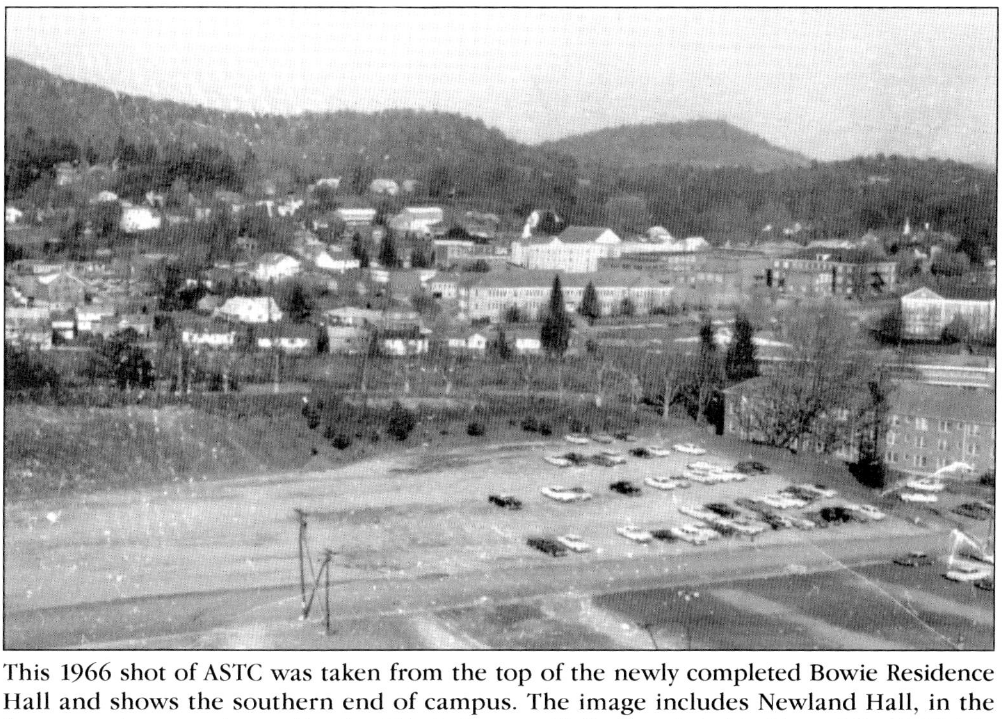

This 1966 shot of ASTC was taken from the top of the newly completed Bowie Residence Hall and shows the southern end of campus. The image includes Newland Hall, in the foreground next to the parking lot; Edwin Duncan Hall, directly behind it; and Smith-Wright Hall, across from Edwin Duncan on the right. Chapell Wilson Hall is to the left behind the row of houses.

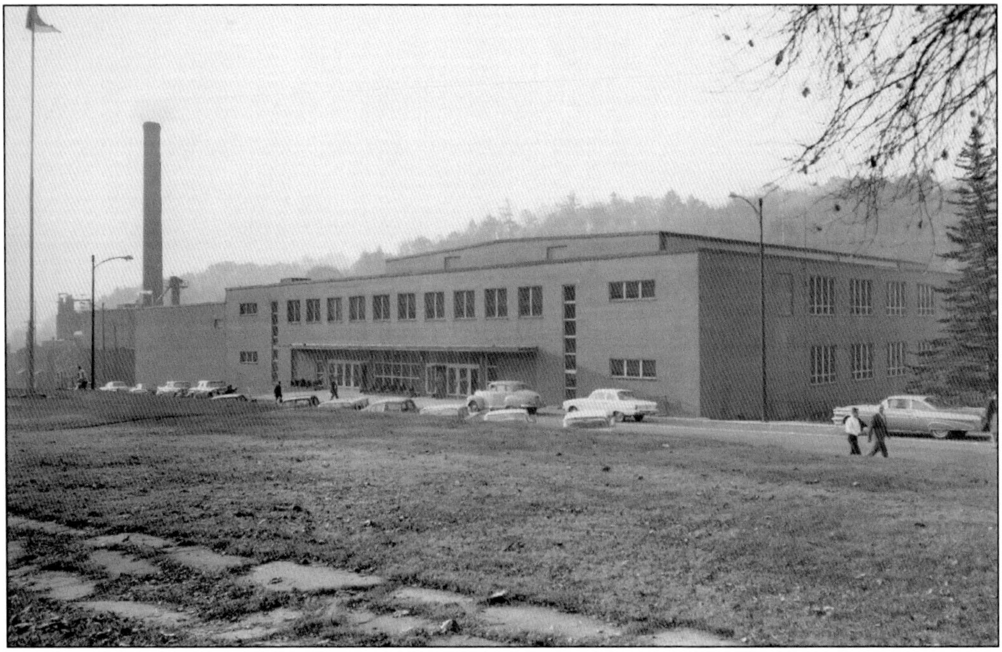

Broome-Kirk Gymnasium was completed in 1955 and named in honor of coaches Robert Broome and John Kirk. Coach Broome was a 1940 graduate of Appalachian State Teachers College, an assistant professor in health and physical education, and head football coach from 1947 to 1956. Coach Kirk was also an Appalachian alumnus, graduating in 1948 with a bachelor's degree and receiving a master's in 1950. He was an assistant professor in social studies and an assistant football coach.

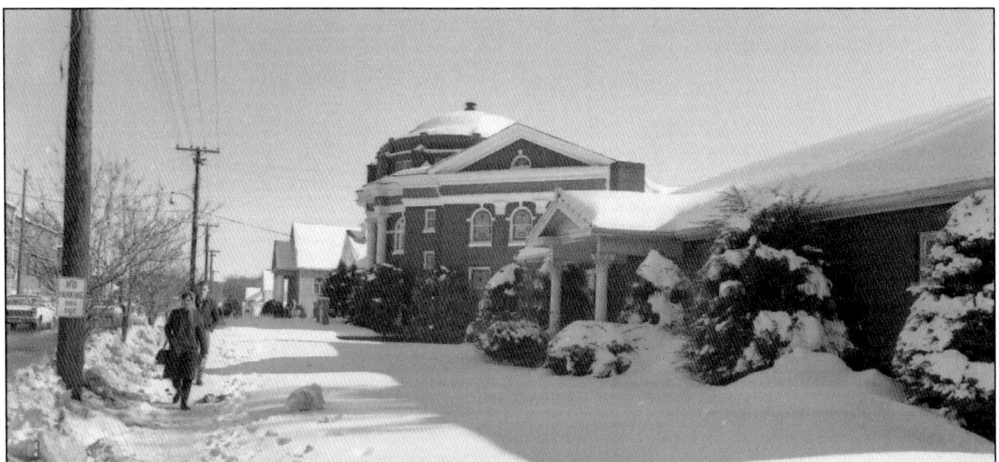

This wintery view of King Street (left) was taken in the 1960s. In the center is Boone Methodist Church, now the Turchin Center for the Visual Arts. This structure was damaged by fire in the early 1980s and then rebuilt. The First Baptist Church is just visible to the left of the Methodist church. College Street is located on the far side of the Baptist church.

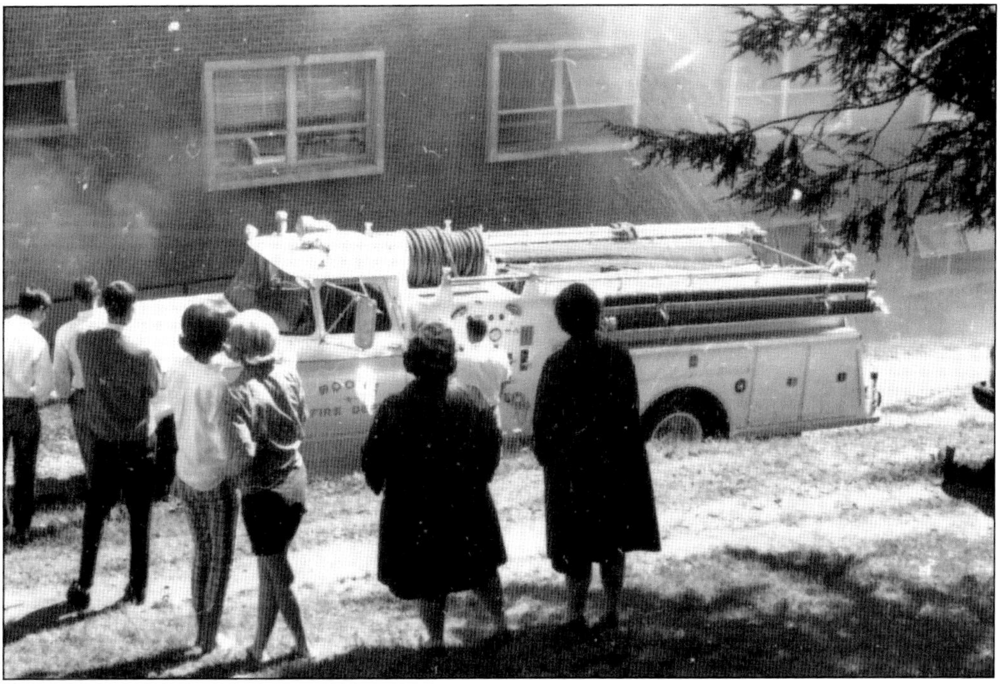

East Residence Hall is one of the older buildings on the Appalachian campus. Built in 1952, the building first served as a women's dormitory that held 204 residents. An additional wing was added in 1959, and the building is now a part of the Pinnacle Residence Hall community and houses the honors program offices. This 1966 fire in East Hall started in the sanitary engineer's department and was confined to the main entrance of the building.

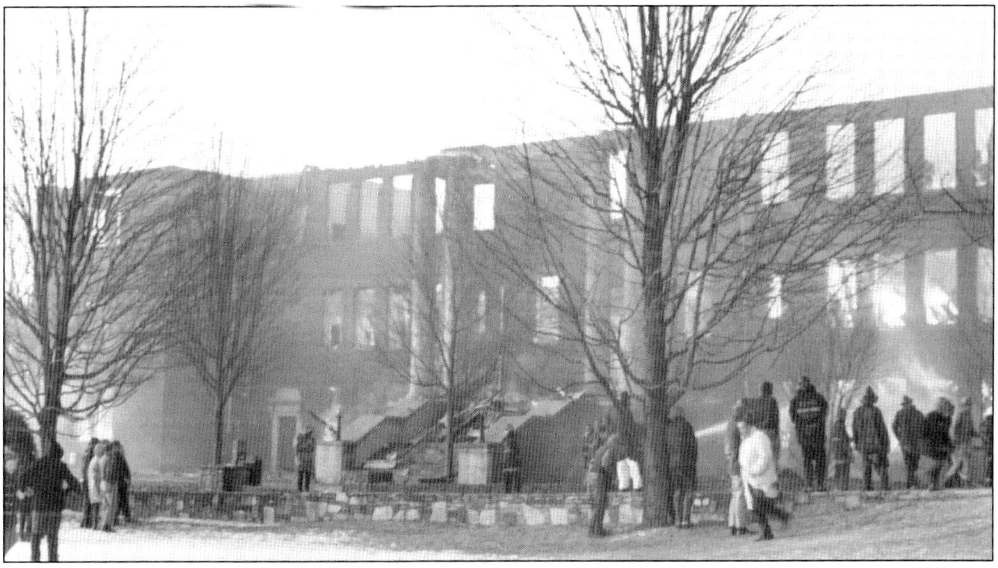

Firefighters battle the blaze that destroyed the second administration building on December 29, 1966. At the time of the fire, the building housed administrative offices and the academic offices of the English and foreign languages departments, as well as the offices of *The Appalachian* newspaper and the *Rhododendron* yearbook. Many of the school's records were lost. After the fire, offices were temporarily relocated to White Hall.

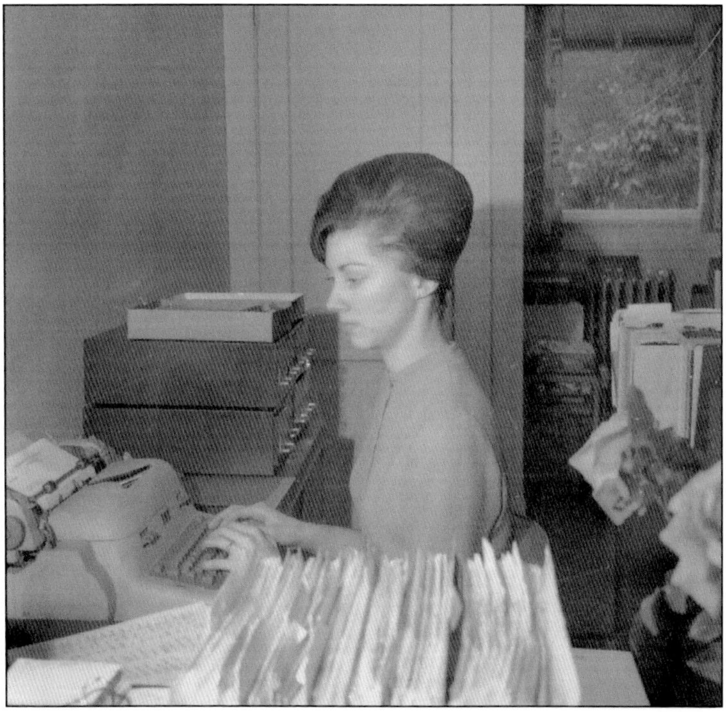

Carolyn Taylor Heavner is hard at work in President Plemmons's office in March 1966. Heavner was a staff member at Appalachian State Teachers College for 34 years. She was an administrative staff member and then the assistant to president William H. Plemmons and chancellors Herbert Wey, John E. Thomas, and Francis T. Borkowski.

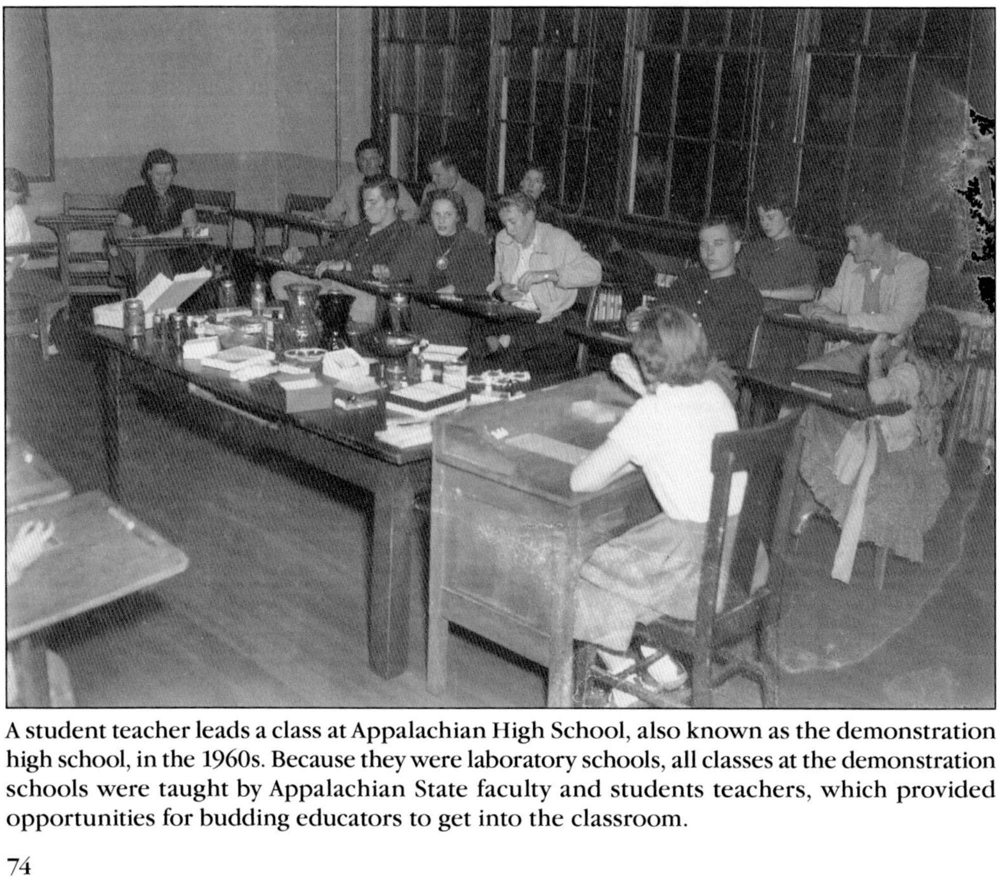

A student teacher leads a class at Appalachian High School, also known as the demonstration high school, in the 1960s. Because they were laboratory schools, all classes at the demonstration schools were taught by Appalachian State faculty and students teachers, which provided opportunities for budding educators to get into the classroom.

Dr. Julian Yoder stands in front of a map of North America. A 1933 graduate of Appalachian in math and science, Dr. Yoder taught physical, economic, historical, and political geography, as well as American history, for 41 years. He retired from the university in 1974, having served as the chairman of two departments. Dr. Yoder was professor emeritus of geography until his death in 2006.

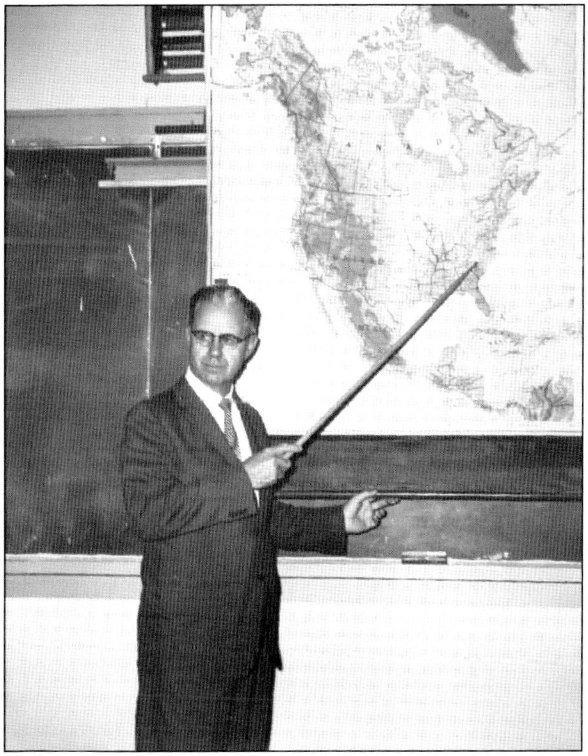

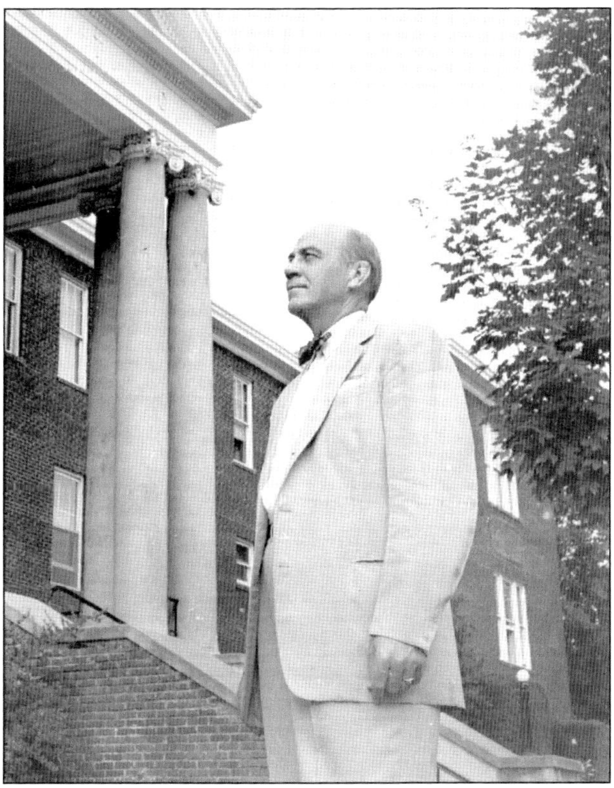

Appalachian State president William Howard Plemmons stands in front of the entrance of the second administration building. Plemmons was president of ASTC and ASU from 1955 to 1969. Under his administration, many outdated campus buildings were replaced with more modern facilities, including Varsity Gymnasium, the B.B. Dougherty Administration Building, the old Belk Library, and many of the current dormitories.

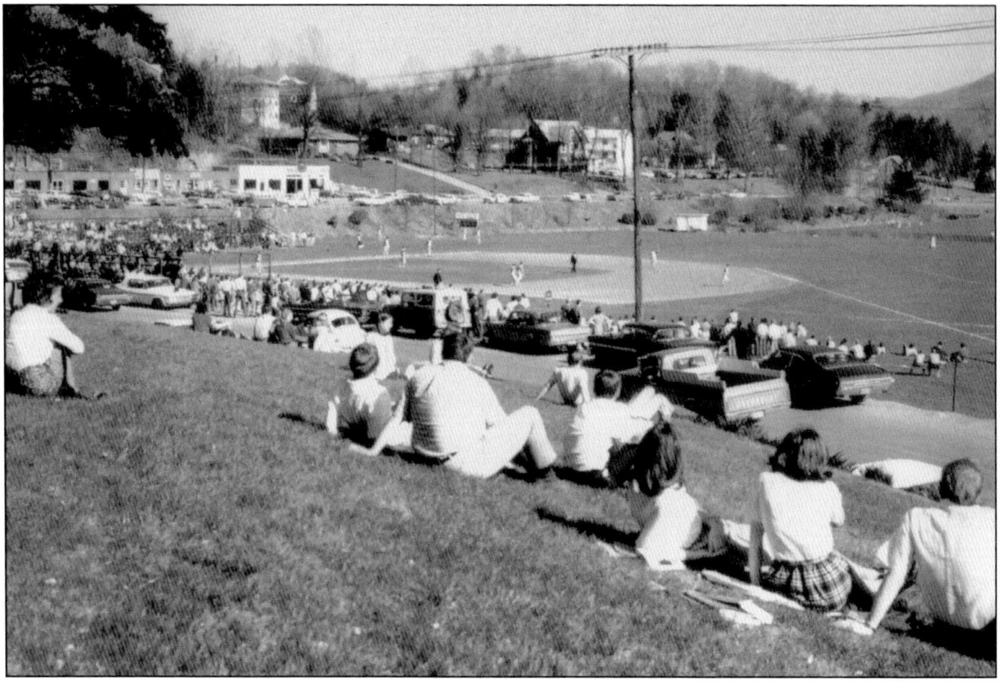

Above, students watch a baseball game at ASTC in 1965. Below, the soccer team practices on Lackey Field, with the B.B. Dougherty Administration Building in the background. The original baseball field was located southeast of campus at the current location of Durham Park, at the corner of Blowing Rock Road and Rivers Street, and was later moved west of the football stadium in the late 1990s. It was dedicated as Red Lackey Field in 1987 in honor of E.G. Lackey, who graduated from Appalachian in 1937 and served on the board of trustees for 18 years. Beaver Field at the Jim and Bettie Smith Stadium now sits behind the former Broyhill Conference Center.

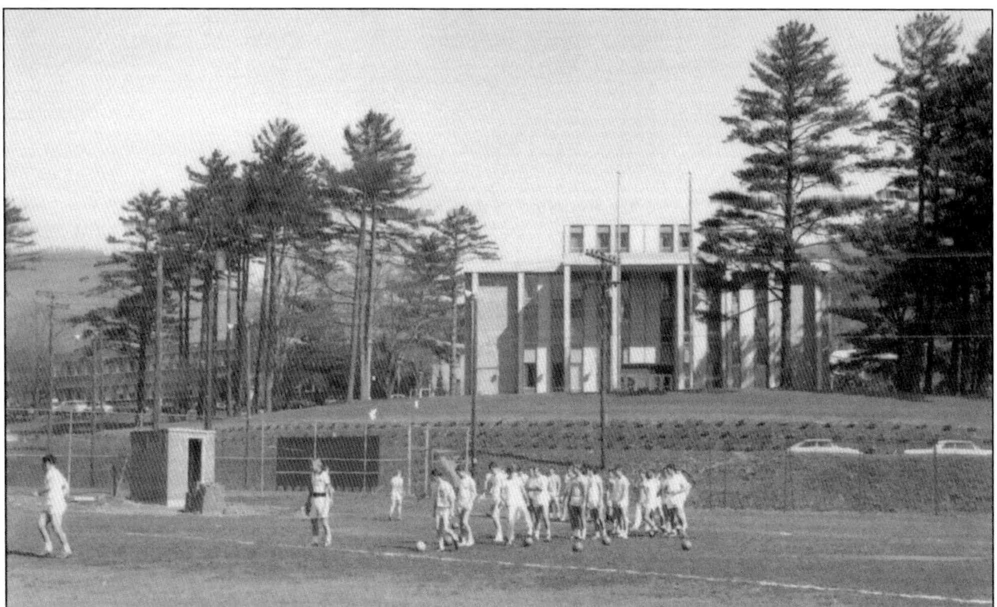

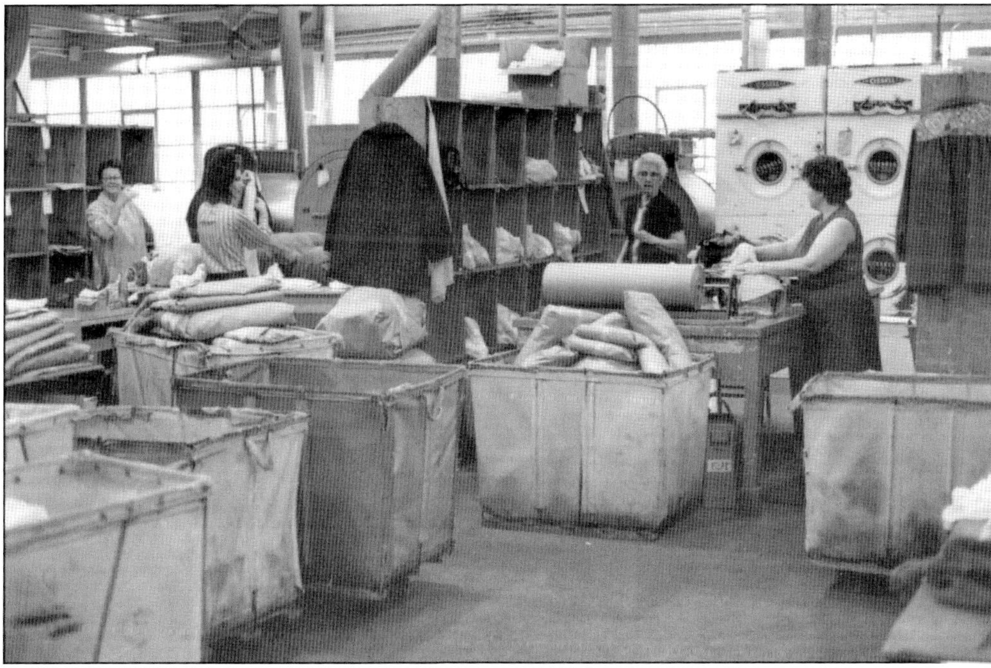

In the early years, Mondays were laundry days and no classes were held. Beginning in 1914, the Appalachian campus provided laundry services to students. Campus Laundry picked up bags of laundry left by students, who paid a fee each semester for the service. In 1949, the Student Services annex was built and housed the campus laundry. The campus ceased providing laundry services in the mid-1990s.

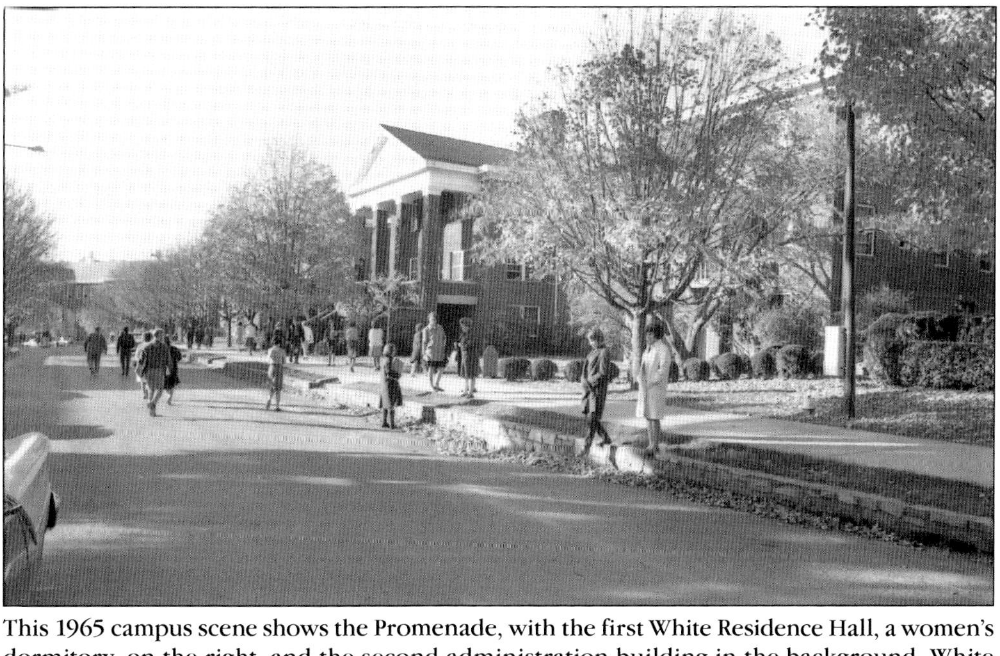

This 1965 campus scene shows the Promenade, with the first White Residence Hall, a women's dormitory, on the right, and the second administration building in the background. White Hall, along with the Lovill Home and Dauph-Blan Hall, was demolished to expand Sanford Mall, which was originally called Founders Mall.

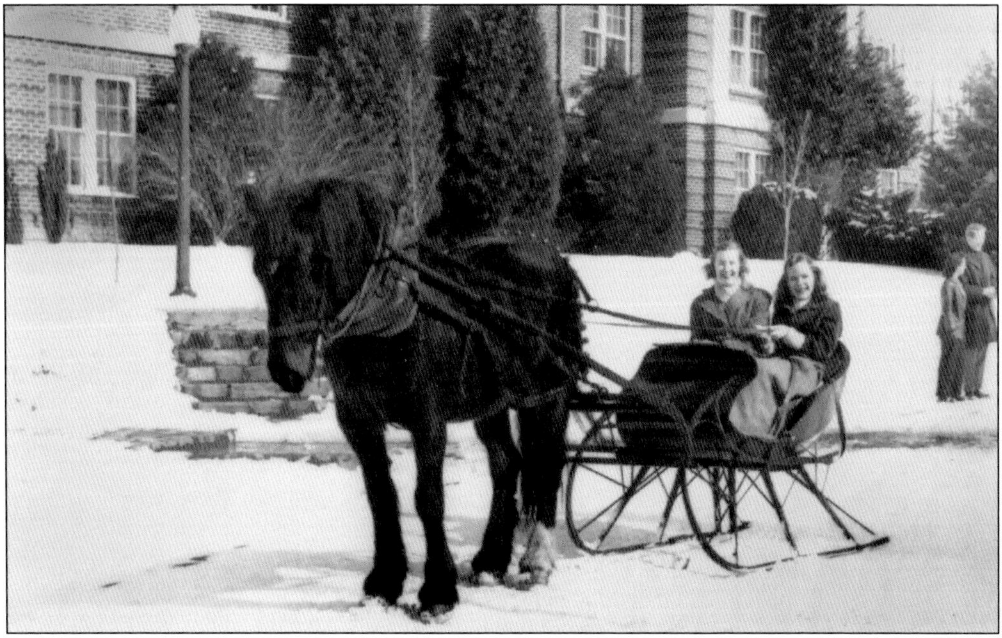

This 1960s photograph shows two students pausing during a sleigh ride to have their picture taken on the Promenade. They are stopped in front of Dauph-Blan Residence Hall, which was built in 1929 and served as a women's dormitory. Later named Watauga Hall, it was torn down in 1980.

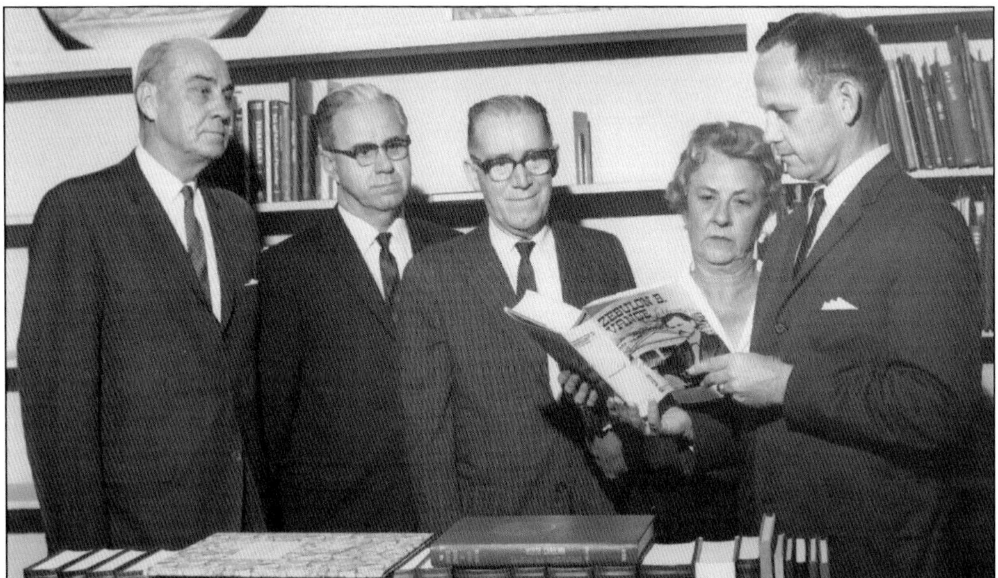

This group image shows, from left to right, William Howard Plemmons, president; Dr. Julian Yoder, Department of Social Studies chair; William L. Eury, library director; and Annie Whitener, wife of Daniel Jay Whitener, and her son Carr Choate (C.C.) Whitener. They are in the D.D. Dougherty Library looking at history books donated in honor of D.J. Whitener, a history and social studies professor at Appalachian beginning in 1932 and the dean of the College of Arts and Sciences from 1955 to 1964.

Professors Daisy (left) and Graydon Eggers (right) were a husband-and-wife team that taught in the English department at Appalachian. Graydon began teaching in 1927 and served as the departmental chair from 1947 to 1969; Daisy started in 1954 and taught until her retirement in 1982. She headed ASU's cooperative study program with Warren Wilson College for many years.

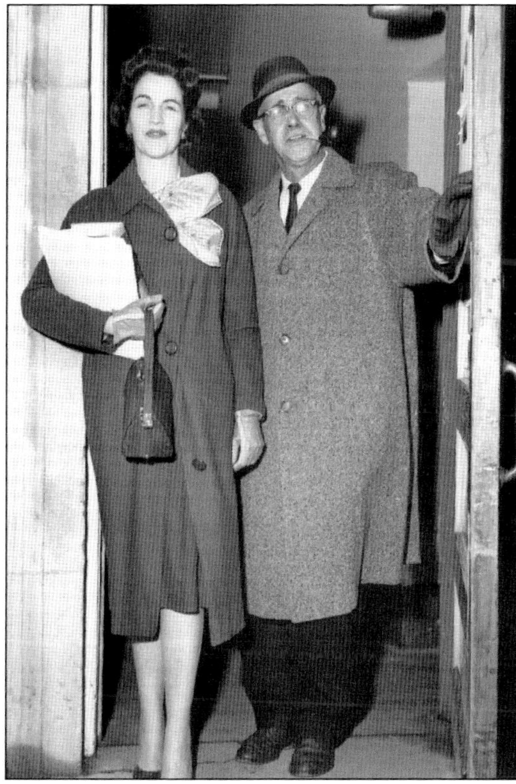

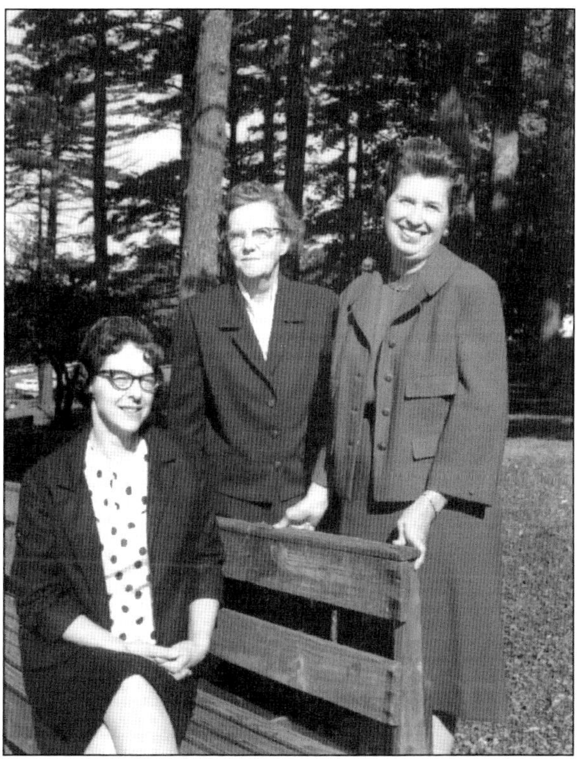

Maxi Edmisten (center) poses in this photograph with a Mrs. Church (left) and Helen Yoder, the wife of former Appalachian geography and history professor Dr. Julian Yoder. Edmisten received her bachelor's (1931) and master's (1954) degrees from Appalachian and served as the dean of women from 1956 to 1971.

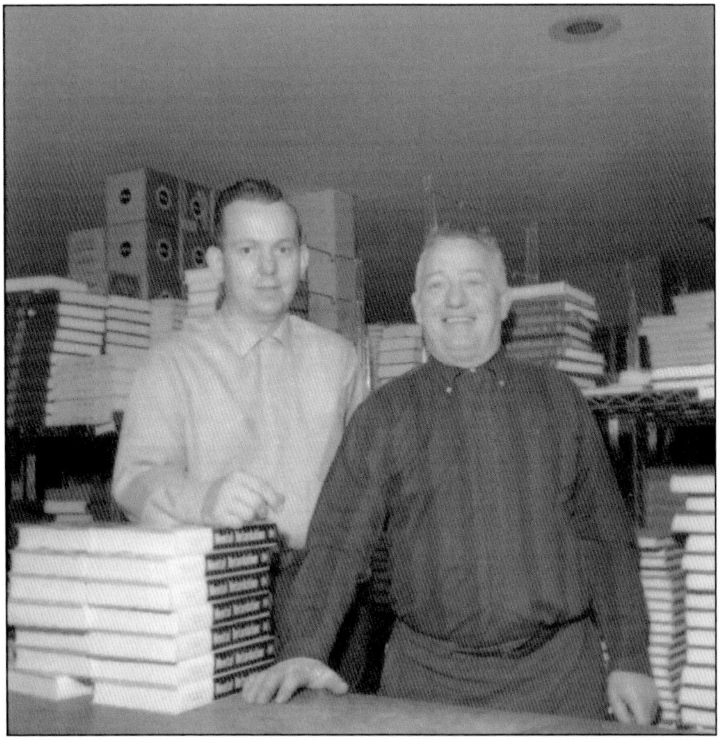

Howard J. "Twin" Cottrell (right) is surrounded by books at the college bookstore. Cottrell attended Appalachian as a student and began working at the school in 1939. He served as the college bookstore manager from 1942 until his retirement in 1971. His twin brother Raleigh worked as a campus security officer. Next to him is Wade Meadows, who was also a bookstore employee.

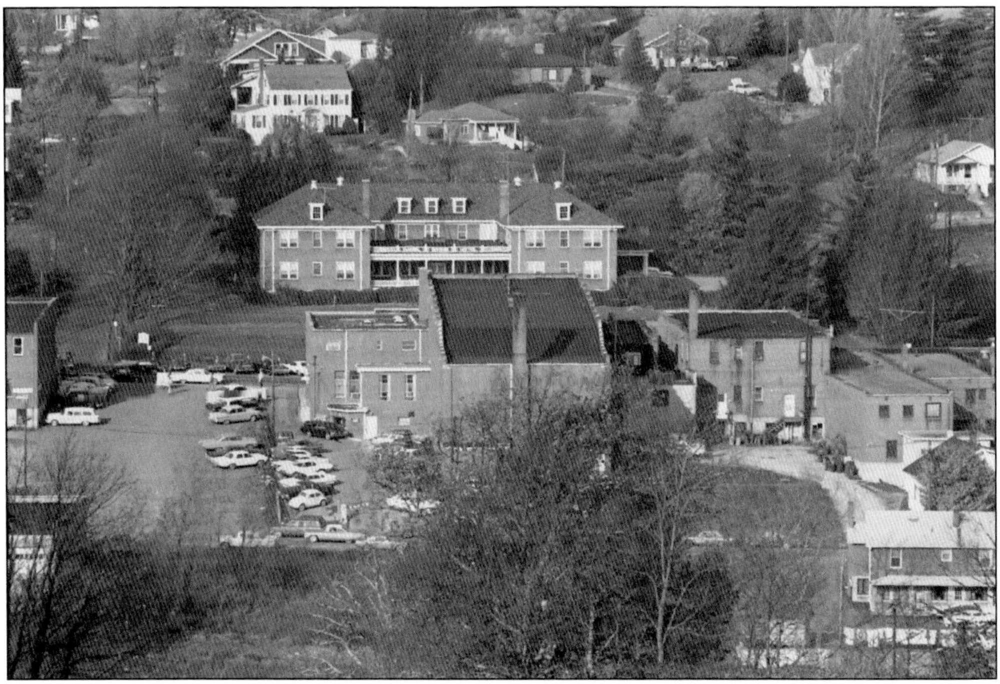

Taken from the roof of Bowie Residence Hall looking north to downtown Boone, this photograph shows the Daniel Boone Hotel, built in 1925. Located on King Street, the hotel, with symmetrical wings and five rooftop dormers, was torn down in 1982 despite being listed in the National Register of Historic Places.

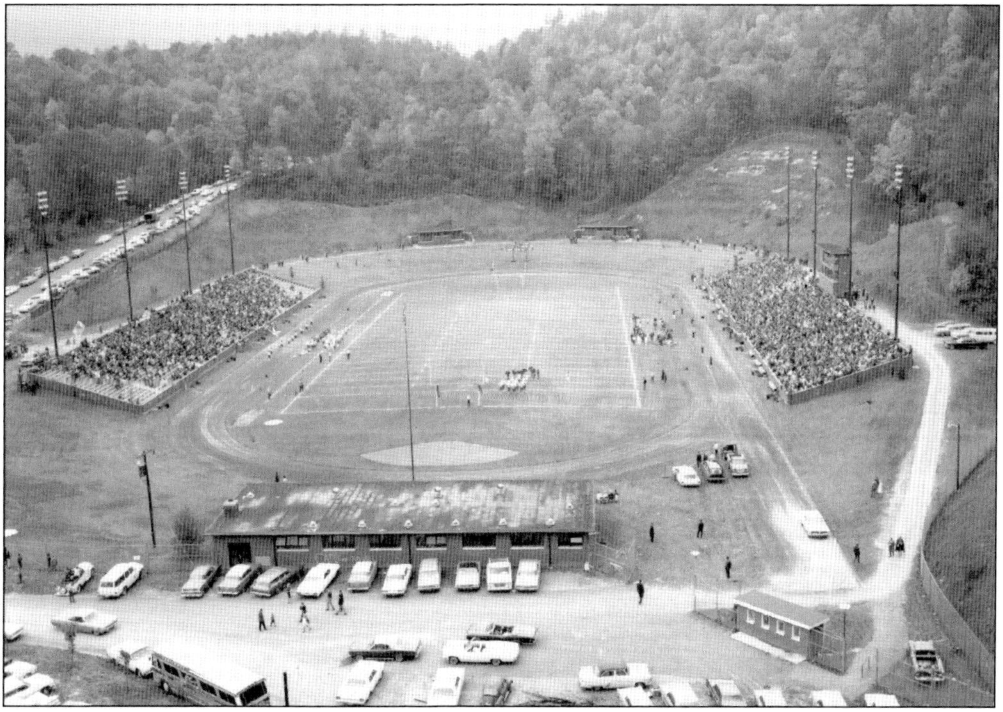

This photograph shows a 1967 ATSC football game against Catawba College, played at Conrad Stadium. Completed in 1962, the stadium replaced the old College Field and was dedicated to William J. Conrad, who became a member of the Appalachian State Teachers College board of trustees in 1941. The stadium was renovated in 1979 and renamed Kidd Brewer Stadium in 1988 to honor the former football coach.

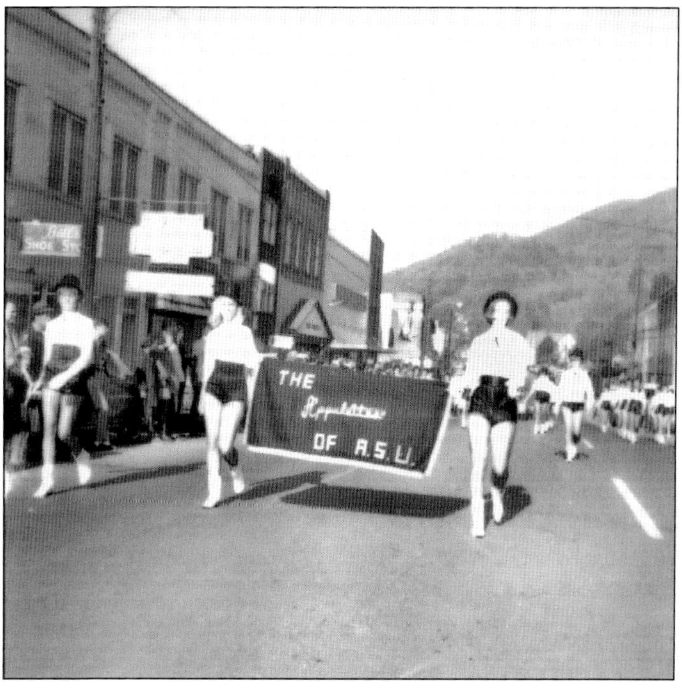

Formerly known as the Mountaineer Marching Team, the Appalettes were originally a drill team but eventually became a dance group. The group often performed off-campus at places like Tweetsie. They are marching down King Street in this 1967 homecoming parade photograph. Local businesses can be seen in the background, including Flowers' Photograph Shop. George Flowers was a photographer in Boone for 30 years.

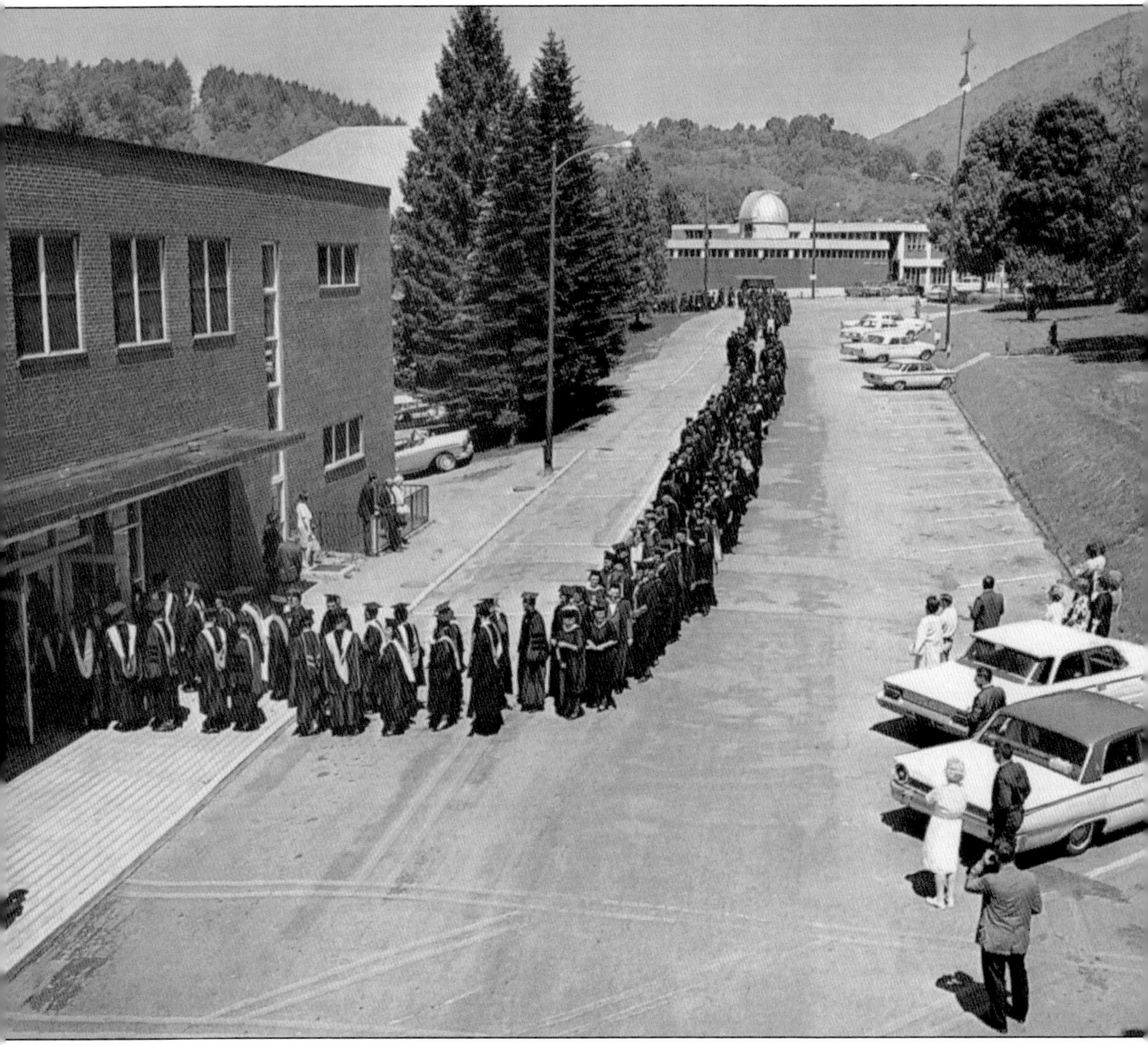

Graduates are lined up outside of Broome-Kirk Gymnasium for commencement in 1966. Approximately 545 seniors received degrees that year, and the class of 1916 attended as special guests to celebrate their 50th anniversary. A year later, ASTC became Appalachian State University.

Three

Appalachian State University

The greatest changes to Appalachian have come in the 47 years since the school became Appalachian State University. This last chapter highlights some of those changes. Technology has shaped the campus and curriculum in ways undreamed of by the school's founding fathers. With advancing computer technology, the Internet, and virtual-learning environments, the campus has brought the classroom to the students. Technology also has provided more opportunities for students to participate in the global community. Enrollment has grown, currently topping 17,000 students, with more than 900 full-time faculty providing instruction.

Climate change and environment and energy issues have influenced the curriculum and management practices on campus with the sustainable development degree program, the Energy Center, and the push for more environmentally sustainable buildings. While still offering quality academic programs for teachers in training, Appalachian has expanded to other areas, including entrepreneurship and health care, creating the Center for Entrepreneurship and the College of Health Sciences.

Finally, the profile of the athletics teams has grown along with the university. The football team in particular has carried the banner for Appalachian State, winning three consecutive FCS national championships and, in 2007, producing a historic victory over the University of Michigan that made national news. But it is not just the football team that excels. Appalachian has swept the Southern Conference's Commissioner's and Germann cups, recognizing the conference's top overall men's and women's sports programs, a record eight times.

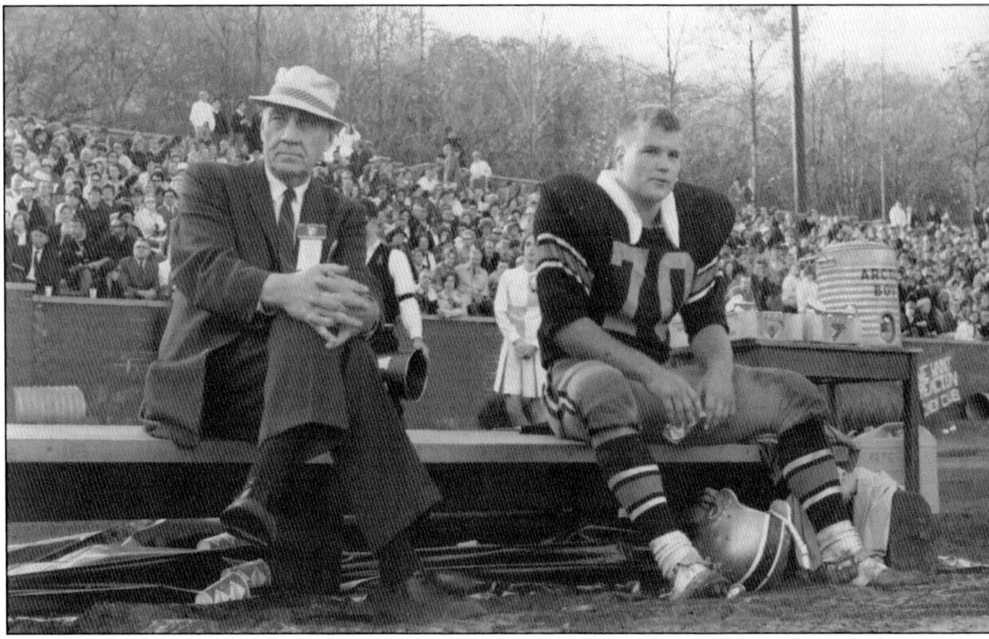

Appalachian State University president William Howard Plemmons (left) watches a football game at Conrad Stadium with Appalachian player Mark Gilliland in 1968. According to the December 6, 1968, edition of *The Appalachian*, the Mountaineers finished the football season with an 8-2 record. They set 16 records, including most points in a single season and most total offense from scrimmage.

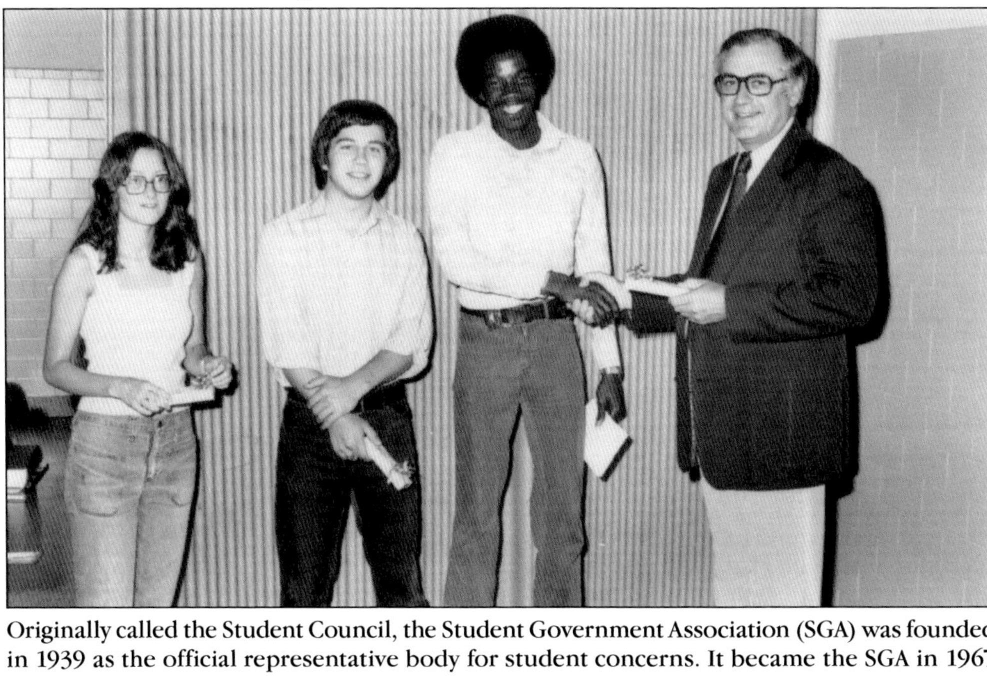

Originally called the Student Council, the Student Government Association (SGA) was founded in 1939 as the official representative body for student concerns. It became the SGA in 1967 when the school constitution was rewritten. Student representatives are elected each fall from each of the different colleges. In this 1974 photograph, former SGA president Robert Leak receives a gift from Ned Trivette, the vice chancellor of business affairs.

James F. "Jim" Jones was a professor of accounting at Appalachian from 1956 to 1992. A departmental chair and coordinator of accounting graduate studies and internships, he also coached the men's tennis team for 18 years and spent more than two decades in athletic administration, including six years (1974–1980) as athletic director. Jones retired with 36 years of service to Appalachian.

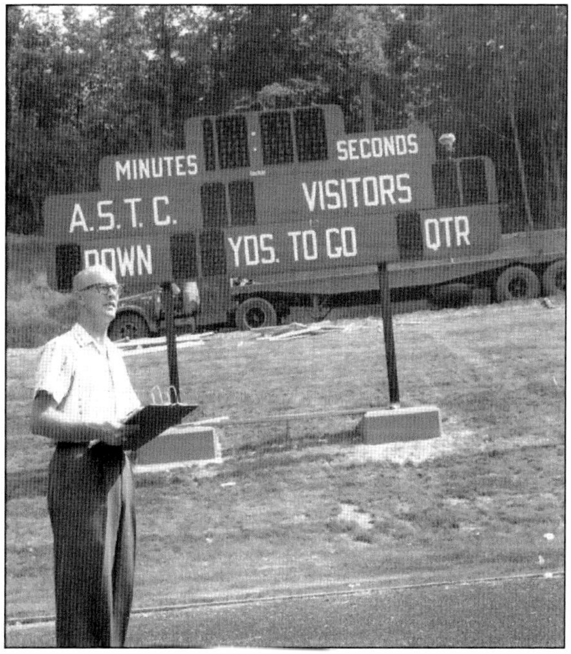

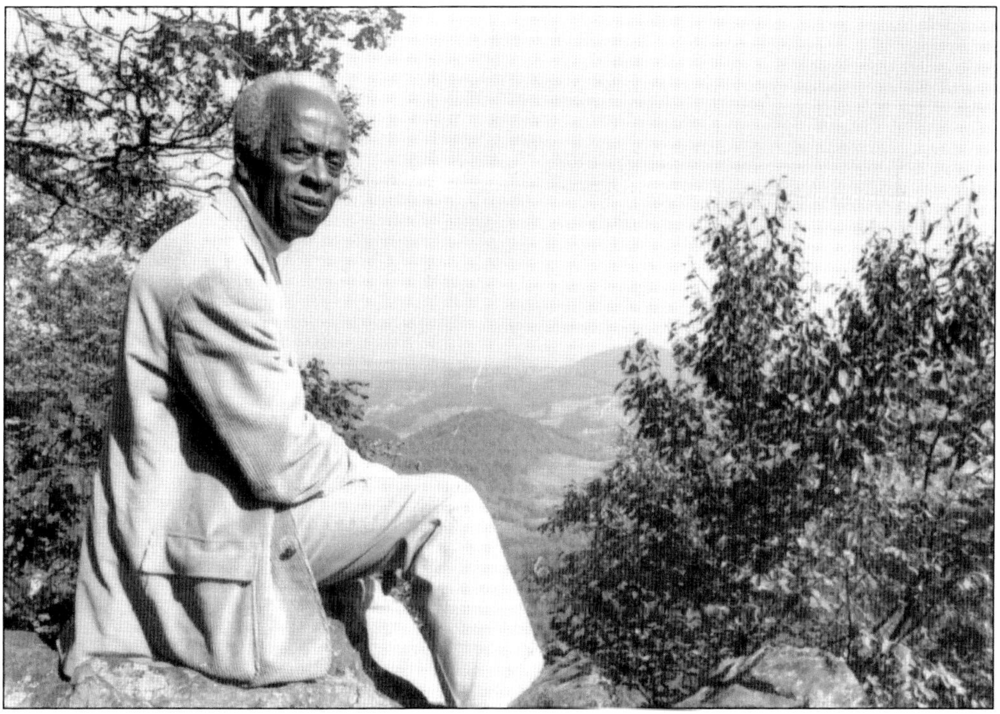

Jesse Jackson, the pioneering children's author whose work often addressed issues of race, served as a lecturer and writer-in-residence in the education department beginning in 1974. His most popular novel, *Call Me Charley* (1945), about a young black boy who integrates an all-white school, was one of the first major children's books with a black protagonist. A year before his death in 1983, Appalachian awarded Jackson an honorary doctor of humane letters degree.

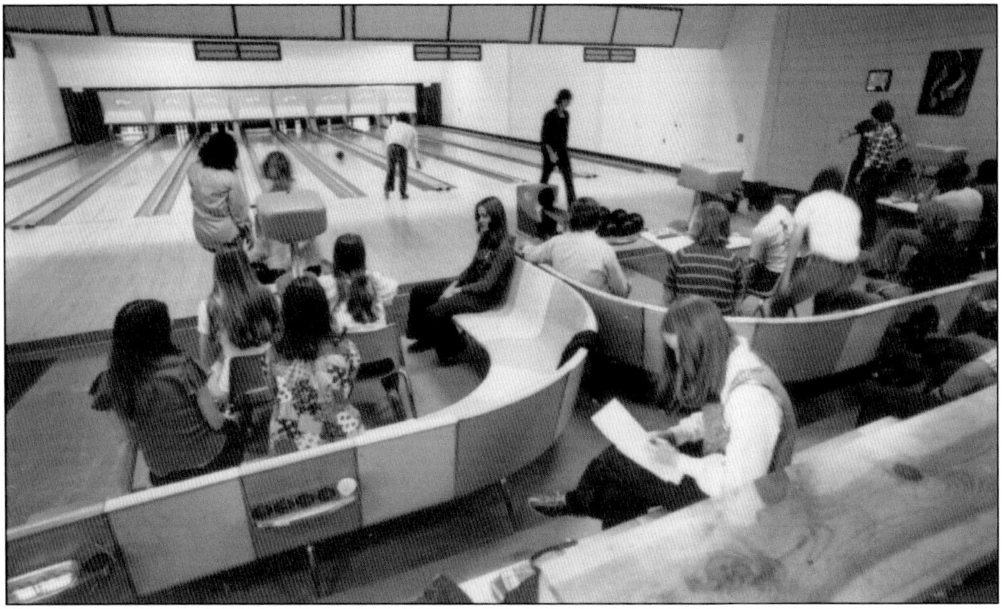

The campus bowling alley, a popular hangout in the 1970s and 1980s, was located in the Plemmons Student Union. Removed in 1998, it was replaced by the current Greenbrier Theater and office space. The Greenbrier is a state-of-the-art theater that shows classic films and is under the management of the Appalachian Popular Programming Society (APPS) Films Council.

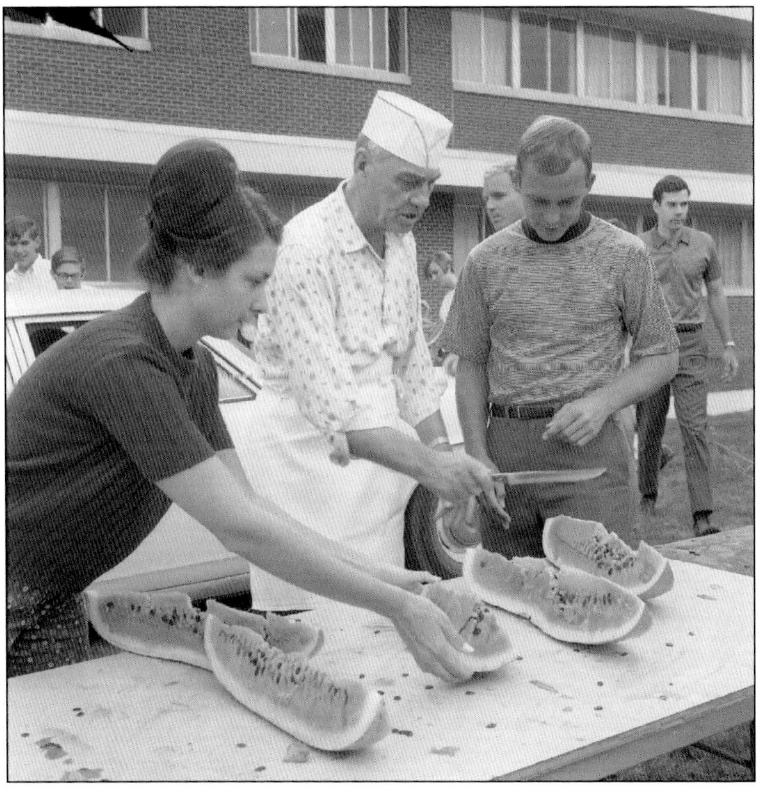

From 1960 through the 1970s, Appalachian held an annual summer watermelon cutting. The first cutting, which was open to faculty, staff, and students, was held in August 1960. Here, President Plemmons slices watermelon for waiting attendees on July 29, 1968, in front of Edwin Duncan Hall.

Appalachian's newly installed third president, Herbert Wey (left), and Ned Trivette speak to a mother and her son. Trivette, a native of Watauga County and an Appalachian alumnus, began his career at Appalachian in 1956 in the business office. He eventually became vice chancellor for business affairs and retired in 1990 with 34 years of service to the university.

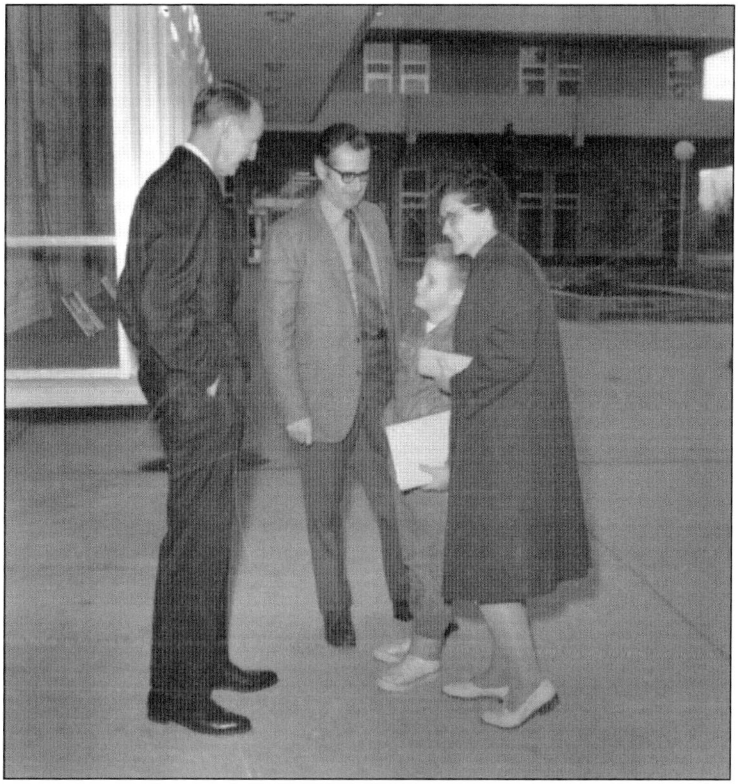

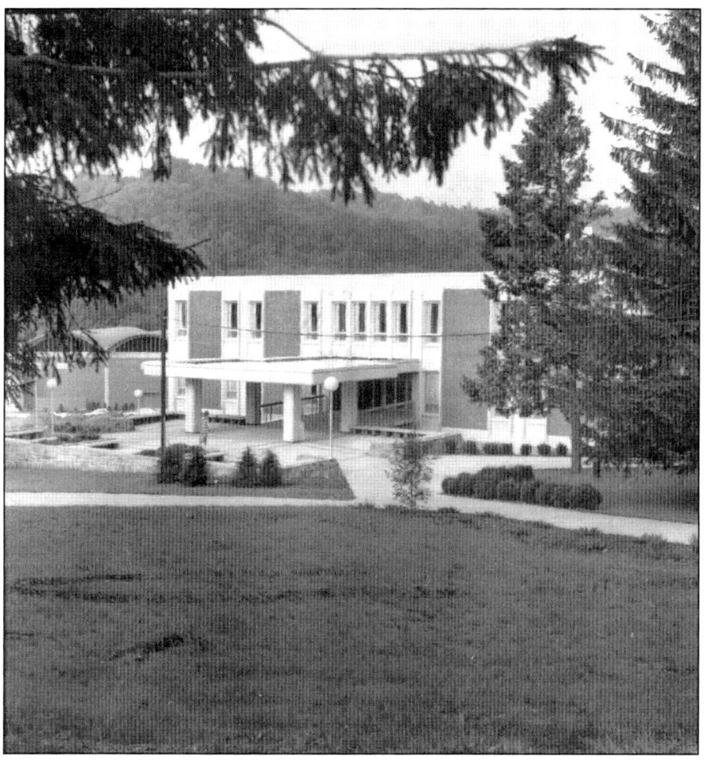

Carol Grotnes Belk Library was completed in 1968. It opened with 86,500 square feet of space and included the Curriculum Laboratory, the Appalachian Room, collection space for up to 450,000 volumes, and student study areas. The building was named for Carol Grotnes Belk, who, with her husband, Irvin Belk of Belk Enterprises, Inc., contributed to many civic and cultural organizations, including Appalachian's library.

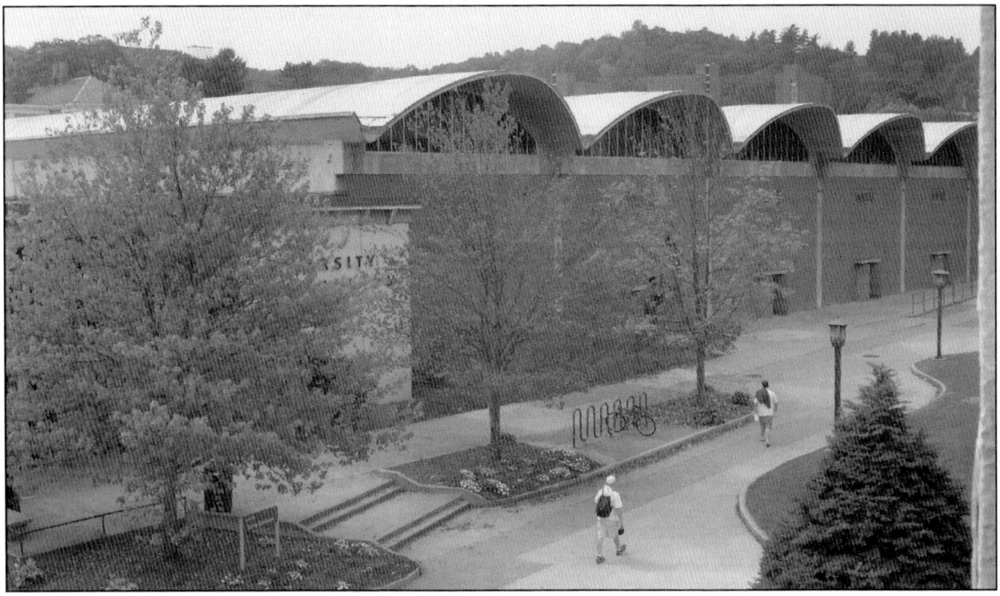

When it was completed in 1968, Varsity Gymnasium was the largest athletic facility west of Charlotte and Winston-Salem, North Carolina. It featured one of the most advanced gymnastics facilities in the South, which was photographed by the Nissen Manufacturing Company for the color cover of its gymnastics catalog. It also housed classroom space as well as the sports arena, and it is still in use today.

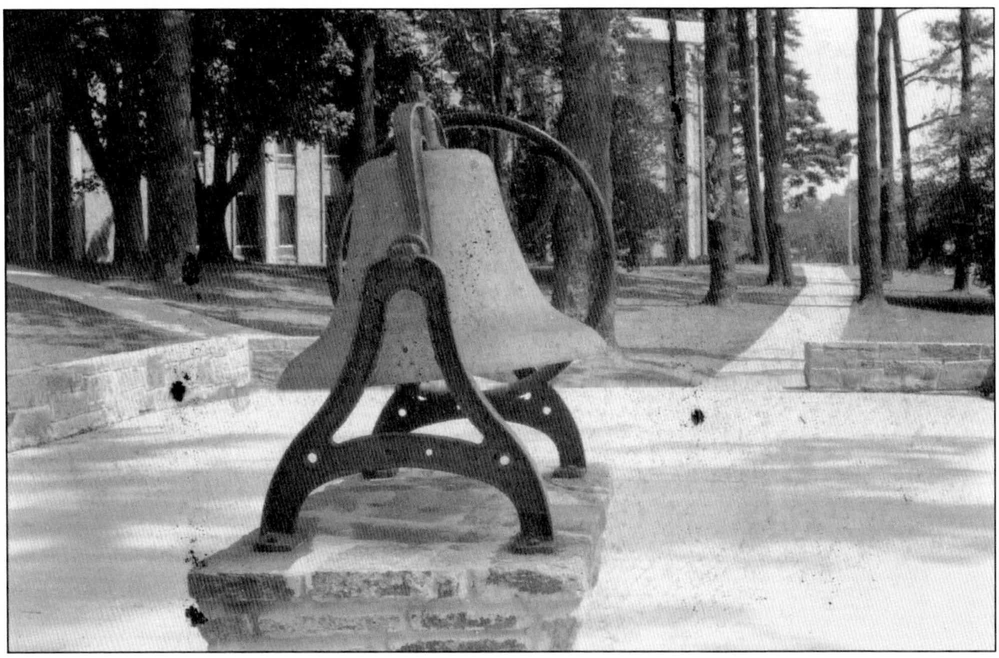

The "Founders Bell" or "Spirit Bell" was a gift to Appalachian State Teachers College from the Men's "A" Club in 1937. The bell originally sat outside of the men's gymnasium and was later moved near the administration building. At some point, the bell was moved again to sit in front of the first Belk Library (now Anne Belk Hall). Early in its history, the bell was rung when the football team won an away game.

Former Appalachian president William Howard Plemmons (center) holds the Appalachian seal as Dr. Herbert Walter Wey (right) waits to be installed as the next president of Appalachian in 1969. Dr. Wey began his career at Appalachian in 1938 as a math and physics teacher in the demonstration high school and served in other capacities before becoming the university's first chancellor, a post he held from 1971 to 1979.

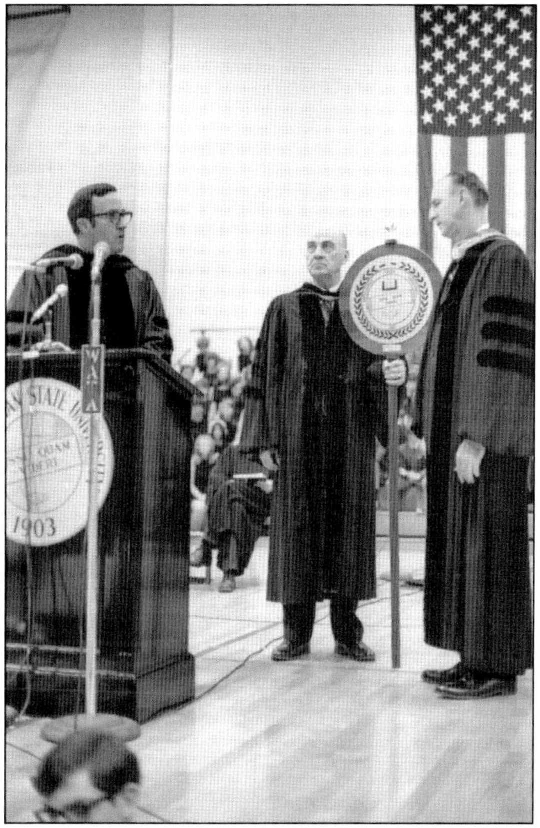

Dancing was prohibited in the early days of Appalachian's history, but by the 1970s, it was not only permitted, but also quite popular. Here, students participate in a dance marathon held in the Plemmons Student Union, with the music supplied by a jukebox on the wall at left.

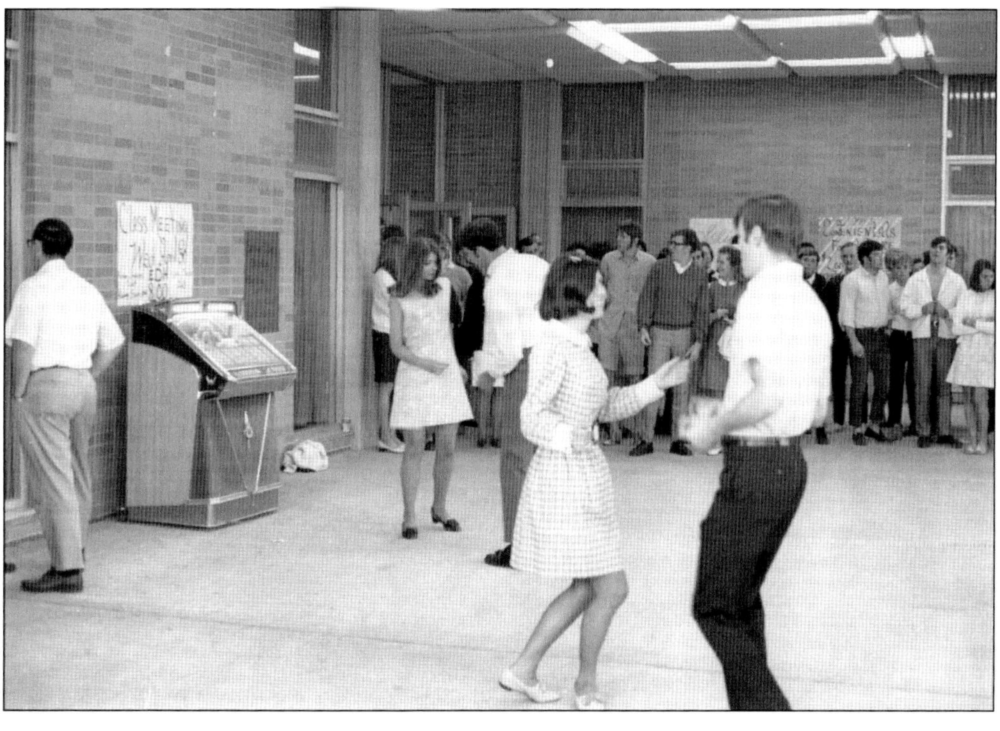

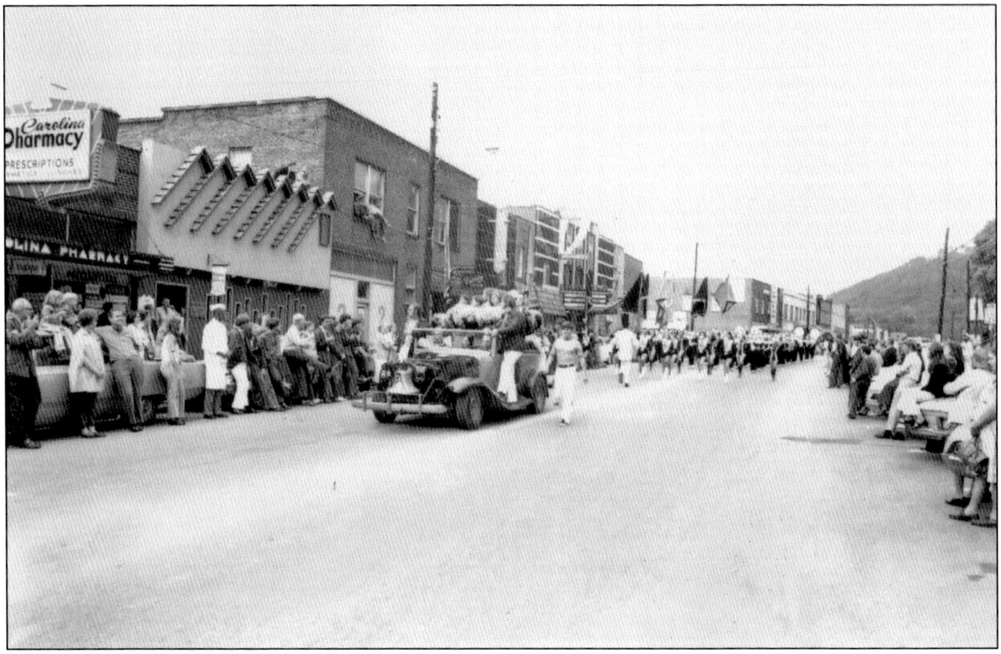

The 1971 homecoming parade makes its way east down King Street as onlookers line the way. Some noted businesses, including the Carolina Pharmacy (far left) and the old Appalachian Theater (fourth building from the left), are visible on the left side of the street.

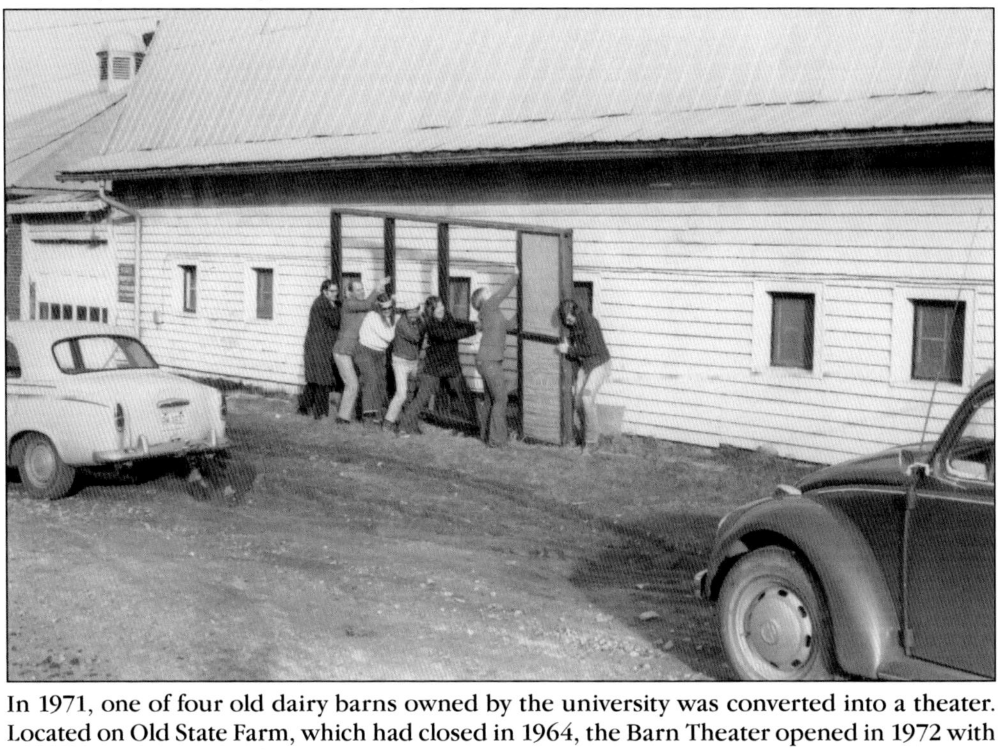

In 1971, one of four old dairy barns owned by the university was converted into a theater. Located on Old State Farm, which had closed in 1964, the Barn Theater opened in 1972 with a seating capacity of 206, a stage, and dressing rooms in the silo. The building was renovated through donations and volunteer labor.

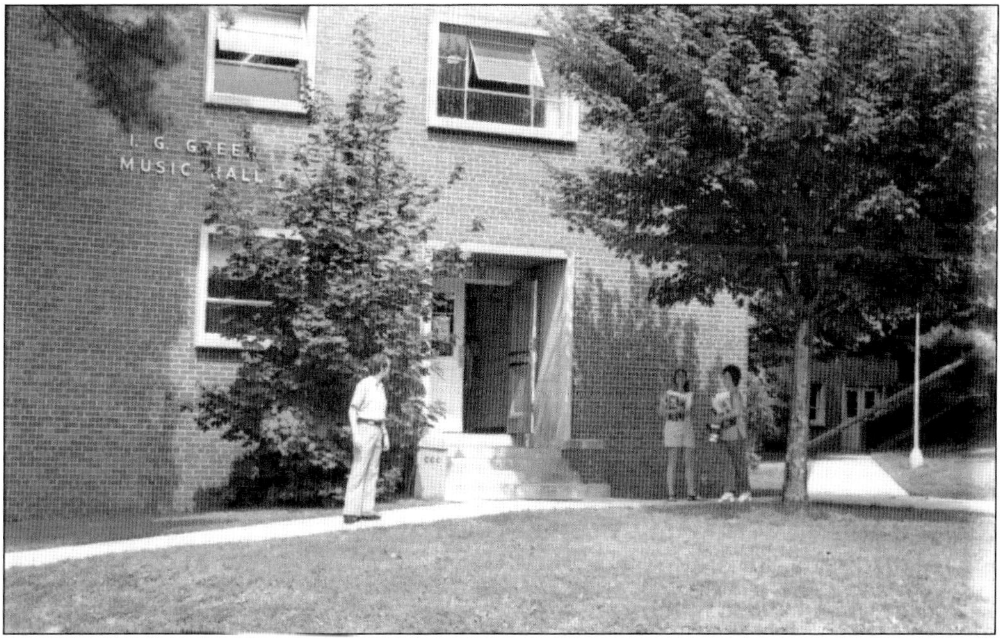

I.G. Greer Hall, shown here in 1975, was named for Isaac Garfield ("I.G." or "Ike") Greer (1881–1967), a professor of history and government at Appalachian State Teacher's College from 1910 to 1932. Constructed in 1950, the building originally housed the music department and included both an auditorium and a music library. Today, it houses student services, international programs, the office of the College of Arts and Sciences, and the Department of Philosophy and Religion. This image shows the northern entrance of the building.

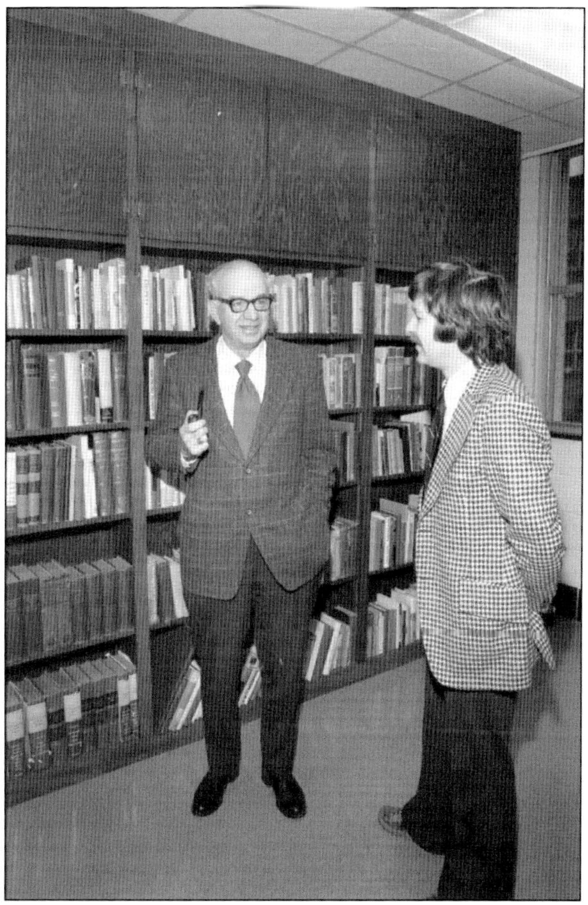

College of Arts and Sciences dean Dr. William Strickland (left) chats with the assistant dean, Leland Nicholls, in this 1974 photograph. Dr. Strickland, who served as dean from 1968 to 1984, began his career at Appalachian as a professor and chairperson of the Department of Philosophy and Religion in 1966, while Dr. Nichols began teaching in the geography department in 1971.

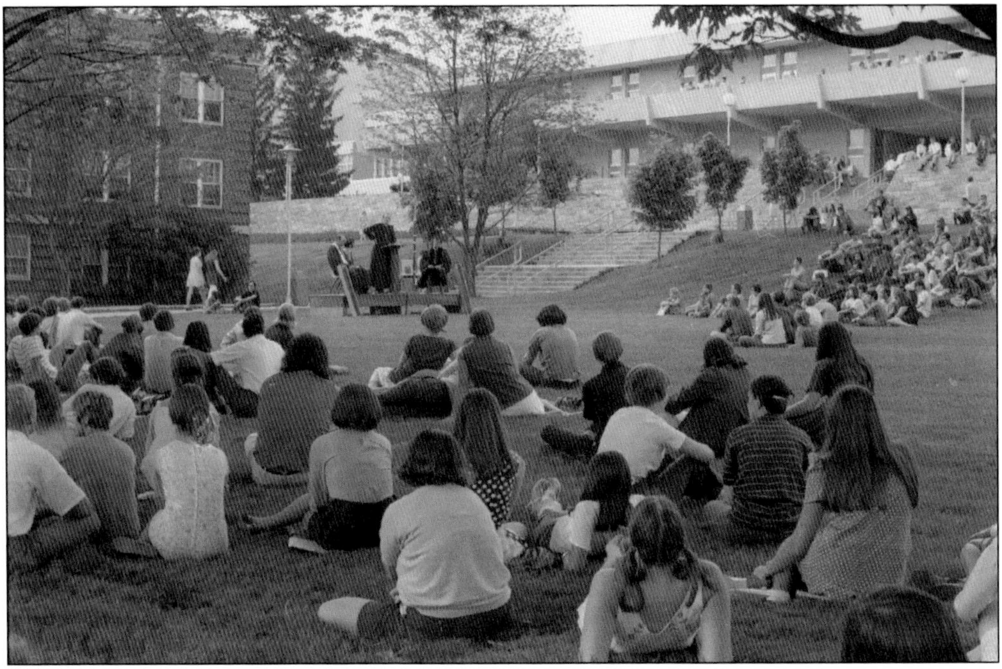

Approximately 300 students attended the Kent State memorial held on Sanford Mall on May 12, 1970. Eight days earlier, in Ohio, four unarmed Kent State University students were killed and nine others wounded by the Ohio National Guard. The memorial at Appalachian included speeches delivered by Rev. Reggie Smith and Rev. Gray Temple.

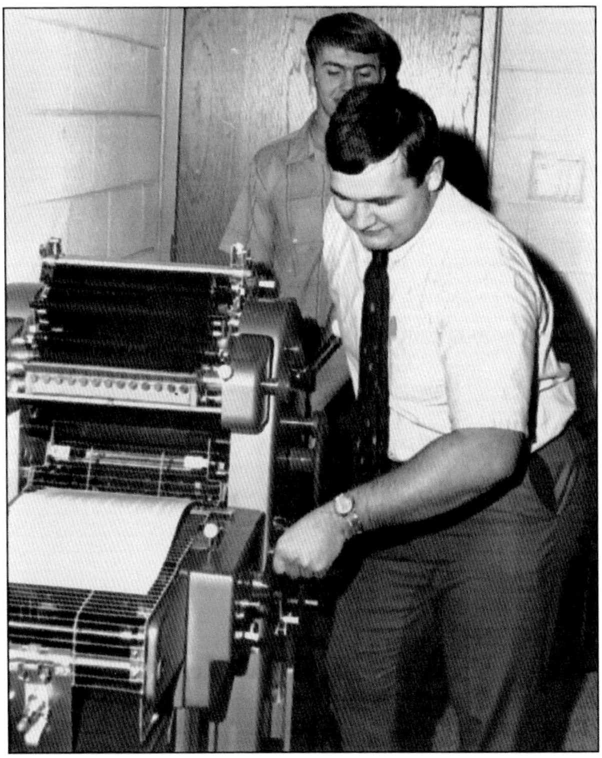

The Student Print Shop was located in Kerr Scott Hall, built in 1961. All printing for student organizations, as well as for the *Rhododendron* and *The Appalachian*, was done here. This April 1971 photograph shows a student using a mimeograph machine.

Charlotte Ross (left), curator of the William Leonard Eury Appalachian Collection at Appalachian State University, inspects a manuscript donated by John Foster West (right), a professor and writer-in-residence in the Department of English, in May 1975. West, a noted Appalachian poet and Pulitzer Prize nominee, donated his manuscript collection to Appalachian. He taught creative writing at Appalachian from 1968 to 1989.

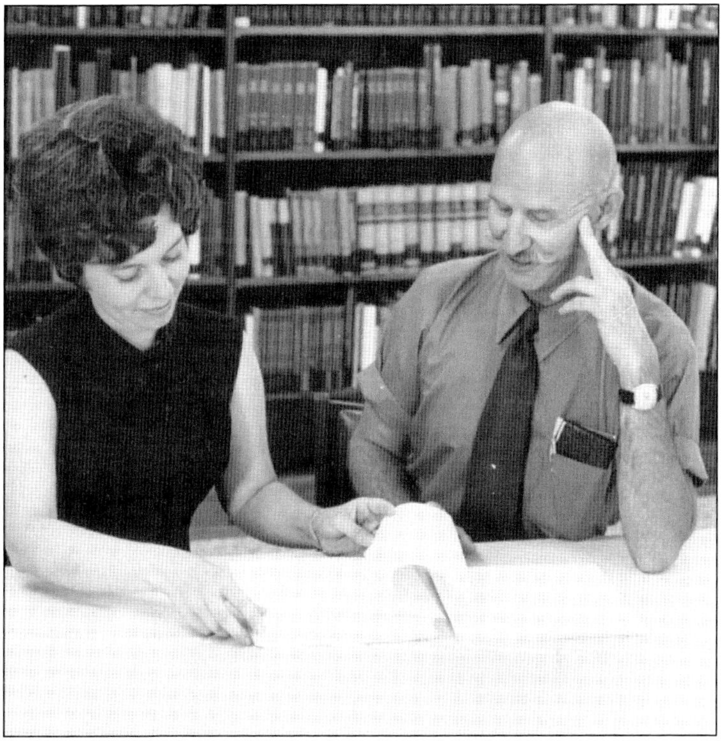

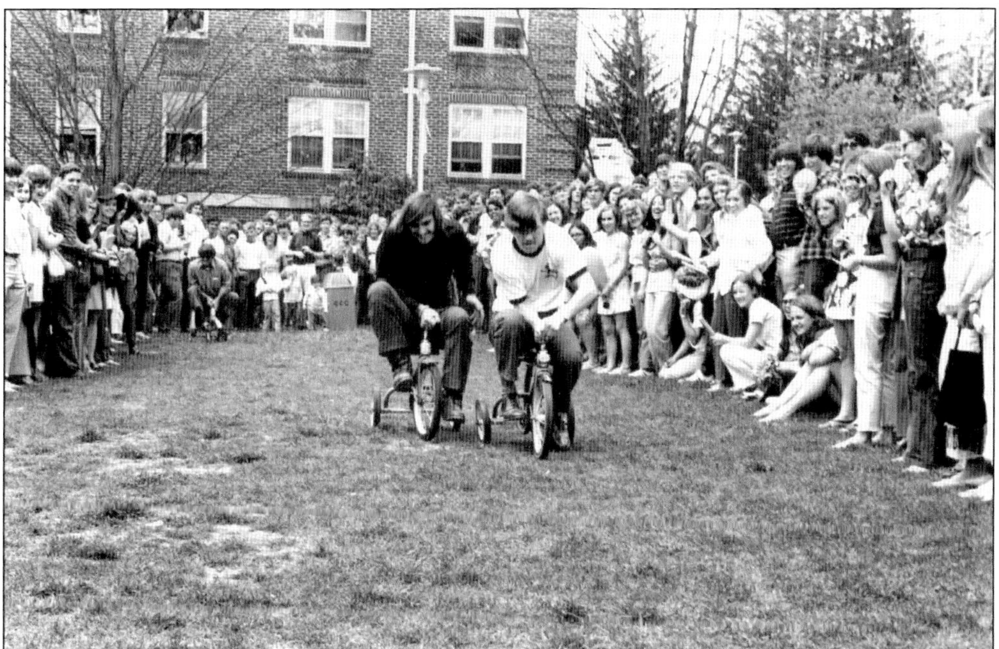

Anti-Suitcase College Weekend, sponsored by the Student Government Association at Appalachian State in August 1977, was initiated so that students would stay on campus during the Labor Day weekend. The event included concerts and games, like the tricycle race shown here.

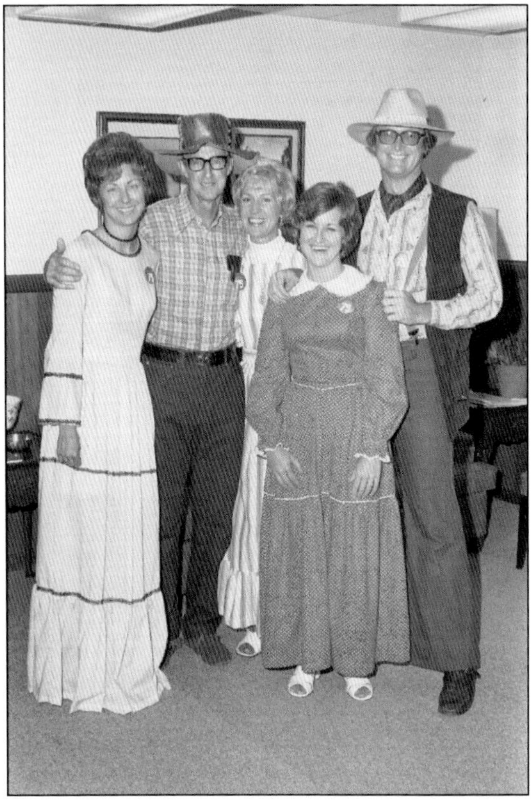

From left to right, Carolyn Taylor, chancellor Herbert Wey, Nancy West, Jeanie Harmon, and assistant to the chancellor Richard D. Howe pose in costume in this 1970s photograph. Dr. Howe served as a professor in the Department of Leadership and Educational Studies in the Reich College of Education and as director of compliance programs from 1979 to 2007.

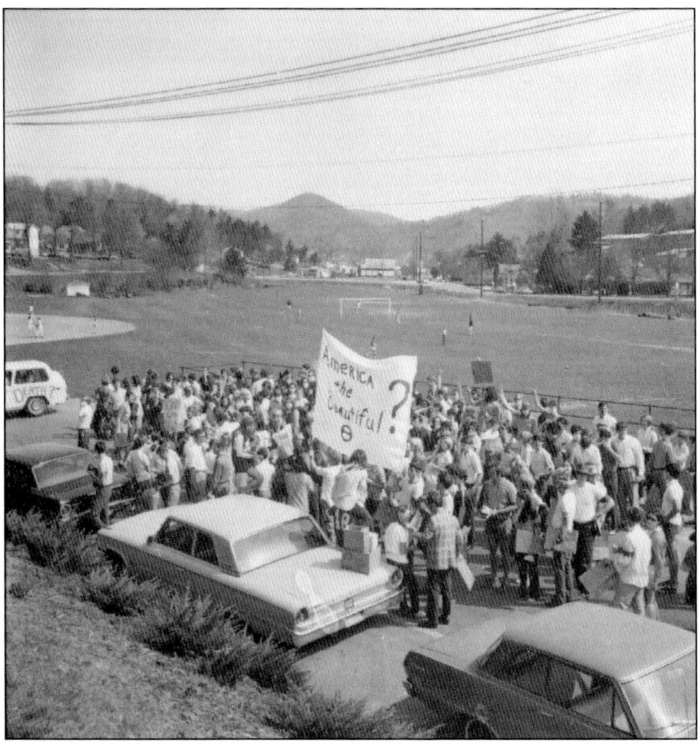

Appalachian has long been environmentally conscious, as reflected in this photograph from the early 1970s in which students gather at the old baseball field to protest pollution. The university had an Earth studies program in the General College from 1979 to 1981, and Appalachian declared 1989 as "The Year of the Environment." Today, ASU is well known for its energy initiatives and for programs such as the Energy Center and the Sustainable Development Program.

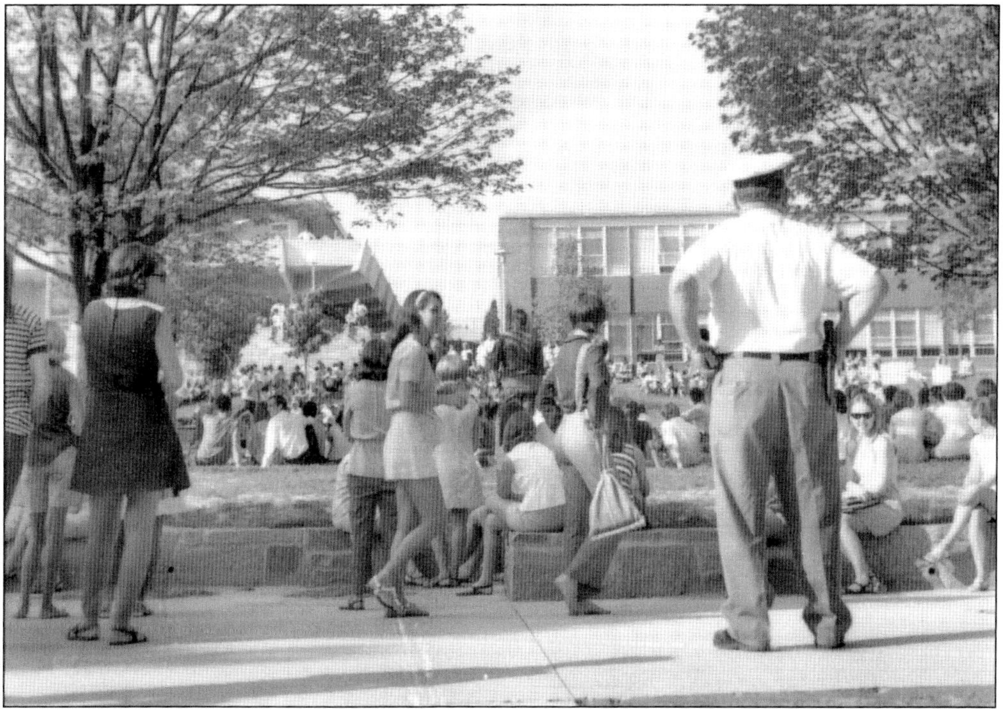

In the 1970s, students from campuses all over the country staged protests of the Vietnam War, the invasion of Cambodia, and other political happenings of the era. This May 14, 1970, student forum sponsored by the Student Government Association was held on the Sanford Mall, with approximately 800 people in attendance. The event hosted various speakers and included protestors, as indicated by the signs in these two photographs. In contrast to some of the protests that occurred on college campuses across the country at this time, ASU's protests were relatively peaceful.

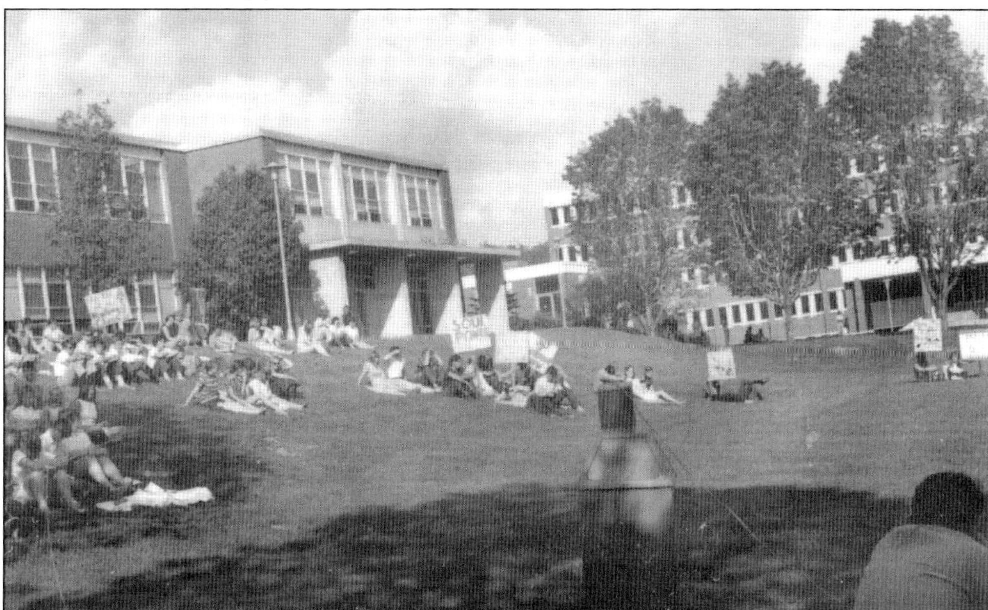

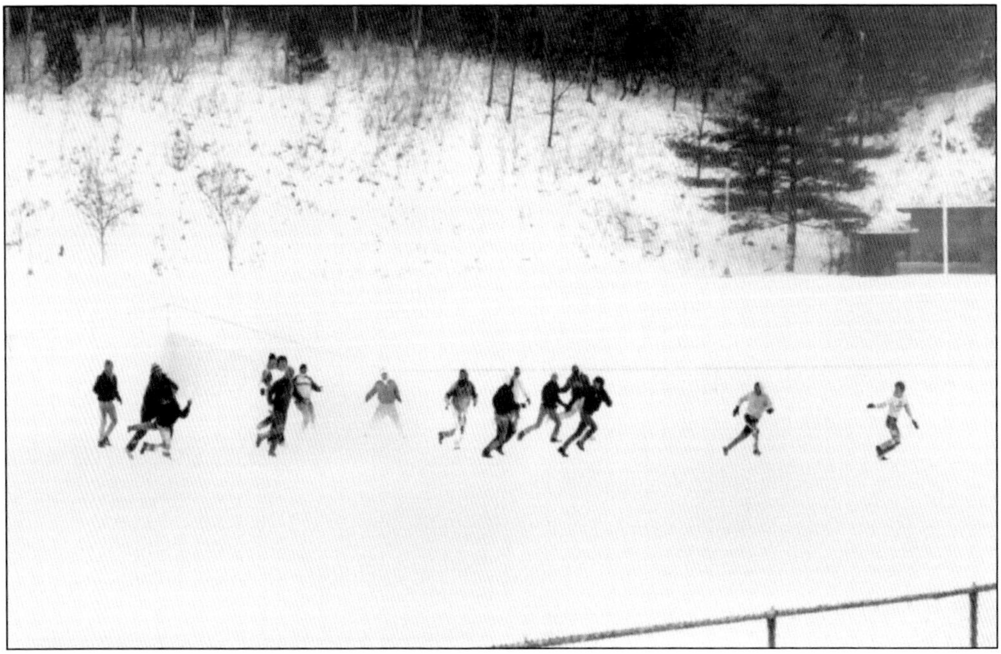

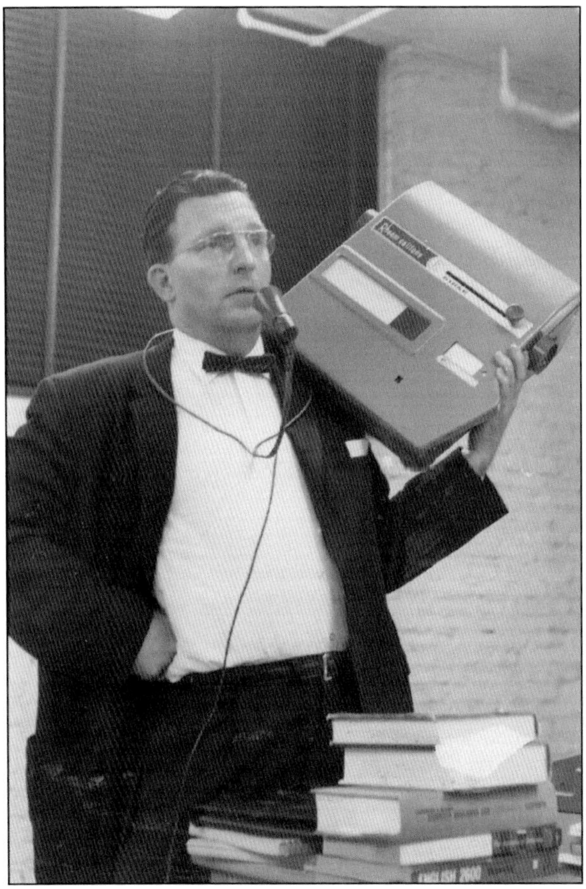

In this 1975 photograph, a snowy game of football is under way on the soccer field as Appalachian students take advantage of the winter weather. Then, as now, the university attracted fans of both outdoor recreation and sports in general. For students in the mid-1970s who were inclined to cheer rather than play, they could watch one of the 18 varsity sports for men and 7 for women offered at Appalachian.

John Alfred Pritchett, a longtime associate professor of education, is credited with organizing the Department of Audio-Visual Education and the Department of Library Science. Pritchett began his career at Appalachian in 1955 and retired in 1991 with 36 years of service to the university. In this image, he demonstrates the Didak 501 teaching machine—an automated test-taking machine that allowed students to self-score—to faculty members.

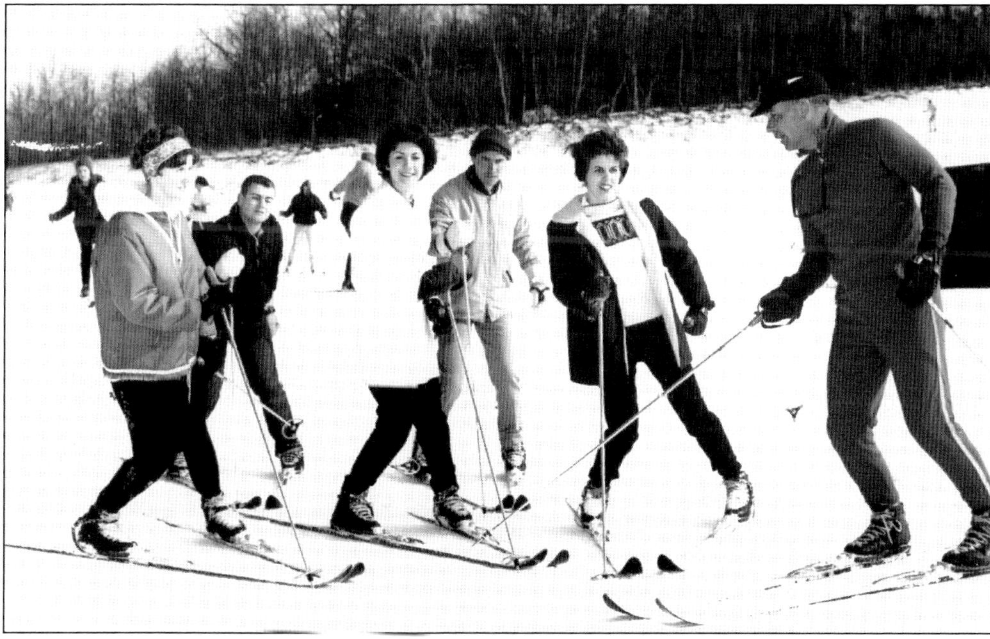

With three ski resorts in the surrounding area, Appalachian Ski Mountain, Ski Beech, and Sugar Mountain (Hawksnest is now snow-tubing only), downhill skiing is a popular winter sport in Boone. The alpine ski team was established in 1969 and continues as an Appalachian State University club. Members of the team receive a lesson from their instructor in this photograph from 1980.

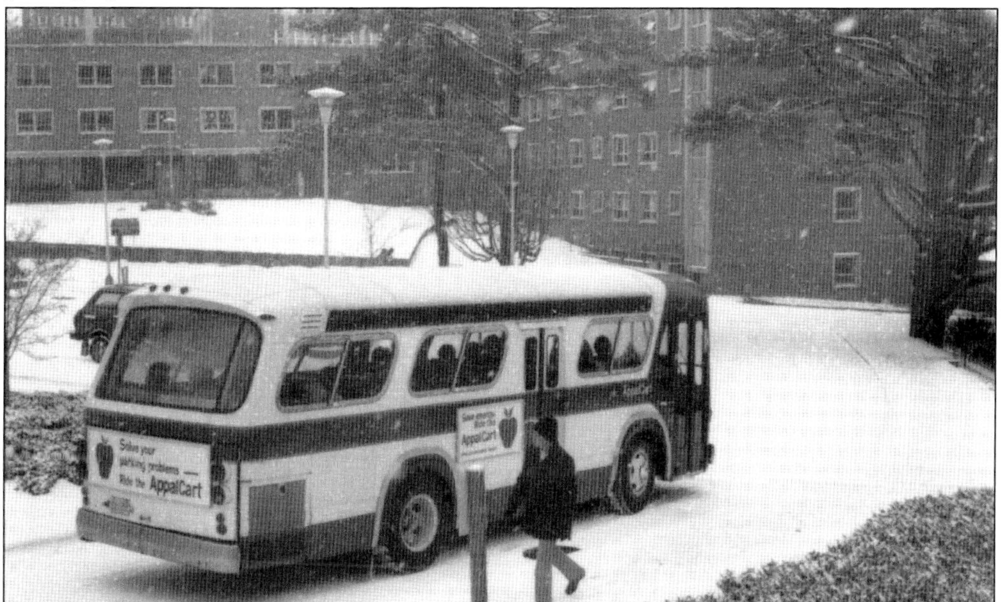

One of the buses from the university's AppalCART transportation system makes its rounds in 1980. At first serving only the campus, AppalCART routes were extended to the surrounding community in 1981 when it merged with the Watauga County Transportation Authority. AppalCART still provides transportation for Appalachian students and Watauga County citizens.

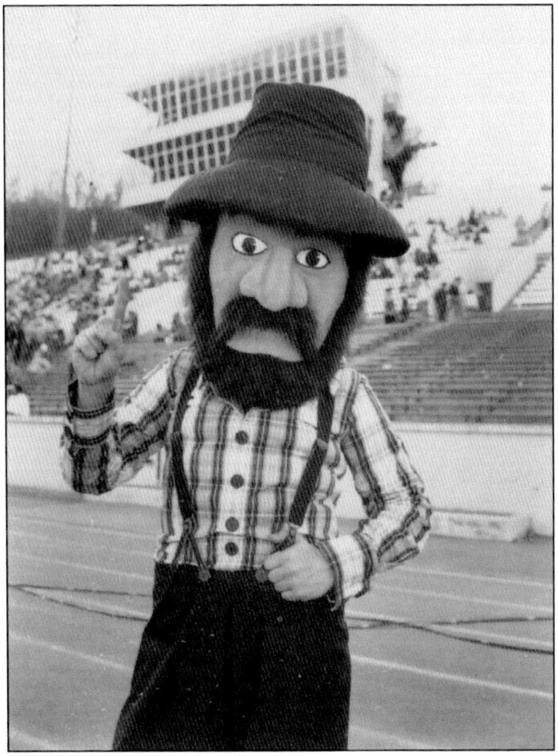

Yosef, pictured at left in 1983, has undergone several image changes since his creation more than 70 years ago. With his gun, pipe, and moonshine jug, Yosef was conceived as a stereotypical mountaineer. Appalachian decided to clean up his image in 1994, a year when big tobacco was much in the news, by dropping the pipe. He underwent another change in 1999 that was a little too toned-down for many Appalachian fans. The university then went back to the drawing board and came up with the rugged fighting mountaineer seen below.

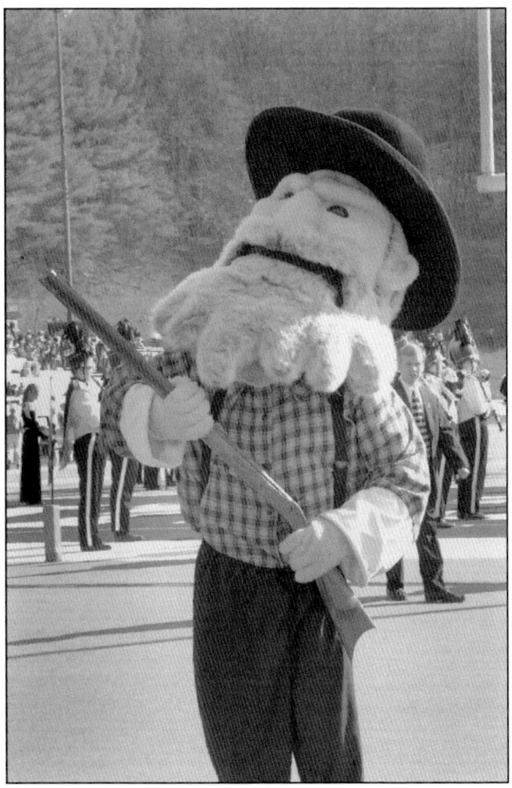

Prof. Rogers Whitener taught English at Appalachian State from 1959 to 1989 and was a world-renowned folklorist. He had numerous folklore publications and is seen here signing a special issue of the *North Carolina Folklore Journal* that reproduced selections from Whitener's weekly column for the *Watauga Democrat*, "Folk-Ways and Folk Speech." The event took place at Boone Drug on September 26, 1981.

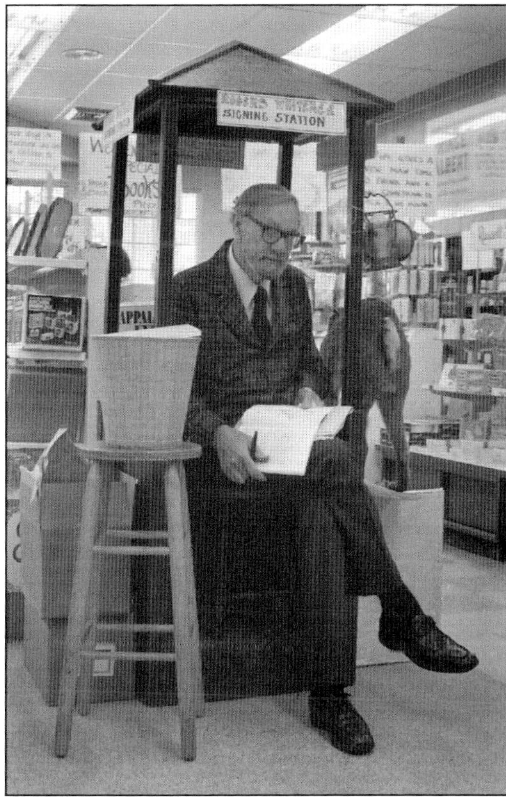

Robert E. "Bob" Snead, former executive assistant to the chancellor, sits in his office. Snead, who earned his bachelor of science (1951) and master of arts (1957) degrees at Appalachian, also served as director of alumni affairs and vice chancellor for development and public affairs during his more than 30 years at the university. In 1970, he helped establish the Appalachian State University Foundation, Inc., which manages development efforts for the university.

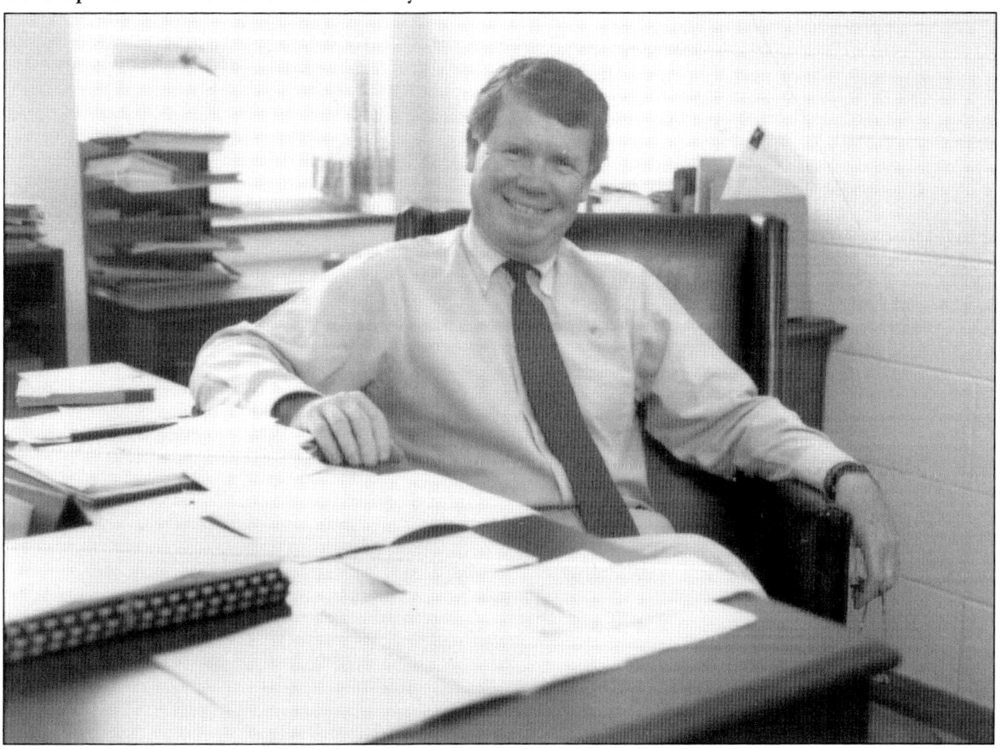

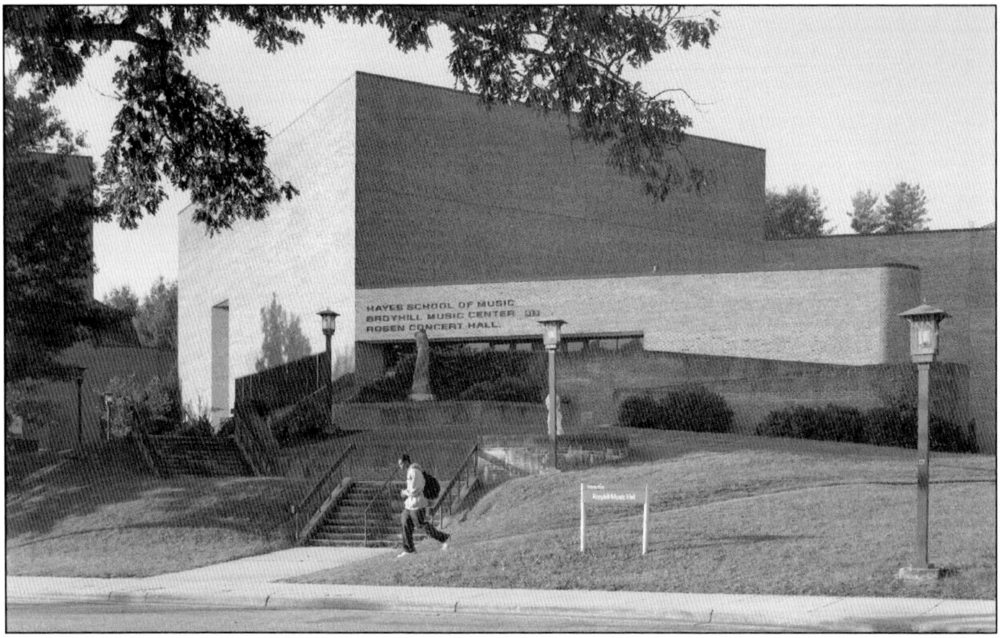

The Broyhill Music Center, located on Rivers Street, is the home of the Hayes School of Music. The building offers more than 90,000 square feet of space, housing a 125-seat recital hall, the 440-seat Rosen Concert Hall, a 5,000-square-foot music library, a record studio, multiple rehearsal halls, an opera studio, small ensemble rehearsal rooms, more than 50 practice rooms (all with pianos), and many offices and classrooms.

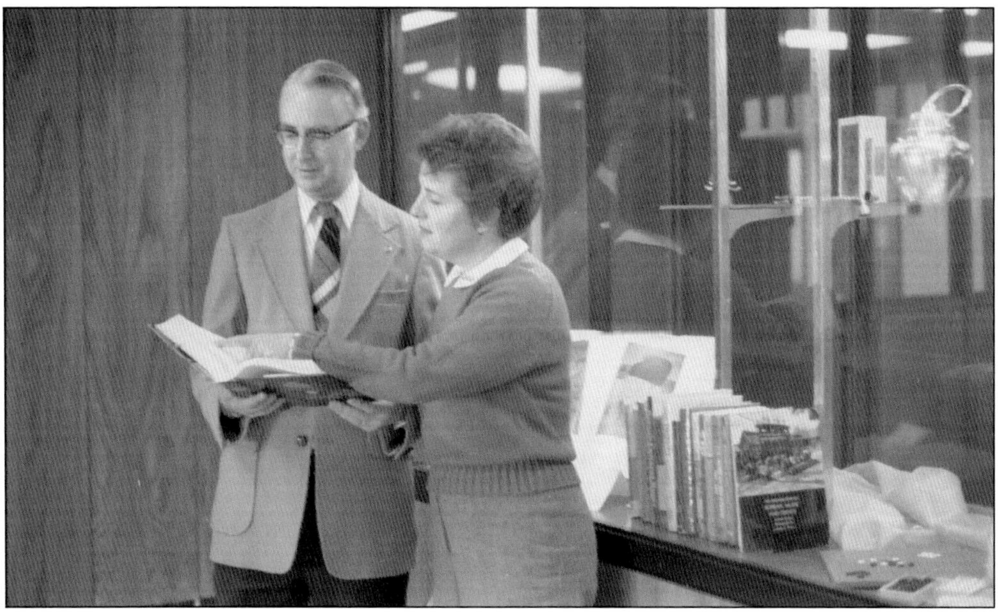

Richard Barker and Bettie Bond inspect a book at the old Belk Library. Barker joined Appalachian in 1956 as a circulation librarian and became the university librarian in 1973, holding that position until his death in 1991. Dr. Elizabeth "Bettie" Bond began teaching history at Appalachian in 1971. In 1981, she helped establish the University Archives and Records Center, serving as its coordinator.

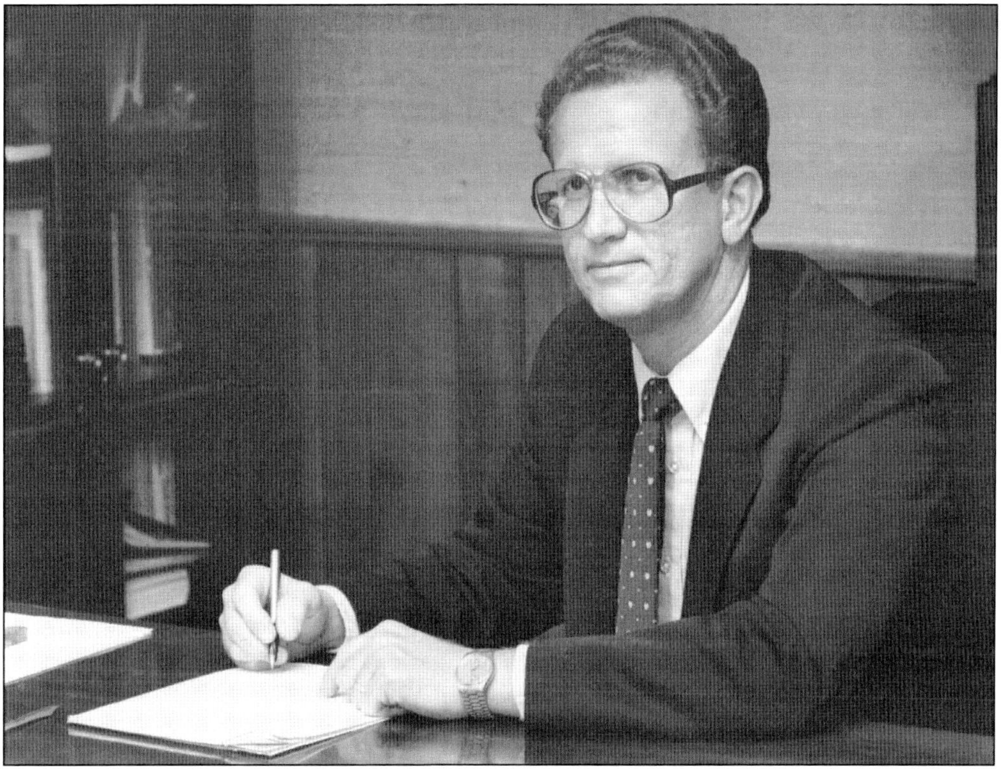

Dr. Harvey R. Durham joined the math department in 1965 and later became its chair before becoming associate dean of the faculty. He was associate vice chancellor of academic affairs from 1974 to 1979 and was promoted to provost in 1989. In 1998, Dr. Durham became executive vice chancellor, and he served as acting chancellor at Appalachian in 2003–2004, after which he retired.

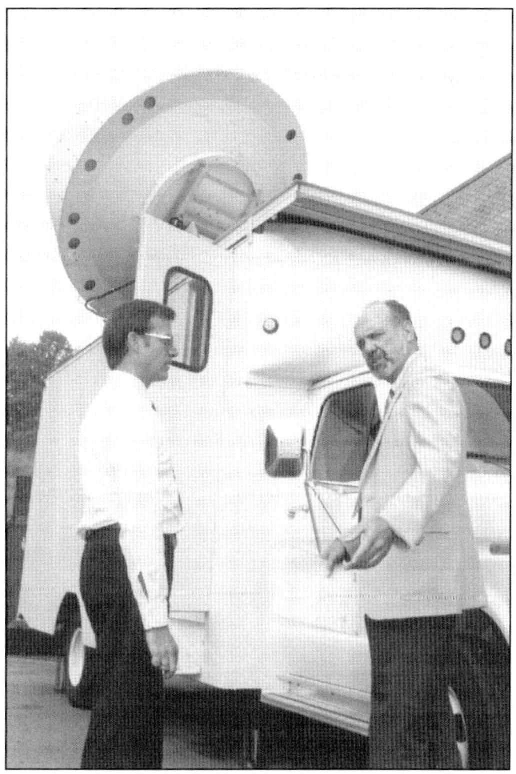

This image shows chancellor John Thomas (right) inspecting the then-new KU-Band satellite uplink mobile unit. The unit was purchased as part of Thomas's initiative to enhance telecommunications on campus. The uplink project provided faculty, staff, and students with distance-education opportunities and transmitted educational programming to other schools in North Carolina.

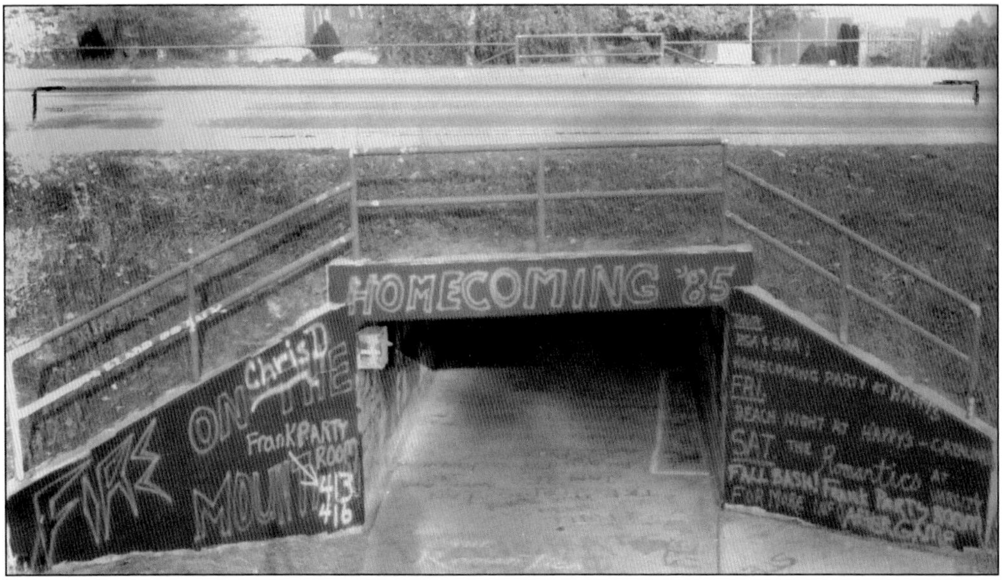

The Rivers Street Tunnel was constructed to provide safe passage for pedestrians crossing the busy thoroughfare. It also became a means of communication as students started to use it for graffiti. That tradition continues, although the university long ago developed a policy concerning what can and cannot be painted on the tunnel. In this photograph, students have advertised homecoming 1985.

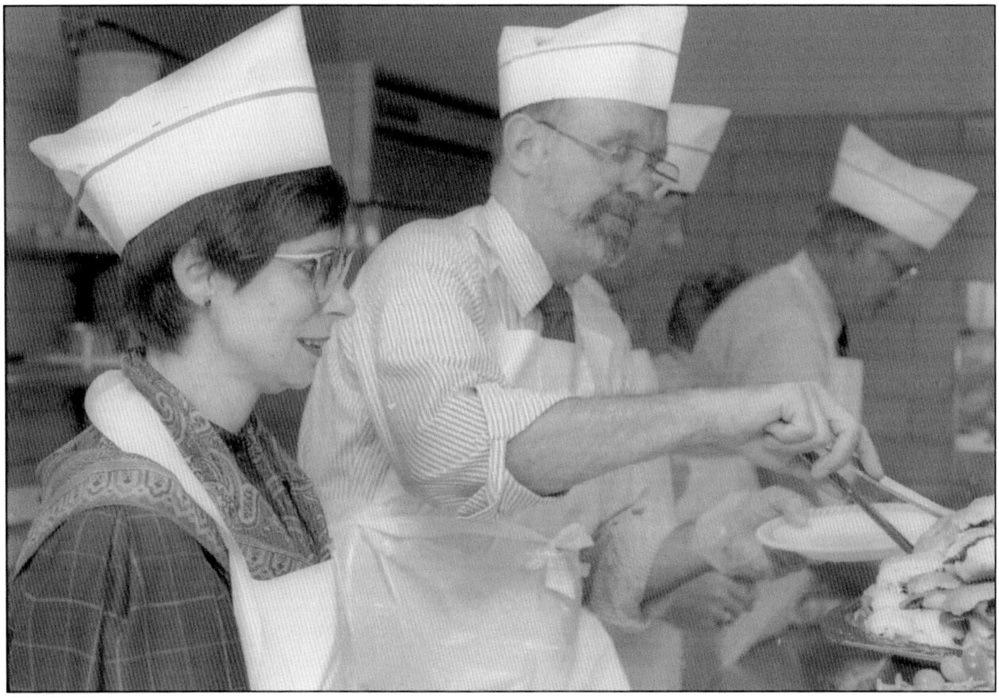

Another tradition at Appalachian is the annual Staff Appreciation Breakfast, at which members of the university staff are the guests of honor and service awards are handed out. Part of Staff Appreciation Day, the breakfast recognizes the staff's contributions to the university community. Here, at the 1985 event, Chancellor Thomas serves up a meal.

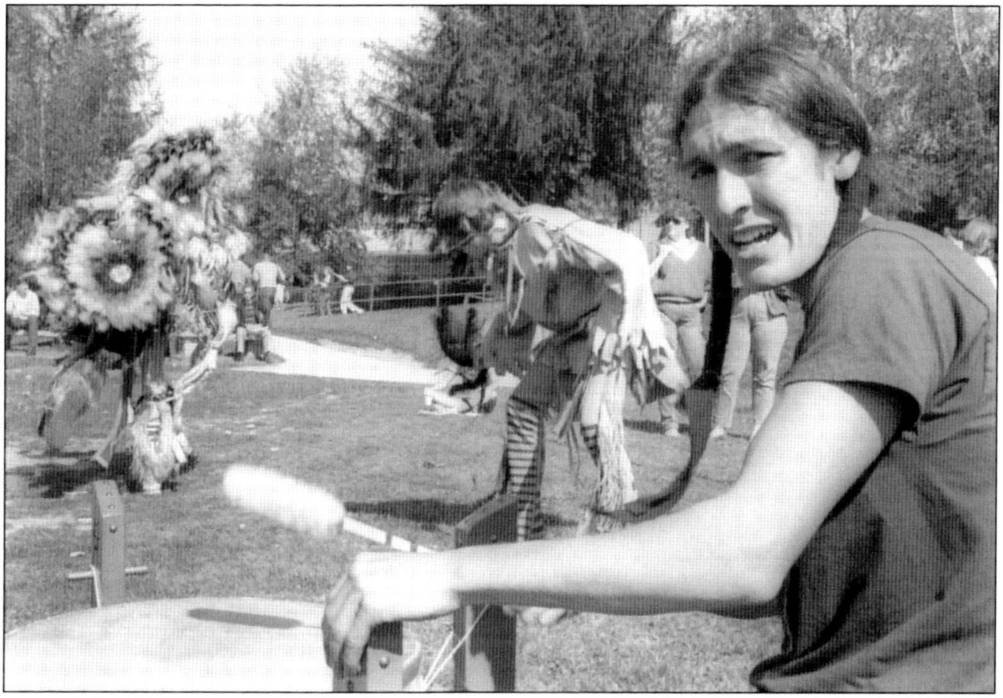

This image shows a performance at the Native American Festival, held on Sanford Mall in 1985. Sponsored by the Native American Council at Appalachian State University, a student-run organization, the festival promoted Native American history, identity, and culture.

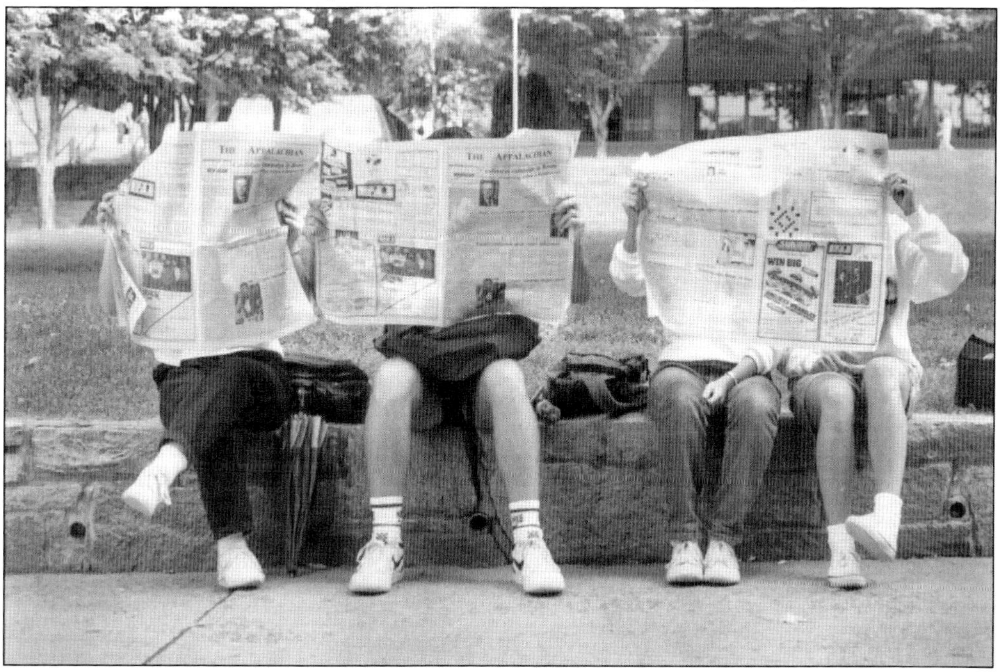

Students pose holding up copies of *The Appalachian* in 1986. *The Appalachian* was first published in 1934 and has been a student-run newspaper ever since. It is now published twice weekly, covering campus events and providing a forum for student commentary.

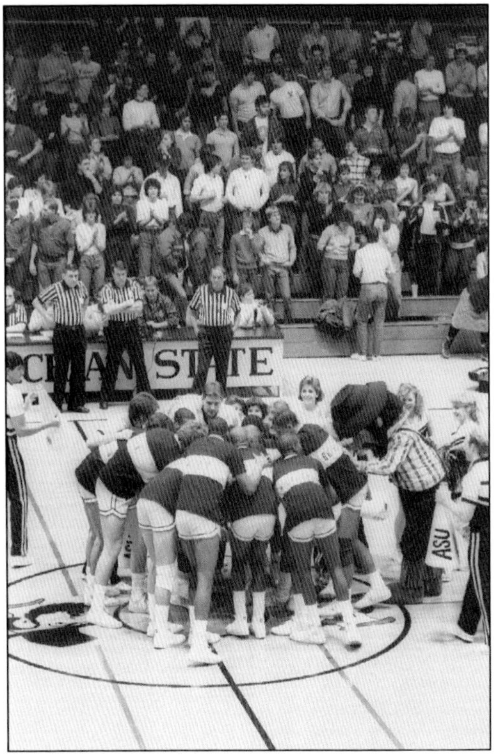

The men's basketball team huddles with Yosef at this 1985 game. That season, led by head coach Kevin Cantwell, the Mountaineers scored more than 100 points for the first time since 1978. Cantwell coached at Appalachian from 1981 to 1986.

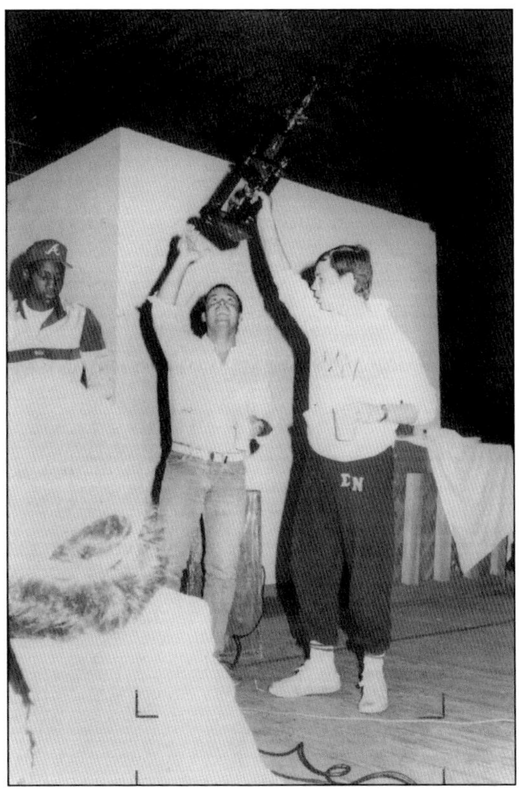

Members of the ASU fraternity Sigma Nu display their trophy at H'Appy's during Greek Week 1986. The first Greek sorority and fraternity were approved in 1972, and in the years that followed, Greek Week became an annual spring event. H'Appy's was a Winn-Dixie grocery store that had been converted to a music venue on campus in 1965. It was renamed Legends in 1988. Legends still provides a venue for student programs, which are chosen by the student-led Appalachian Popular Programming Society.

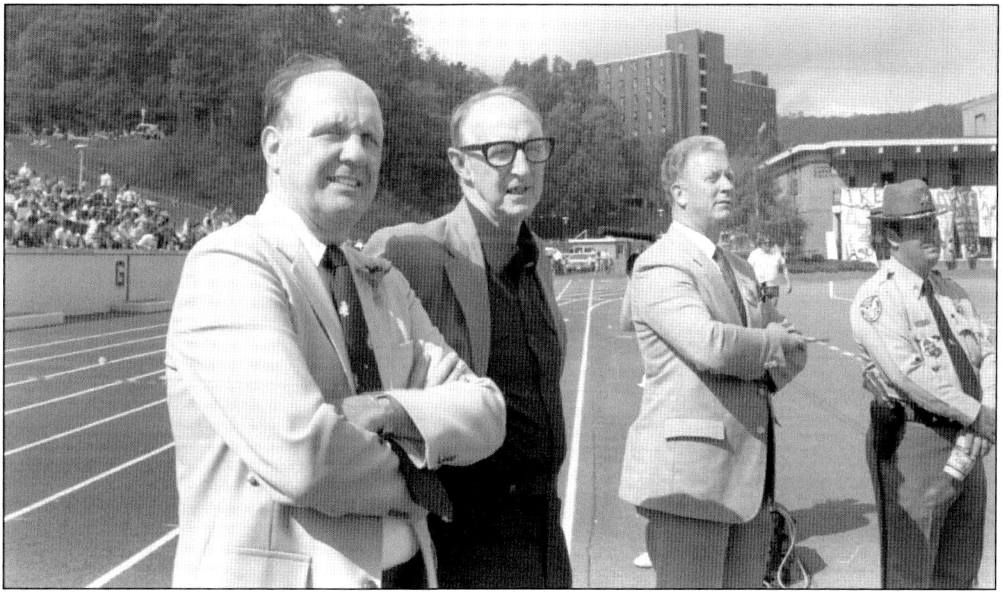

Chancellor John Thomas (left) and former chancellor Herbert Wey stand together on the sidelines watching a 1986 football game. James "Red" Lyons, former Watauga County sheriff, is standing to the far right. Wey retired in 1979 and passed away in 1999. Dr. Thomas retired as chancellor in 1993.

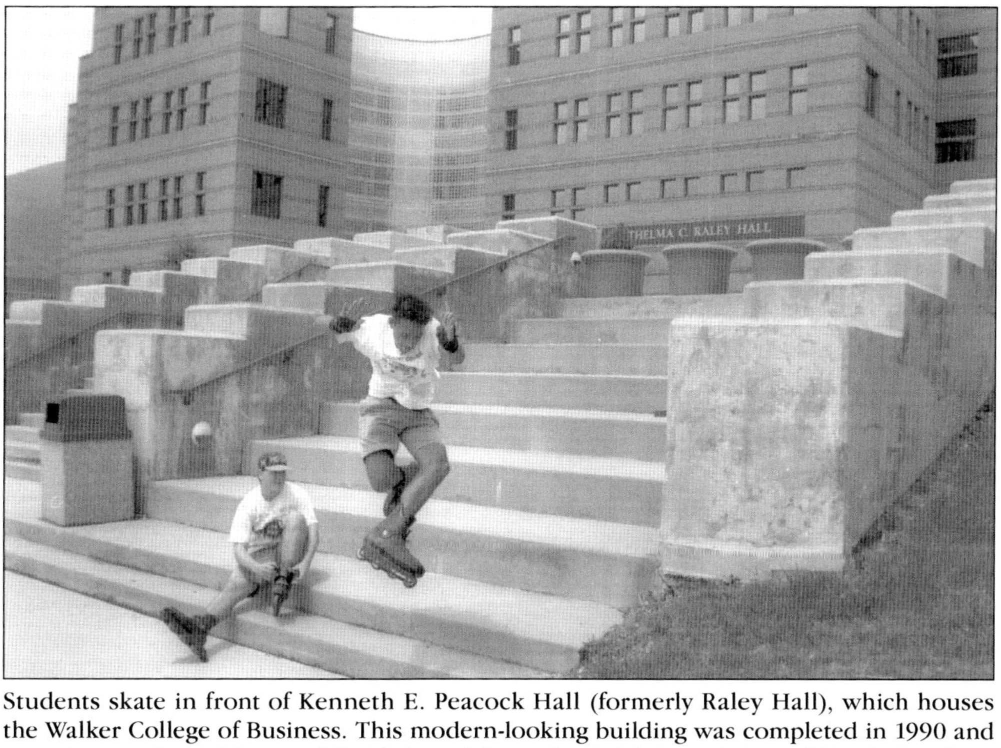

Students skate in front of Kenneth E. Peacock Hall (formerly Raley Hall), which houses the Walker College of Business. This modern-looking building was completed in 1990 and won that year's Architectural Brick Award from the Brick Association of North Carolina. The Walker College of Business currently offers nine undergraduate majors as well as two graduate degrees in accounting.

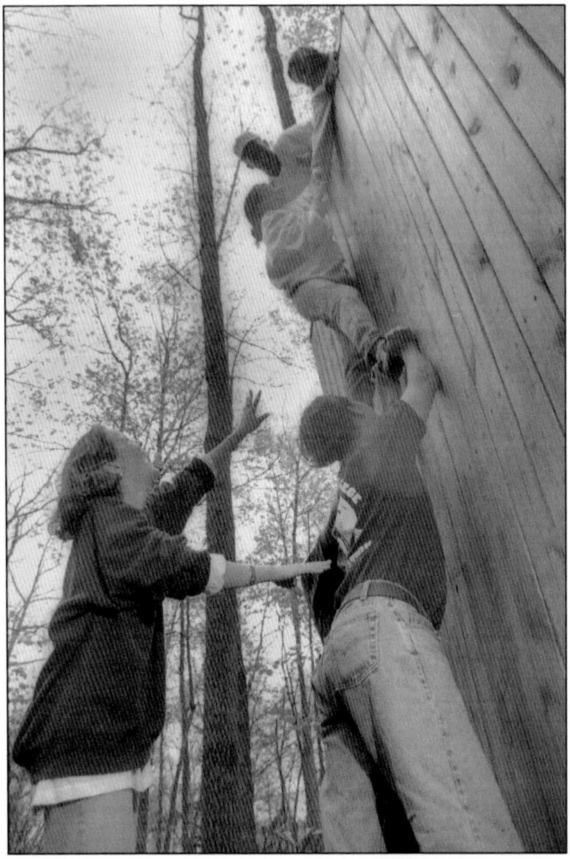

Students attempt to scale a wall as a part of Outdoor Programs activities in 1995. Outdoor Programs began in 1973 and provides outdoor learning experiences such as rafting, skiing, and hiking to students, faculty, and staff. The department, which is part of University Recreation, also offers an instructor development program and various certification courses.

Clockwise from lower left are Edwin Duncan Hall, Kenneth E. Peacock Hall (formerly Raley Hall), and Chapell Wilson Hall. The parking lot on the left runs alongside Rivers Street, visible in the upper left corner. Constructed in 1938, Chapell Wilson Hall is the oldest building of the three and once housed Appalachian High School.

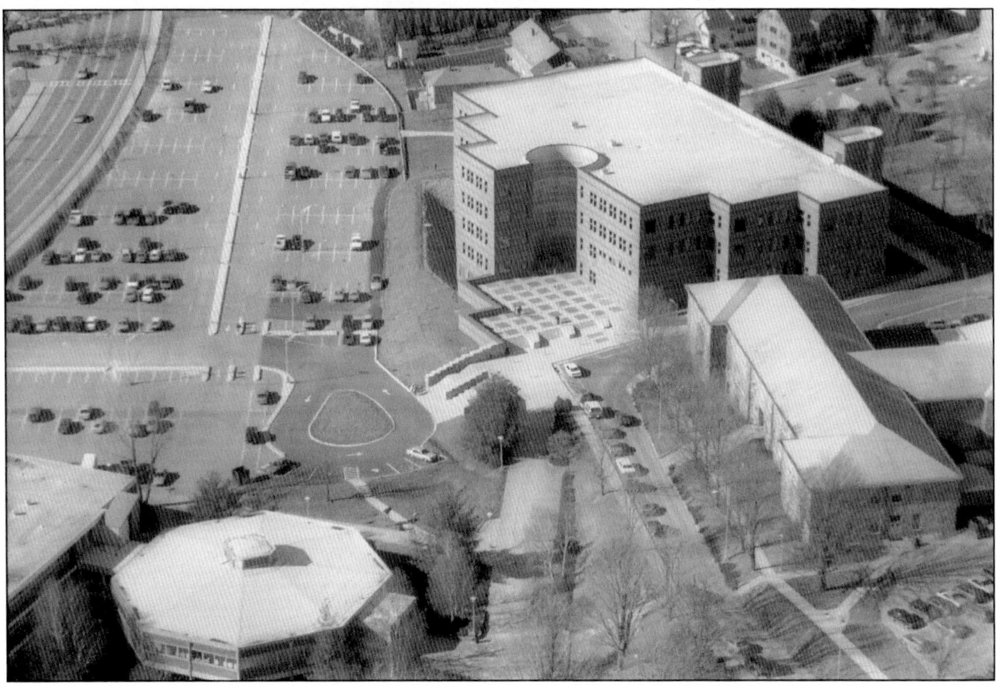

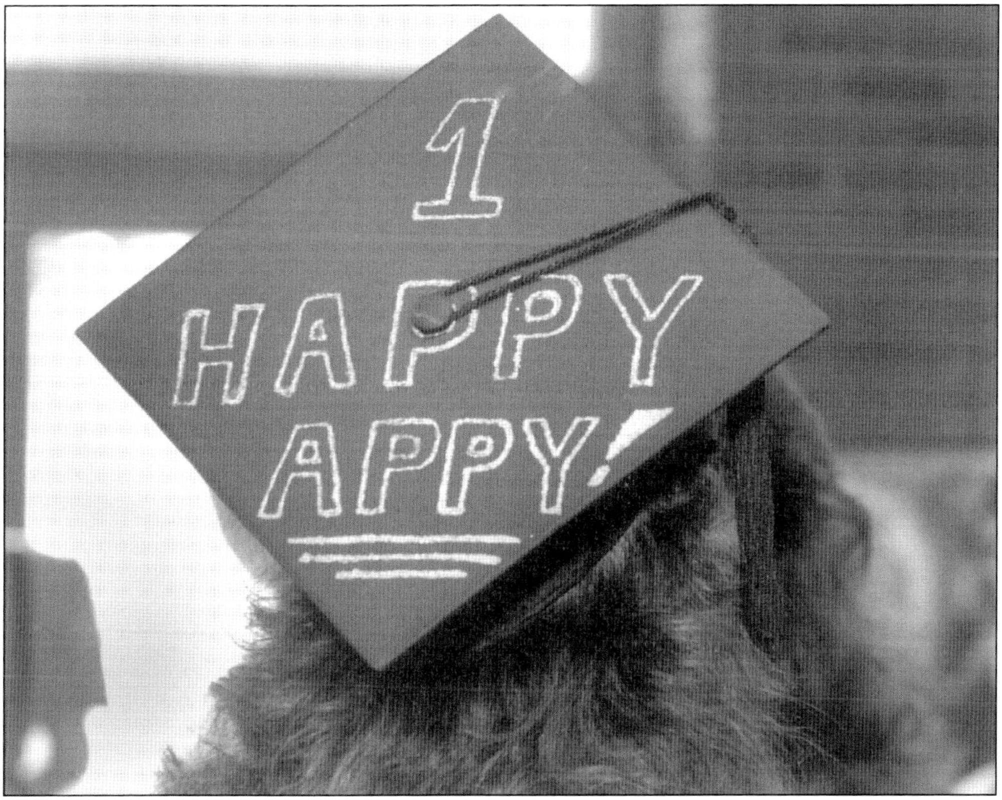

This 1991 graduate advertises her enthusiasm for ASU and her excitement at graduating. The phrase "Happy Appy" has more recently been used to promote Appalachian's faculty and staff health program.

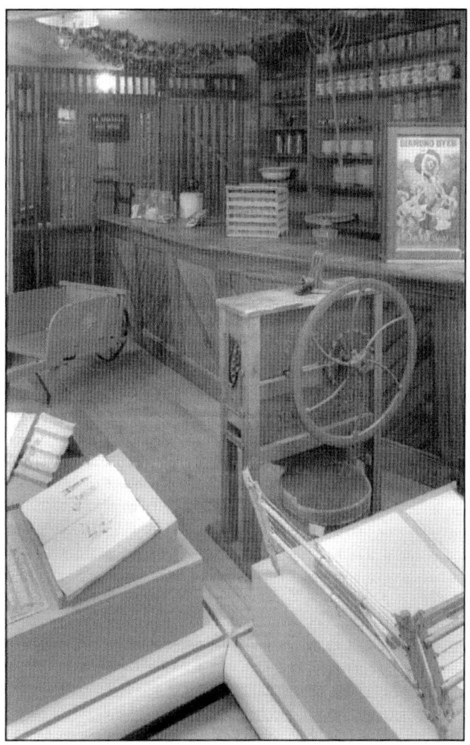

The Appalachian Cultural Museum opened in 1989 to tell the story of Southern Appalachia. The museum hosted many exhibits and events on topics such as stock car racing, the Beech Mountain Land of Oz park, and Appalachian Christmas. The museum closed in 2006.

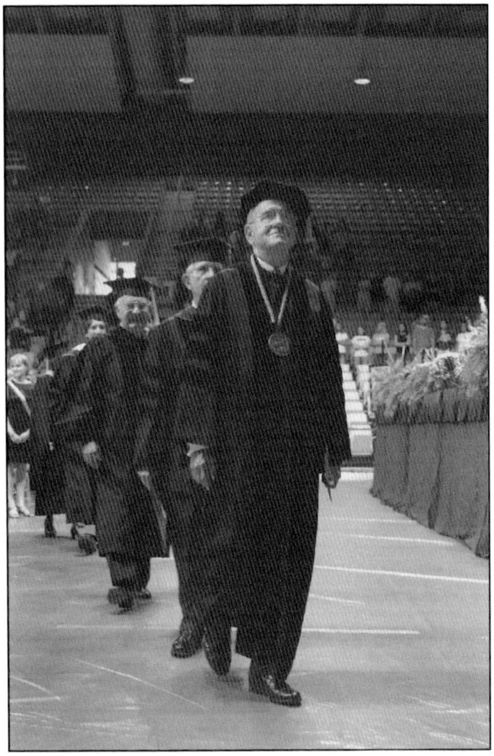

At left, Dr. Francis "Frank" Borkowski, the fifth chancellor of Appalachian, leads the guests of honor in the 2002 convocation march. Below, Chancellor Borkowski shakes hands with a student in 1995. During his 10-year tenure, which ran from 1993 to 2003, Borkowski pushed for diversity, student development, and cultural exchange at Appalachian. Under his watch, the university also added the Holmes Convocation Center (2001), a new science building (2003), Durham Park (2004), and the Alumni Center (1996).

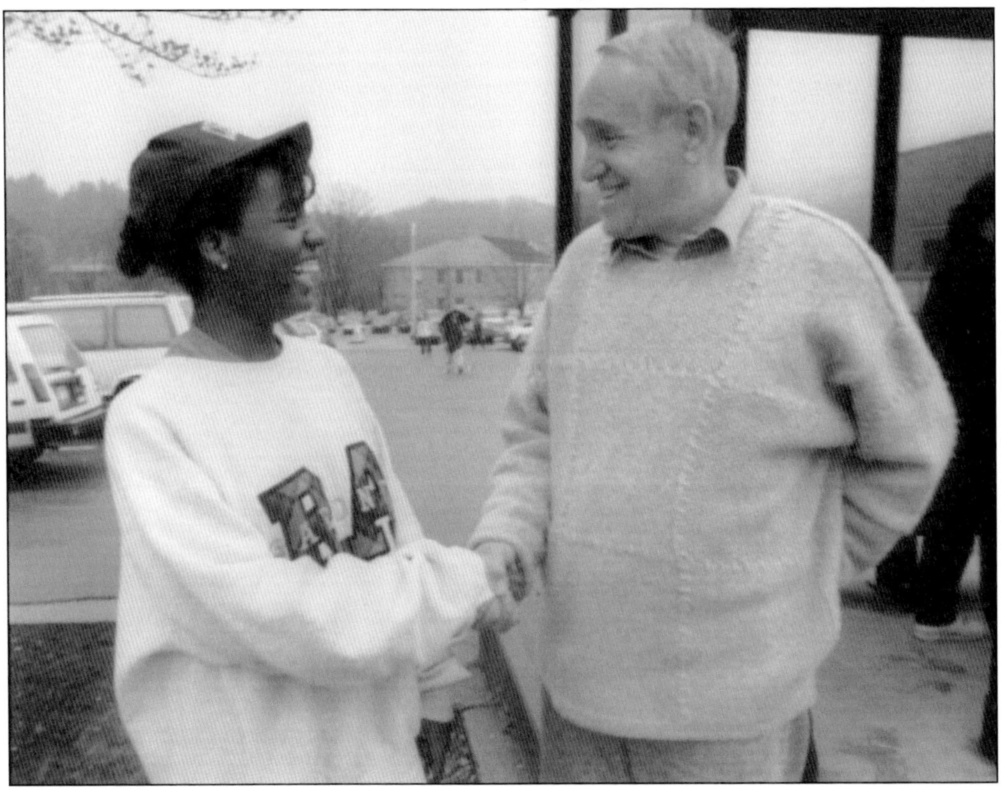

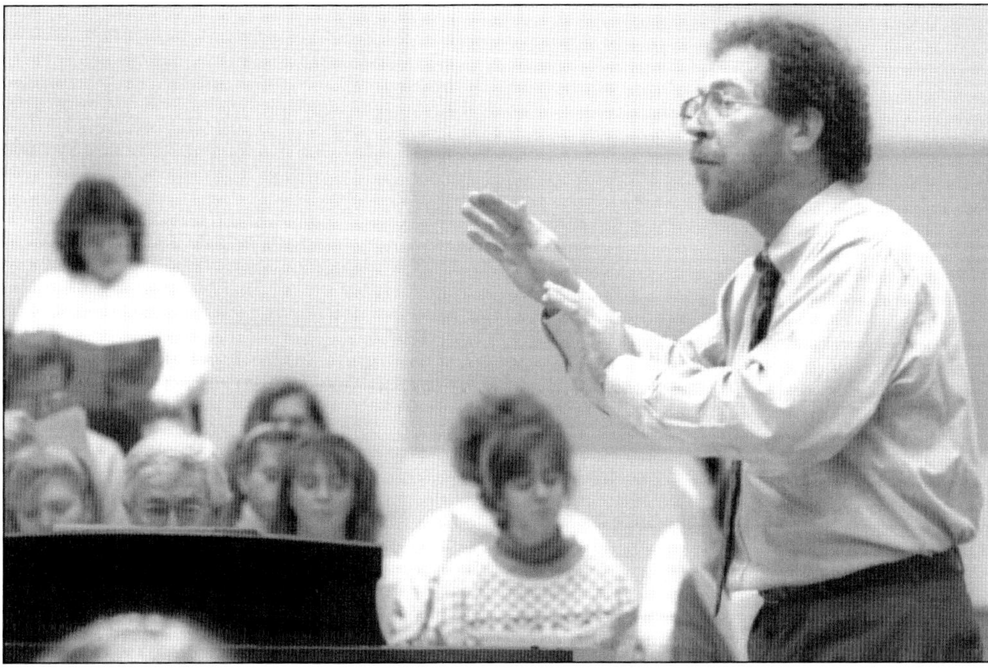

Dr. Robert Clinton Parker, who received a bachelor's degree in music education from Appalachian, joined the faculty as assistant dean of the College of Fine and Applied Arts in 1972. He served as director of the Cannon Music Camp and headed or served on many music organizations both on and off campus. Dr. Parker, now a professor emeritus, retired in 2004 as the senior associate vice chancellor for academic affairs after 32 years of service to Appalachian.

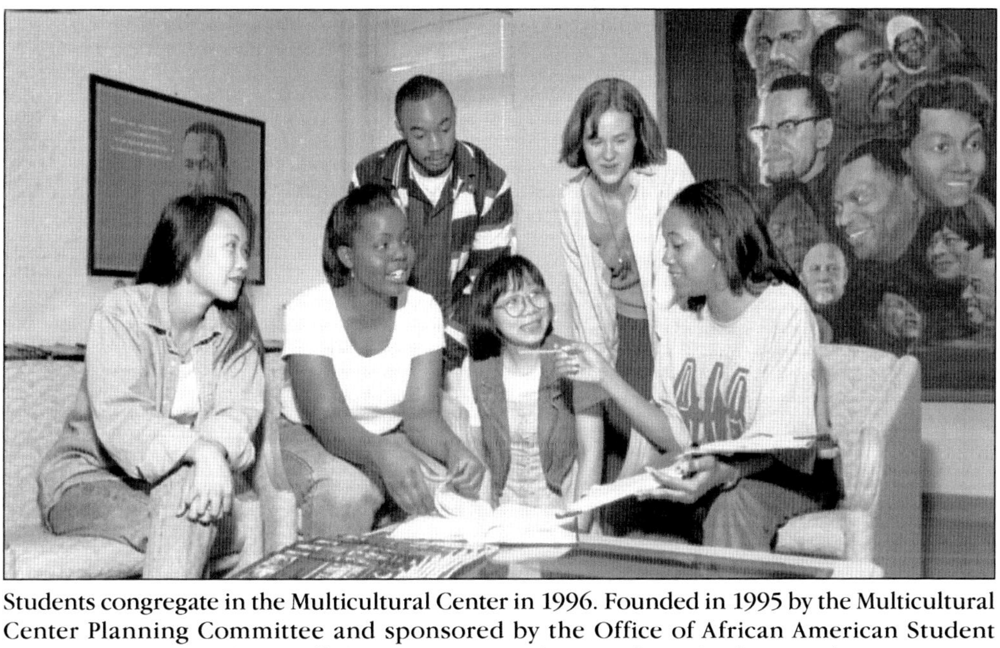

Students congregate in the Multicultural Center in 1996. Founded in 1995 by the Multicultural Center Planning Committee and sponsored by the Office of African American Student Development, the student-staffed center promotes diversity through educational programming. They sponsor multiple events throughout the year, including "Find Yosef a Holiday," the Intercultural Lunch & Learn, and the Multicultural Perspective Weekend.

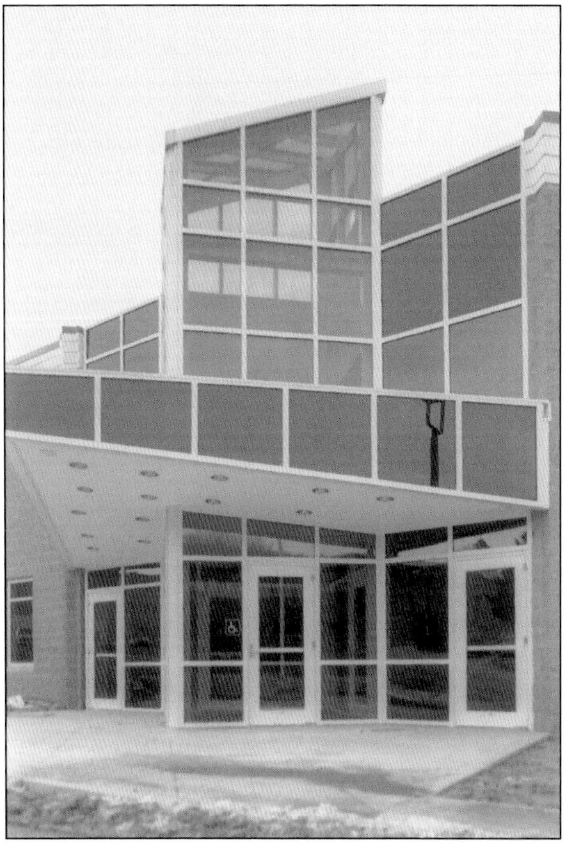

In 1994, Chapell Wilson Auditorium was renovated and opened as Valborg Theatre. The building is named for the late Valborg Sinkler Crossland, who left a bequest to the university. Used by the Department of Theatre and Dance, the Valborg is the University Theater's main stage, seating 334 theatergoers.

The 1995–1996 women's basketball team, coached by Linda Robinson, went 24-6, winning the Southern Conference title and advancing to the NCAA tournament. It was the sixth conference championship for Robinson, whose record-setting tenure as head coach ran from 1984 to 1997. She later served as both the director of the equity office and interim athletic director.

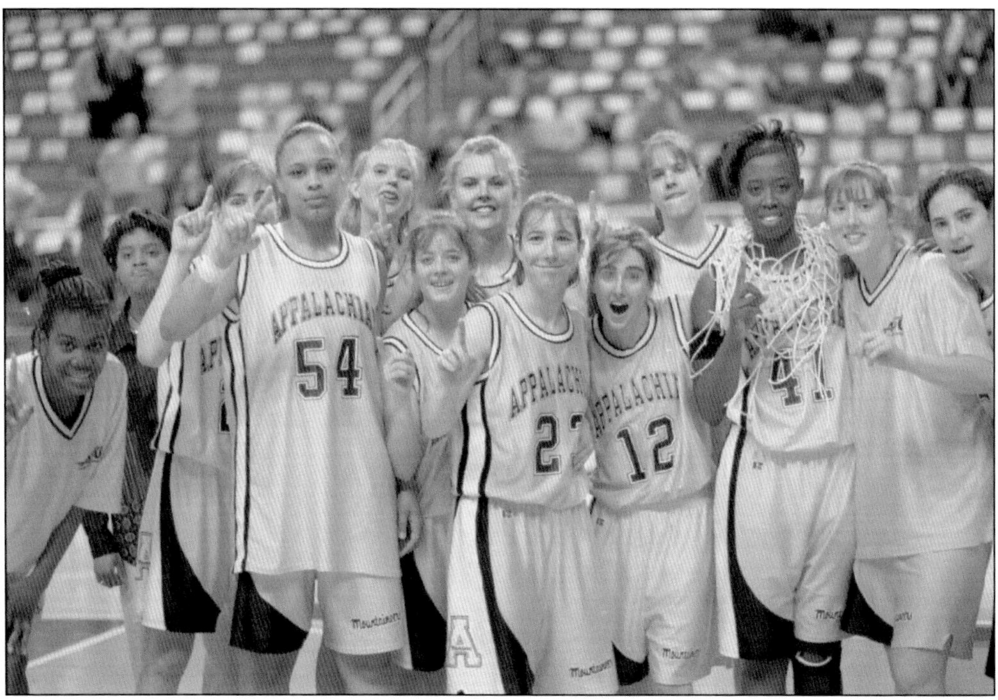

The W.H. Plemmons College Center is seen at right in 1997. Completed 30 years earlier in 1967 and named for university president William H. Plemmons, the building has space for student organizations, conference rooms, a café, a restaurant, and a coffee shop, and it originally housed a bowling alley. The first addition and renovation to the structure was completed in 1995. Another 58,000-square-foot addition was opened in January 2013.

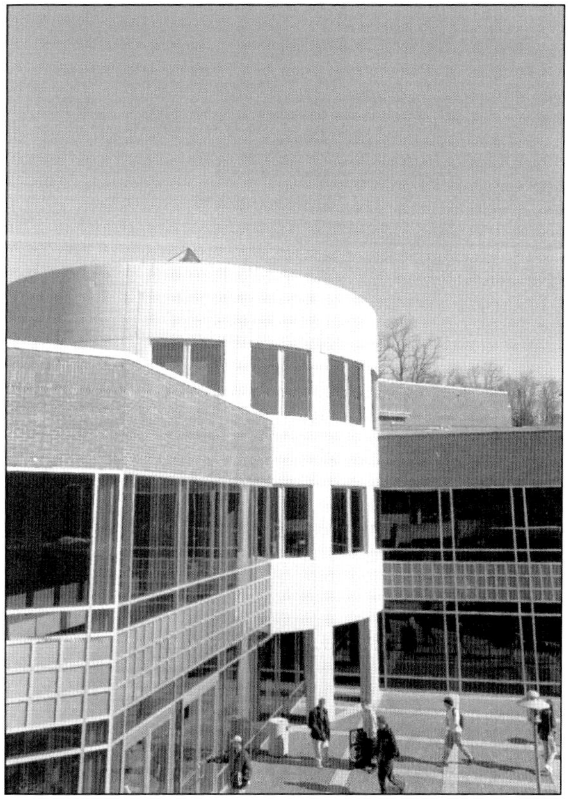

Students stroll in front of Trivette Hall in 1997. Completed in 1991, the dining hall overlooks the duck pond located off Rivers Street and is home to the Park Place Café, McAlister's Select, the Market, and the AppCard offices. The building was named for Ned Trivette, former vice chancellor of business affairs.

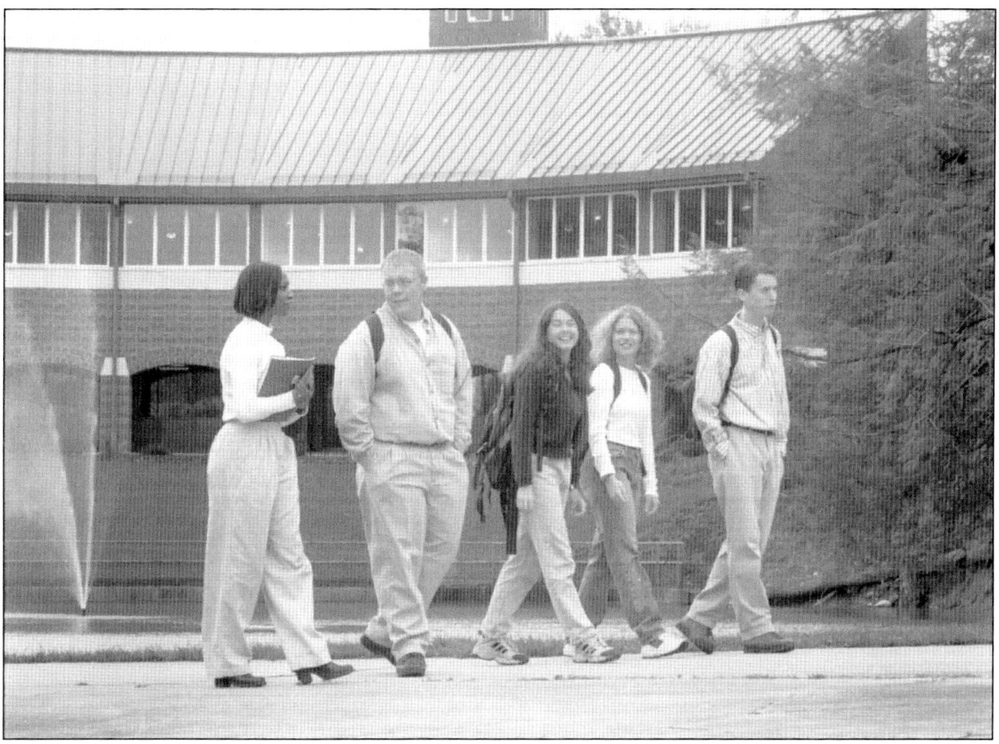

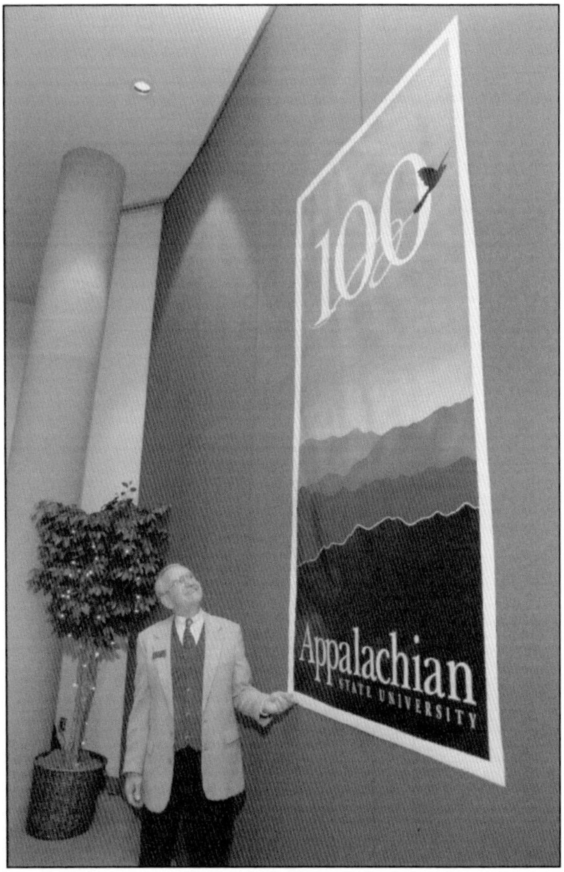

Former chancellor Frank Borkowski stands in front of the logo for Appalachian's centennial celebration in 1999. The Centennial, a yearlong celebration, consisted of a series of events, including a gala, performances, publications, and student projects, lectures, exhibits, and workshops.

Appalachian State University's college radio station, 90.5 WASU, has been in operation for more than 40 years. The station streams at www.WASURadio.com and was one of the inaugural 14 college radio stations to be streamed on iHeart Radio, a free radio service. This image shows former student and current Appalachian associate athletic director David Jackson (left), the "Voice of the Mountaineers," during a show in 2000.

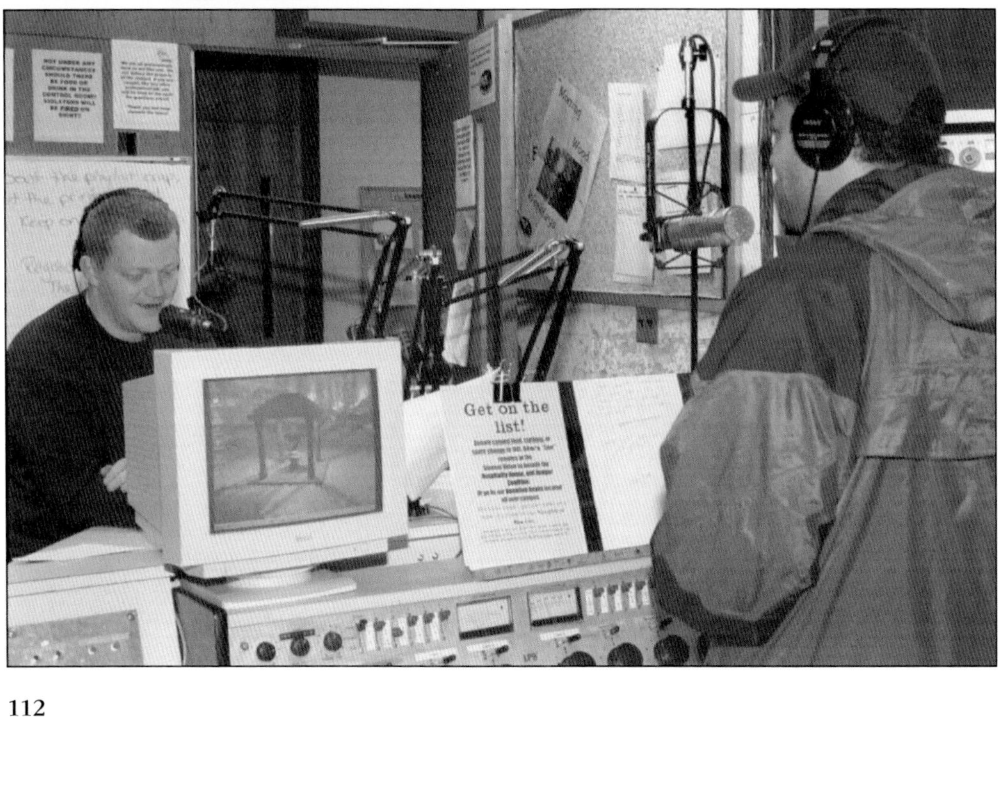

Appalachian Student Ambassadors hold up a sign to welcome alumni. Founded in 1977 by former alumni director Fred Robinette, the Appalachian Student Ambassadors assist with campus tours, alumni events, and the Chancellor for a Day program, among other activities. What started out as a group of 12 students has grown to more than 40 ambassadors committed to service to Appalachian.

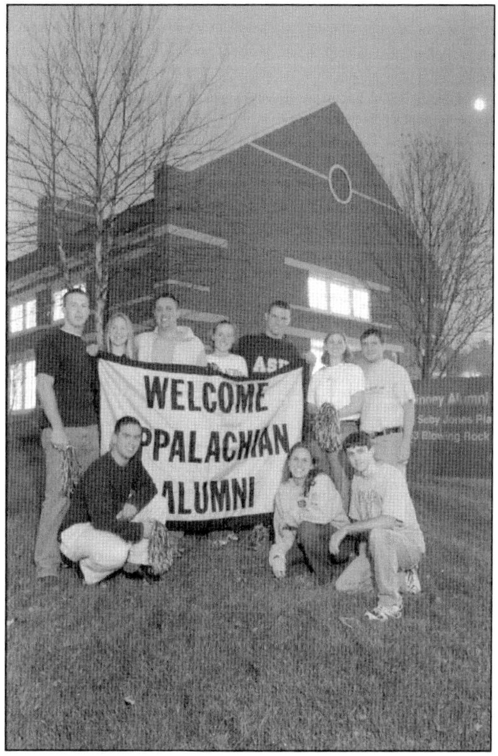

Members of the ROTC Flying Rifles drill team practice on Sanford Mall. The Department of Military Science and Leadership was established in the fall of 1969. The basic military instruction course provides instruction for freshman and sophomore years, while the advanced course is taken junior and senior years. The department also offers a minor in military science and leadership.

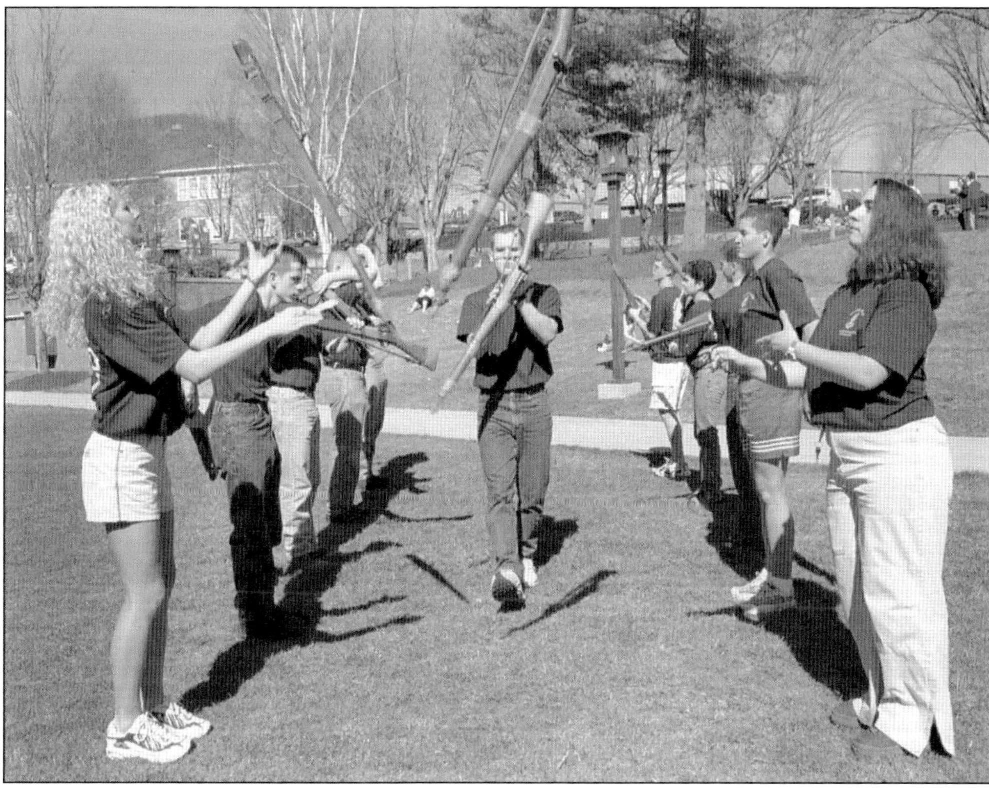

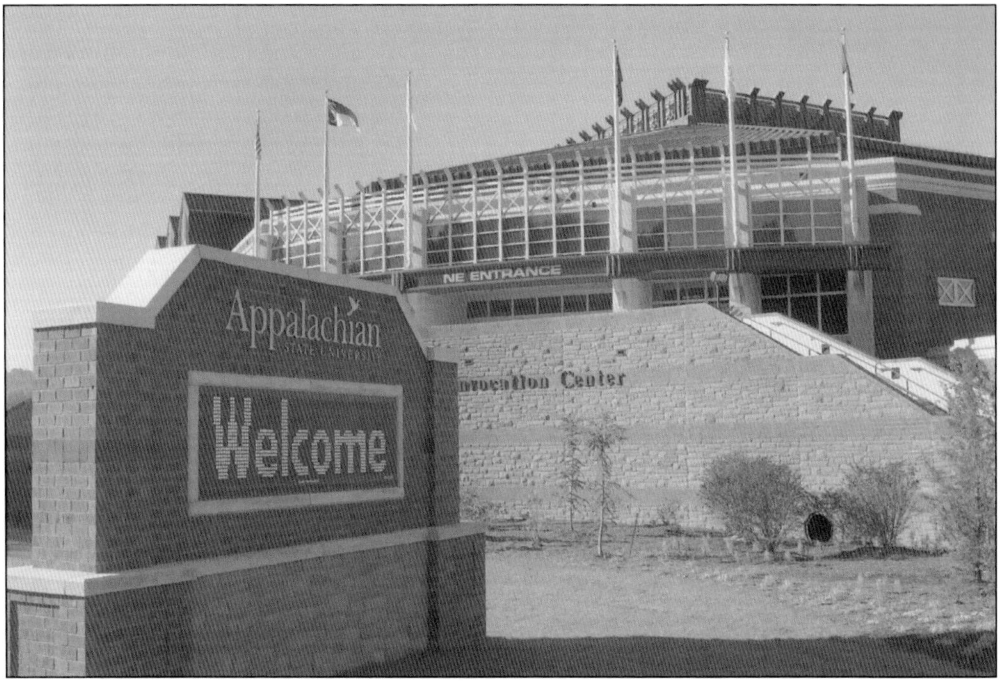

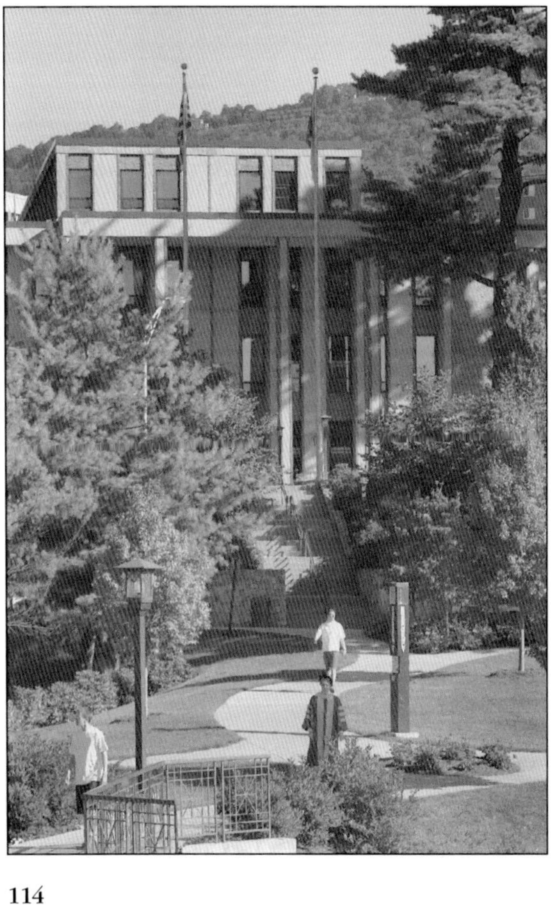

The George M. Holmes Convocation Center was completed in 2000. The 200,840-square-foot structure houses classrooms and offices, as well as the Seby B. Jones Arena, which hosts athletic events, graduation, convocation, and other community and entertainment events. The building is named in honor of George Holmes, an Appalachian graduate and the president and co-owner of the W.N. Ireland Insurance Company. He served 16 terms as the representative for North Carolina House District 92.

The B.B. Dougherty Administration Building, completed in 1968, was erected on the same site as the first administration building, constructed in 1903. The columns on the southern side were designed to mimic the original administration building, and a marble plaque from the old building is incorporated in the current structure. The building is named for university cofounder and president Dr. Blanford Barnard Dougherty. It is pictured here in 2002.

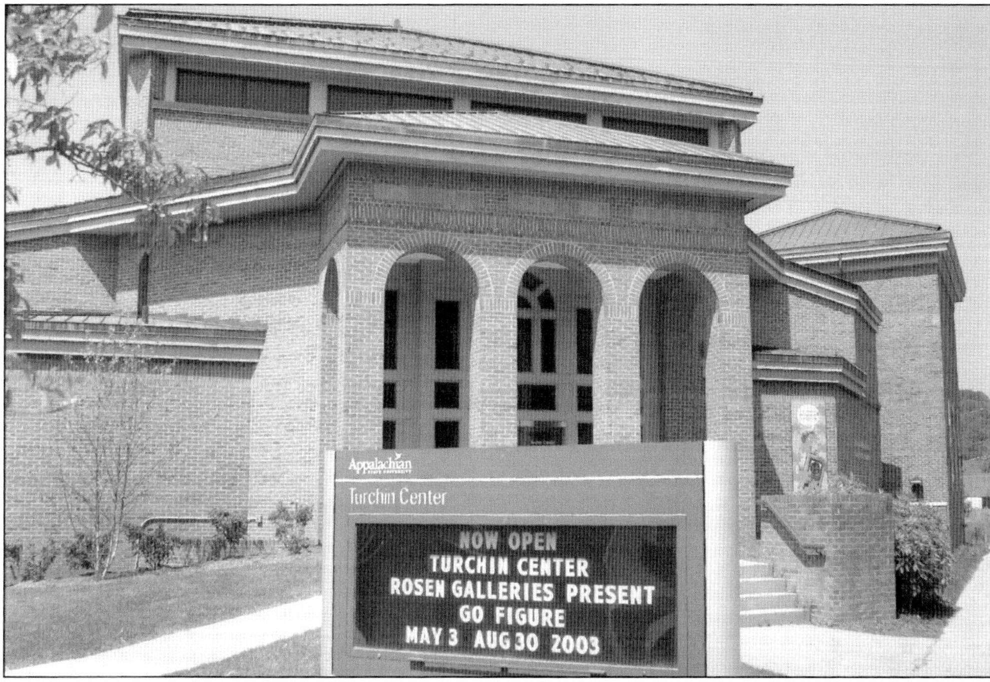

The Robert and Lillian Turchin Center for the Visual Arts is a regional visual arts center that has multiple gallery spaces, administrative offices, and areas for exhibit preparation and storage for the permanent collection. The center offers exhibits as well as other educational programs throughout the year. Robert Turchin, who was president of RLT Investment Corporation, served on Appalachian's board of trustees and was vice chairman of the Appalachian State University Foundation board.

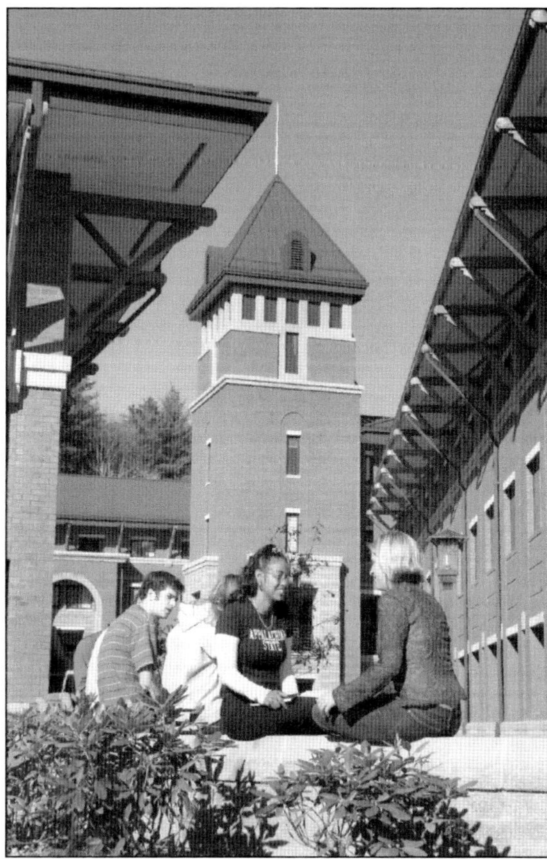

The Living Learning Center (LLC) consists of two buildings. One houses a residential learning community, which includes living space for 312 students, including members of the Watauga Global Community (WGC), North Carolina Teaching Fellows, Language & Culture RLC students, and international exchange students. The academic building houses offices and classroom space for the student groups that reside in the LLC, as well as other academic programs.

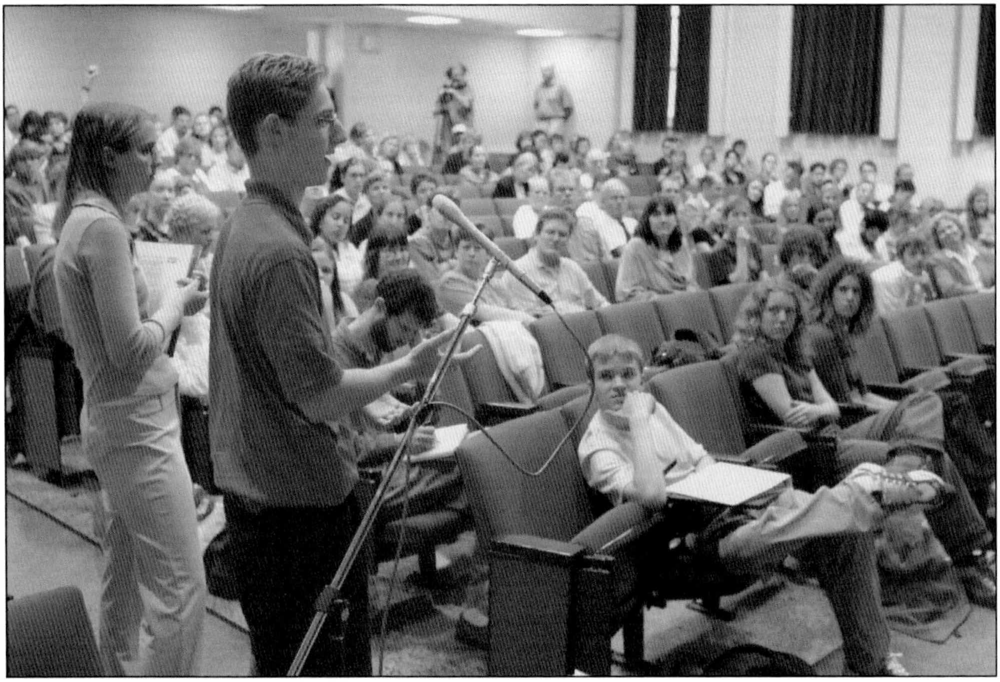

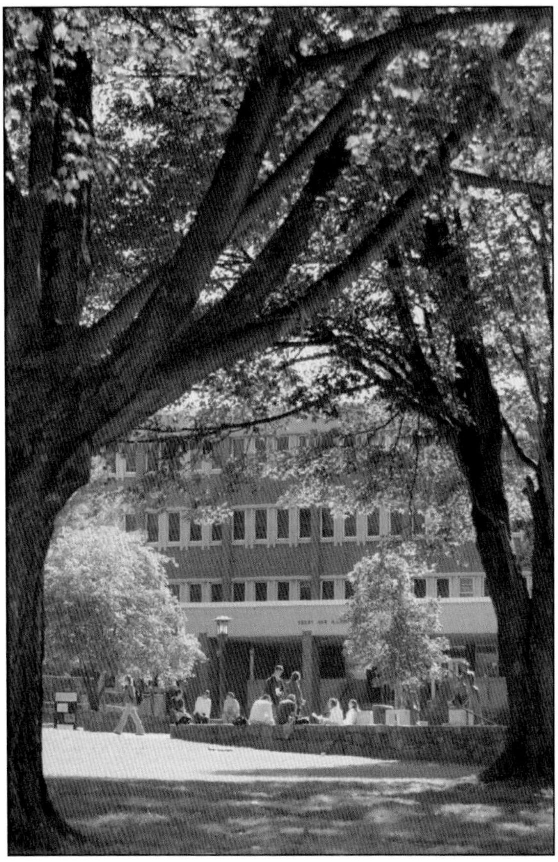

Students participate in a 2003 reading discussion sponsored by Appalachian's Summer Reading Program. The reading program began in 1997 as a part of orientation and requires that all incoming freshman read a book selected for that year. Reading and discussion sessions provide a common experience for freshman and help develop a sense of community. The program is a part of University College.

Terry and Margaret Rose Sanford Hall, completed in 1969, houses the English, anthropology, and foreign languages departments. It sits on Sanford Mall and was named for former North Carolina governor, US senator, and two-time presidential candidate James Terry Sanford, who was also a strong proponent of public education and served as president of Duke University from 1969 to 1985. A professor is holding class in front of the building in this 2003 image.

The Chemistry, Astronomy, and Physics (CAP) Building is the newer of two science complexes at Appalachian. At the time of its completion in 1998, the 118,000-square-foot building was the largest academic structure on campus. In addition to the three physical science departments identified in its name, the CAP Building is also home to the computer science department and labs for the Department of Geography.

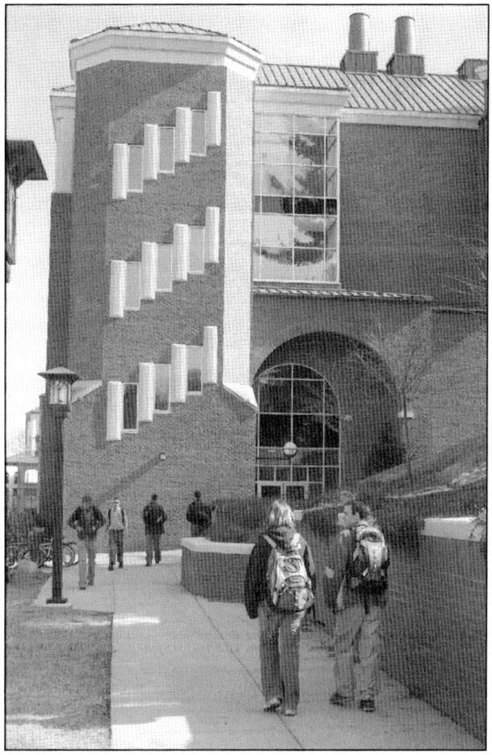

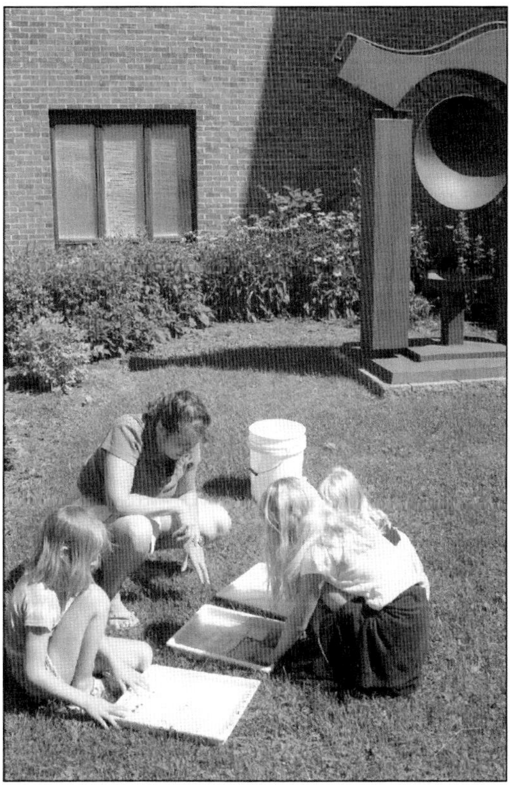

An Appalachian Summer Festival, a multi-arts festival, began in 1984 and is managed by Appalachian's Office of Arts and Cultural Programs. The celebration includes performances in music, theater, and dance, as well as art exhibits and workshops open to the general public. Here, schoolchildren work on art on the lawn of Wey Hall (built in 1976) at one of the Appalachian Summer art workshops.

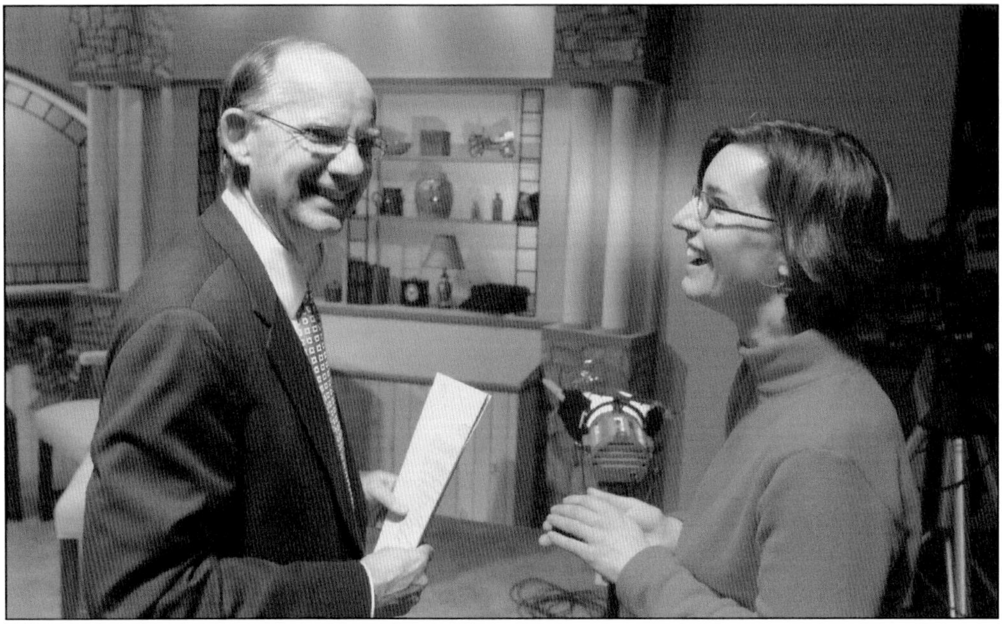

Chancellor Ken Peacock chats with Linda Coutant from University Communications on the set of *Appalachian Perspective*, a 30-minute cable television program hosted by the chancellor and produced by Appalachian State University's Office of Public Affairs and Department of Communications. The program features academic public service programs and noteworthy North Carolinians from across the state.

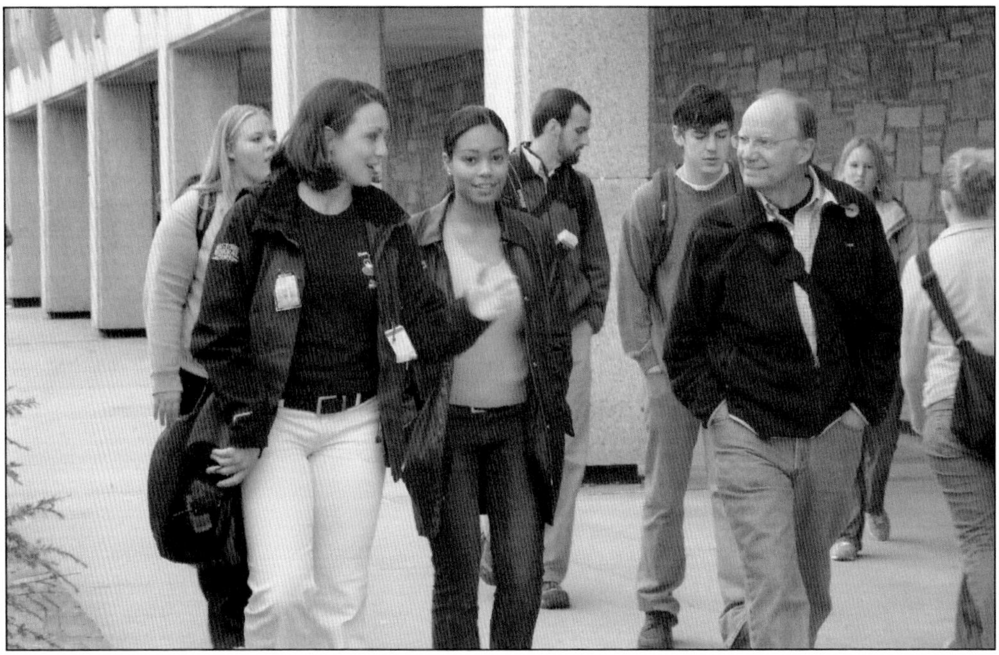

In this 2005 photograph, Chancellor Peacock walks with students during the Chancellor for a Day event, held each year and sponsored by the Appalachian Student Ambassadors organization. Students who participate in the Appalachian Student Ambassadors service projects are selected to switch places with the chancellor for 24 hours.

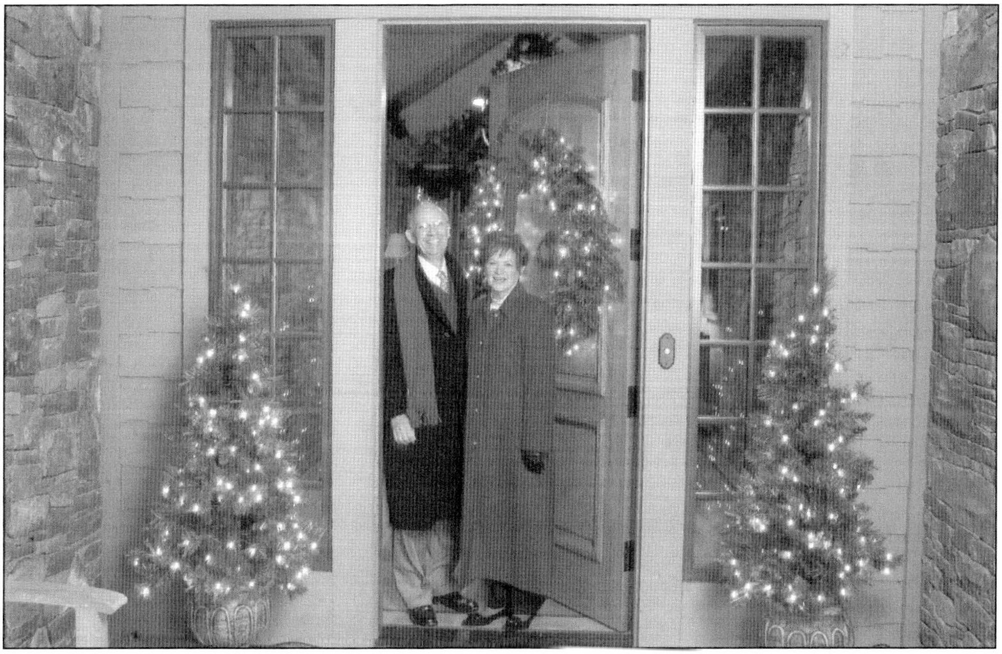

Dr. Kenneth Edward Peacock, Appalachian's sixth chancellor, and his wife, Roseane, are seen here at the Appalachian House on Christmas Day in 2005. Appalachian House, a 9,400-square-foot multipurpose facility located on Bodenheimer Drive, provides space for official university functions and serves as the chancellor's residence. It opened officially in 2000, replacing the old president's house.

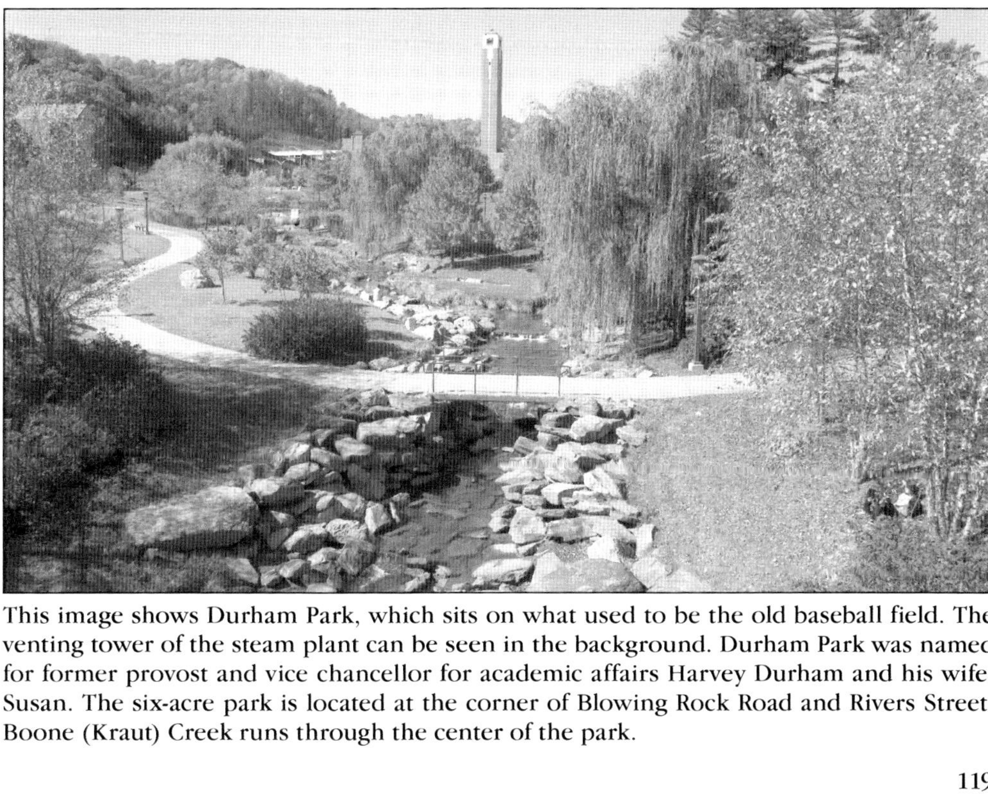

This image shows Durham Park, which sits on what used to be the old baseball field. The venting tower of the steam plant can be seen in the background. Durham Park was named for former provost and vice chancellor for academic affairs Harvey Durham and his wife, Susan. The six-acre park is located at the corner of Blowing Rock Road and Rivers Street. Boone (Kraut) Creek runs through the center of the park.

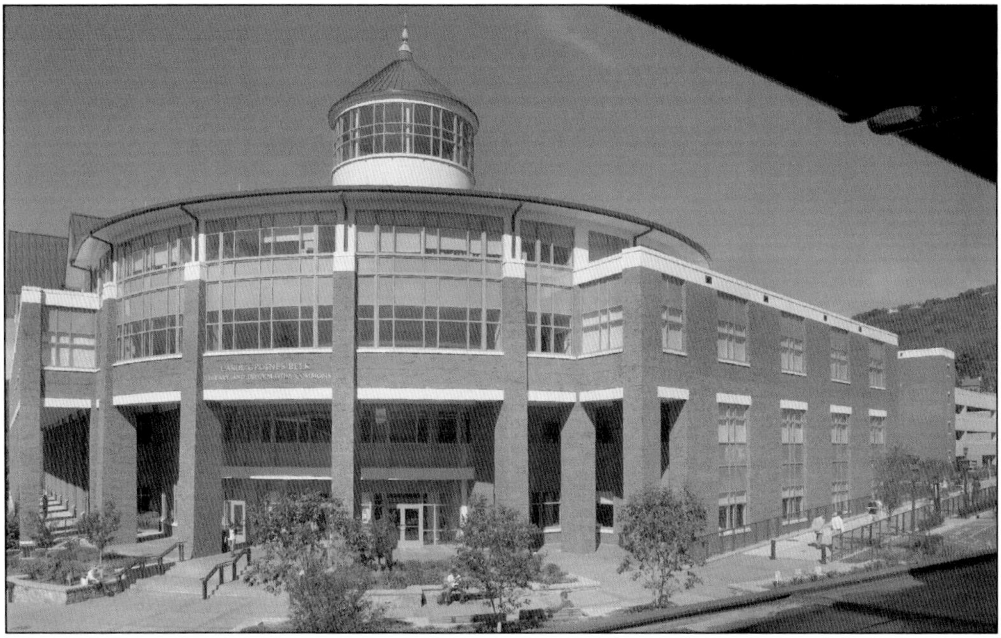

The Belk Library and Information Commons (above) was completed in 2005. Sitting on the highest point on campus, the library provides more than 215,000 square feet for collaborative research and study and includes group study rooms, classrooms, wireless access, and a coffee shop.

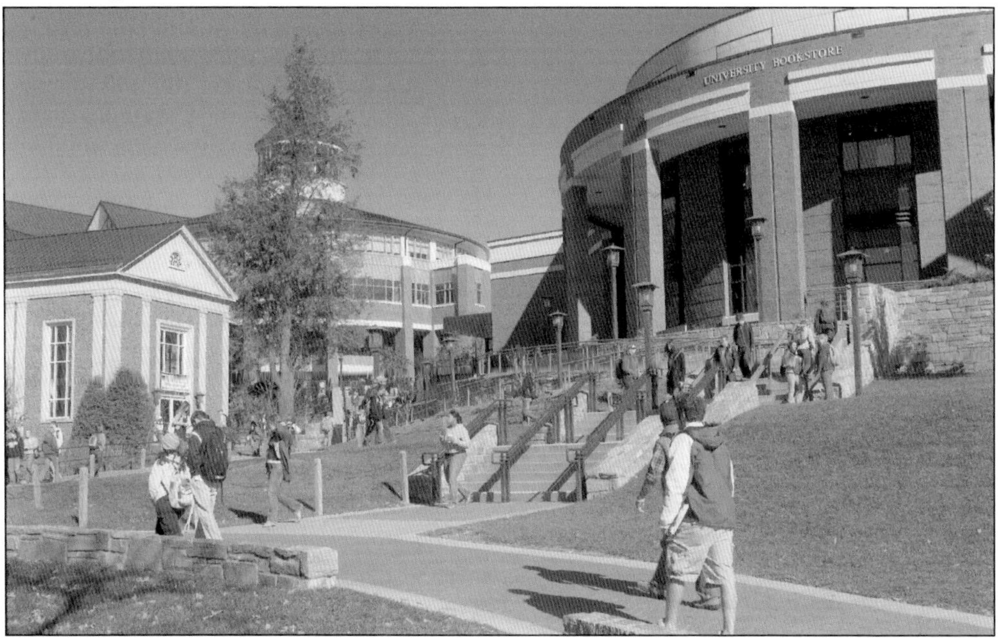

The northwestern edge of the mall is seen above in 2007. The old D.D. Dougherty Library building stands on the left, the new Belk Library and Information Commons is at the center, and the Plemmons Student Union is on the right. The new library and renovations to the student union have dramatically changed the look of this part of campus, but the mall remains much the same and is still a popular place for students to gather on sunny days.

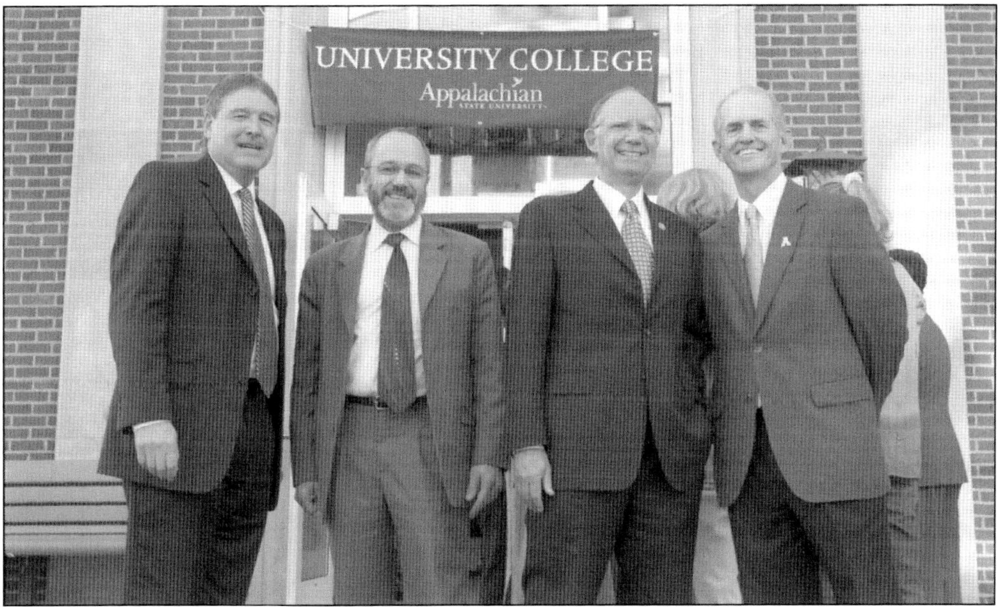

From left to right, Dr. Stan Aeschleman, Dr. David Haney, Chancellor Kenneth Peacock, and board of trustees chairman Jim Deal stand at the opening of University College in 2007. Dr. Aeschleman is a psychology professor and former provost. David Haney, formerly an English professor and the vice provost for undergraduate education, was the first director of University College, which oversees the general education program.

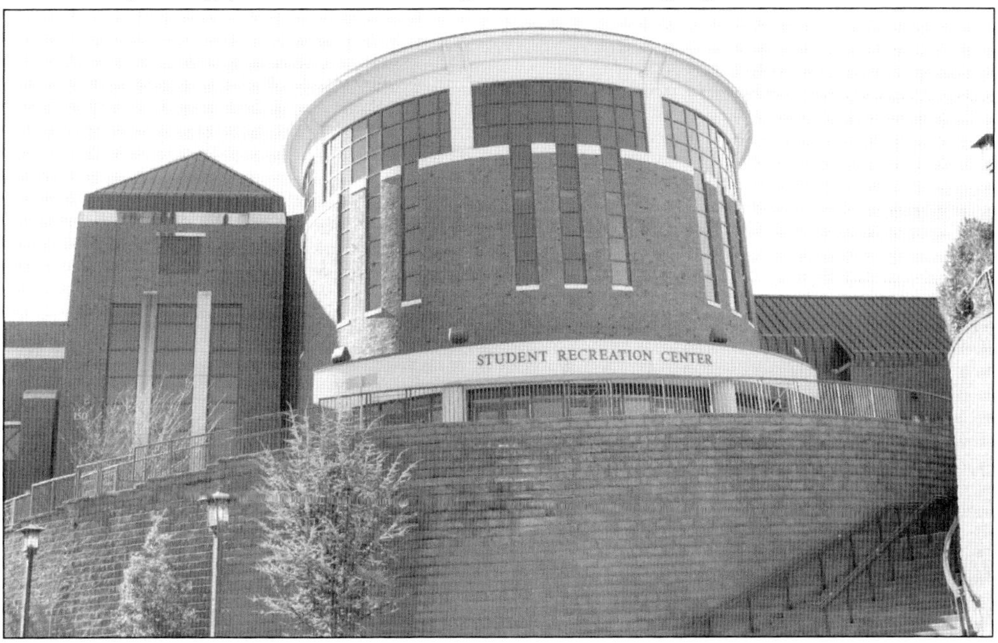

The new University Recreation Center (UREC) opened in 2006. The 120,000-square-foot building includes a 50-meter swimming pool, two gymnasiums, an indoor walking and running track, cardio and weight rooms, and a 50-foot climbing wall. UREC offers educational and athletic programs such as club and intramural sports, aquatics, and camps for students, faculty, staff, and the community.

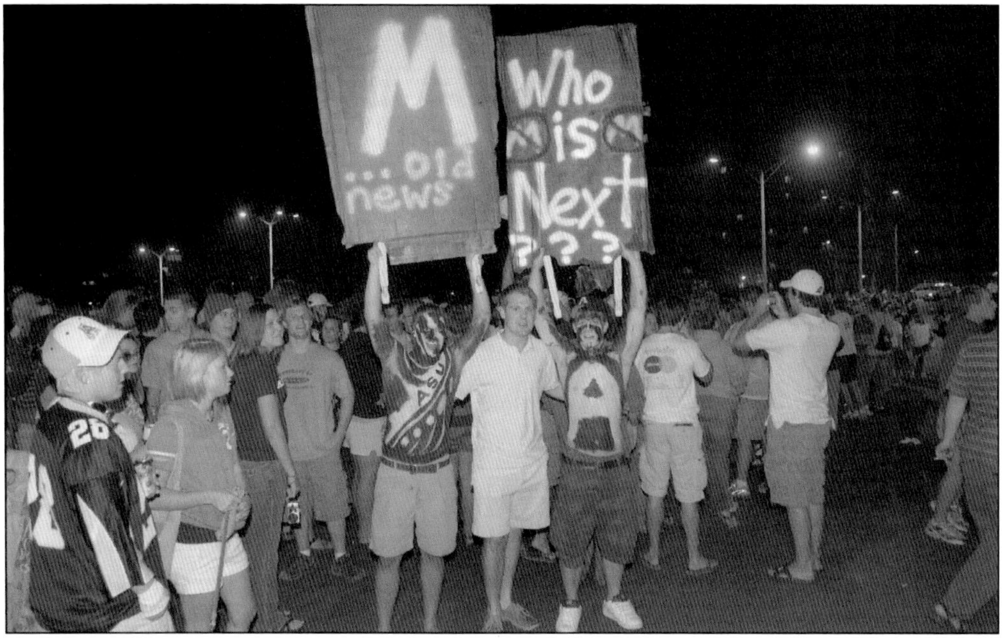

Excited fans gather on campus after Appalachian State's football team stunned the University of Michigan 34-32 in Ann Arbor on September 2, 2007. Appalachian went into the game as the defending FCS champion, having won back-to-back titles in 2005 and 2006; after the victory at Michigan Stadium, the Mountaineers went on to become the first FCS team to win three consecutive championships.

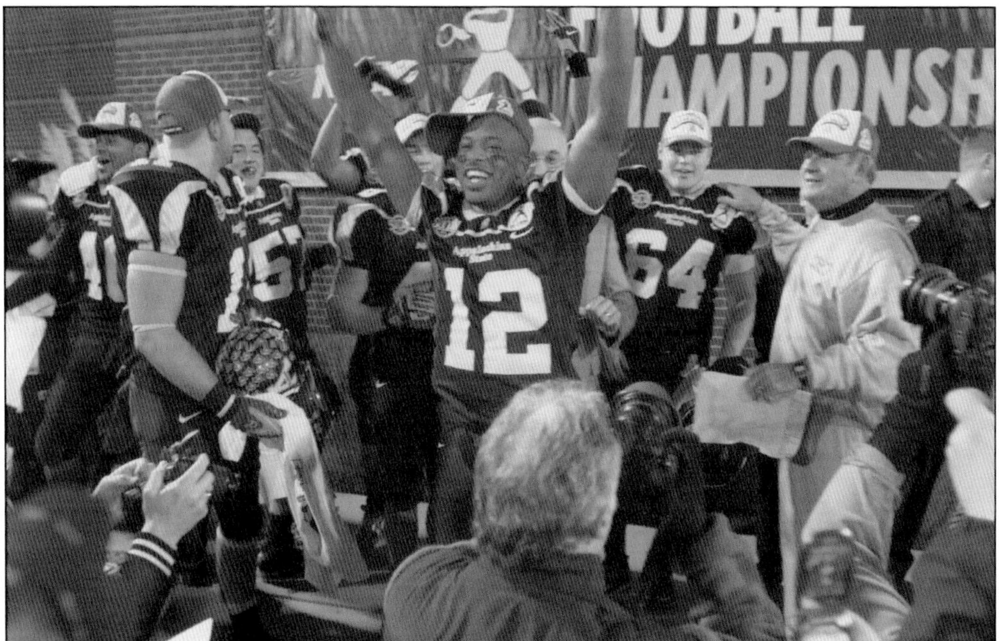

The Mountaineers celebrate their third consecutive FCS championship during a press conference in 2007 while coach Jerry Moore (right) looks on. Moore was head coach of the Mountaineers from 1989 to 2012. In 2014, he was inducted into the College Football Hall of Fame.

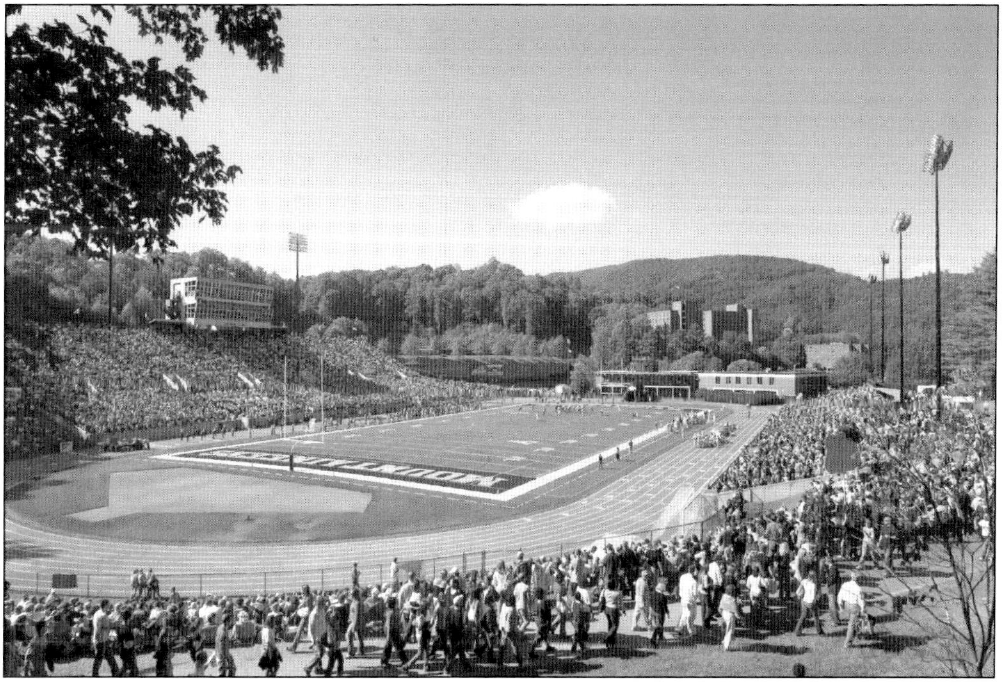

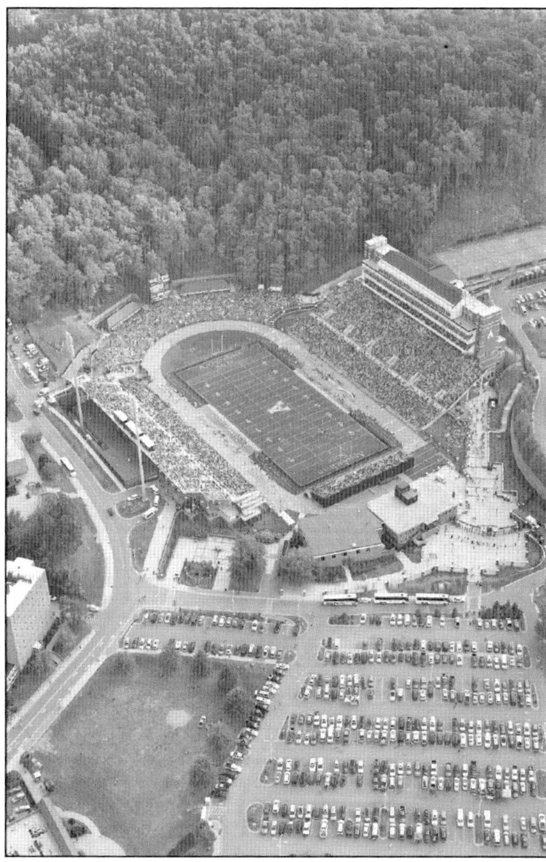

Kidd Brewer Football Stadium, also known as "The Rock," is seen here before (above) and after (right) renovation. Built in 1962 and originally named Conrad Stadium for William Conrad, a former trustee and R.J. Reynolds executive, the football stadium was rebuilt in 1979 and renamed for former head football coach Kidd Brewer, who coached the Mountaineers from 1935 to 1938. The stadium facility supports football, field hockey, and track and field. The most recent renovation of the stadium was completed in 2009 and included the addition of 1,500 seats and the Appalachian Athletics Center, an athletic training facility. The current seating capacity is 21,650. (Both, courtesy of Appalachian Athletics.)

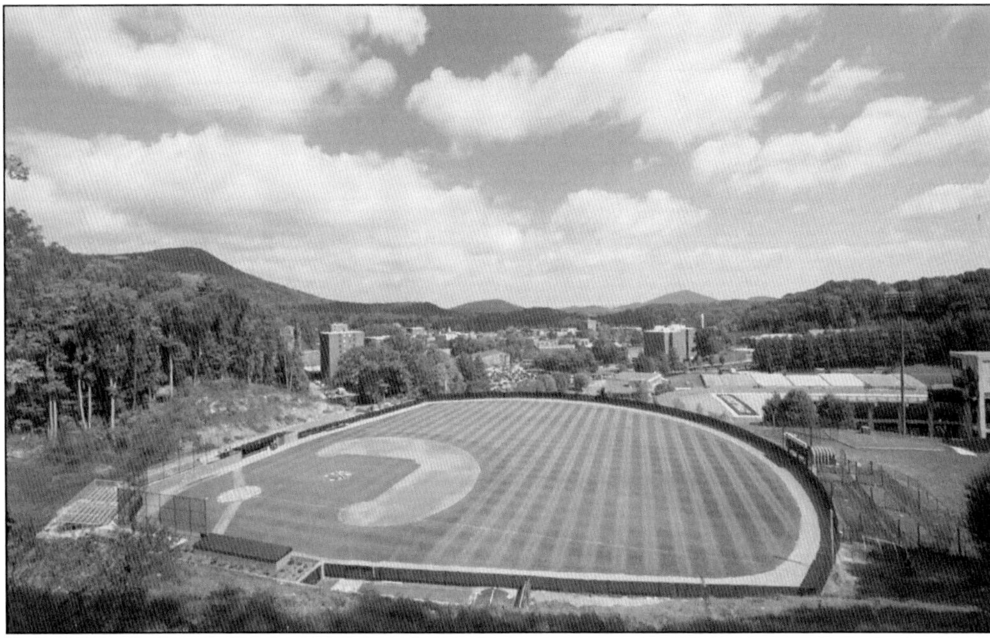

Appalachian's baseball field had three locations on campus. The first field was at the corner of Rivers Street and Blowing Rock Road, now the site of Durham Park. The second field (above) was located west of the football stadium. The most recent complex, Beaver Field (named for board of trustee Donald C. Beaver) at Jim and Bettie Smith Stadium (below), is behind the former Broyhill Inn and Conference Center and opened in 2007. It includes more than 1,000 permanent seats and grass seating to accommodate several thousand more. (Both, courtesy of Appalachian Athletics.)

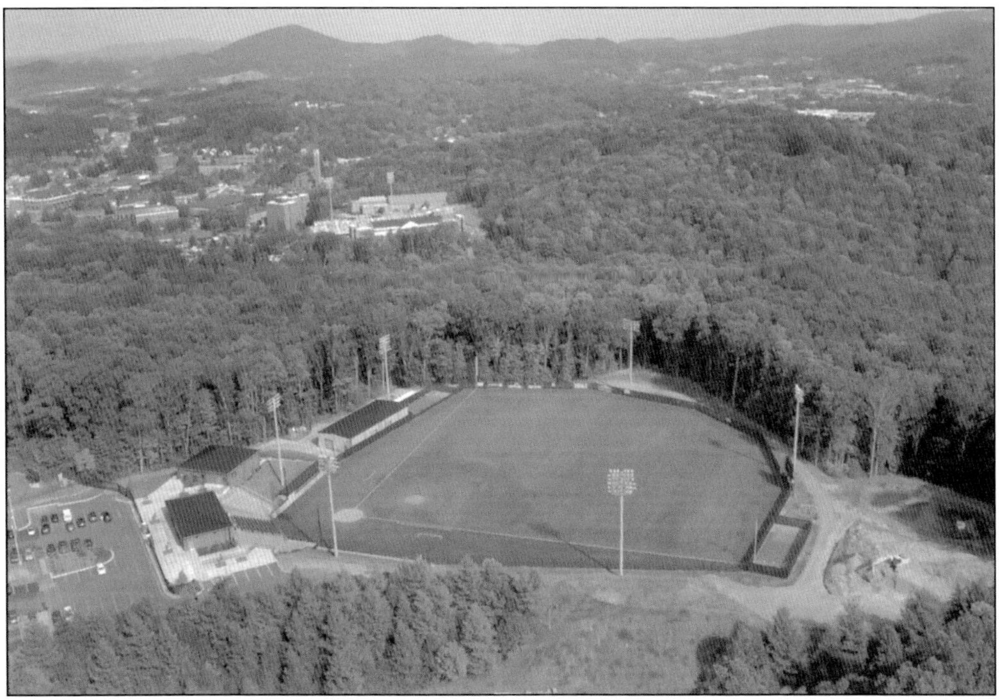

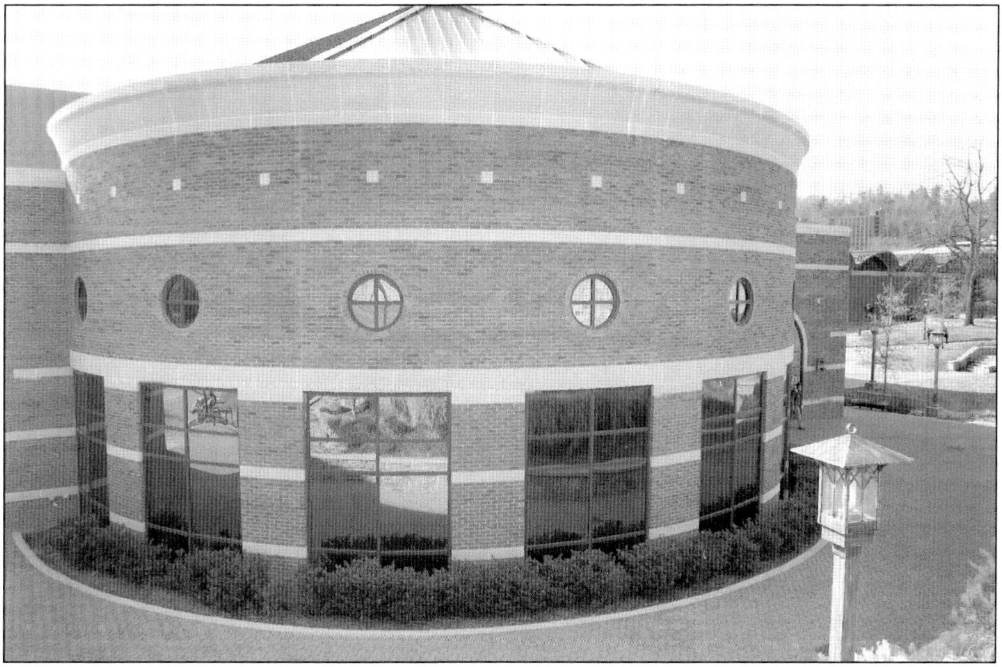

The Central Dining Hall, completed in 2009, was built on the site of the old Welborn Cafeteria, which had stood for more than 80 years. The new building features 84,744 square feet of space, including outdoor seating and a lounge for faculty and staff dining.

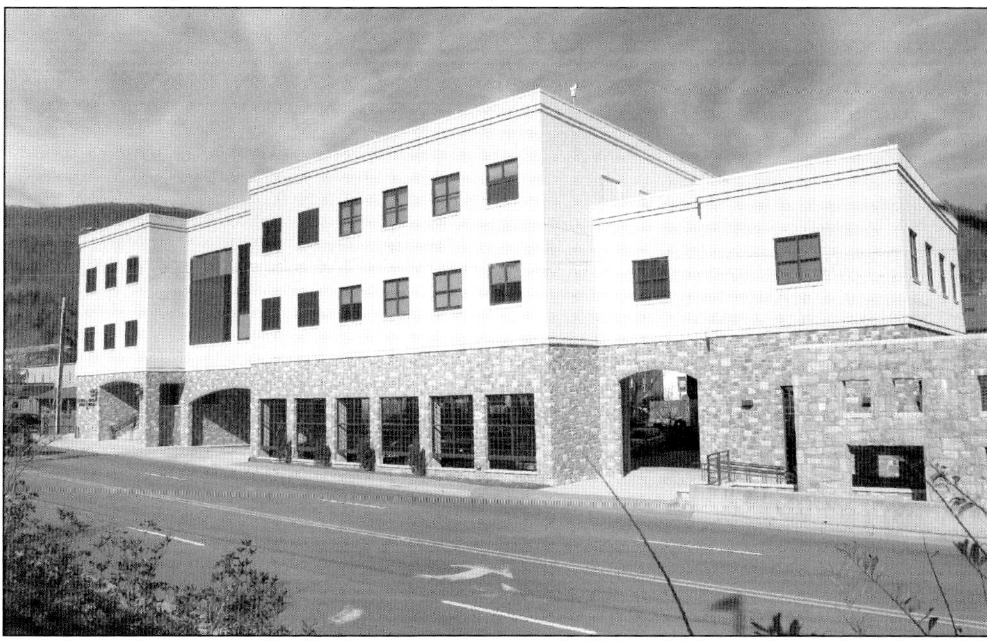

The Beasley Broadcasting Center is the new home for 90.5 WASU-FM, Appalachian's student-run radio station. The new center was built on the corner of Depot and Rivers Streets and opened in 2010. The center was partially funded by a donation from Appalachian alumnus George G. Beasley, who founded the Beasley Broadcast Group, which owns radio stations throughout the country.

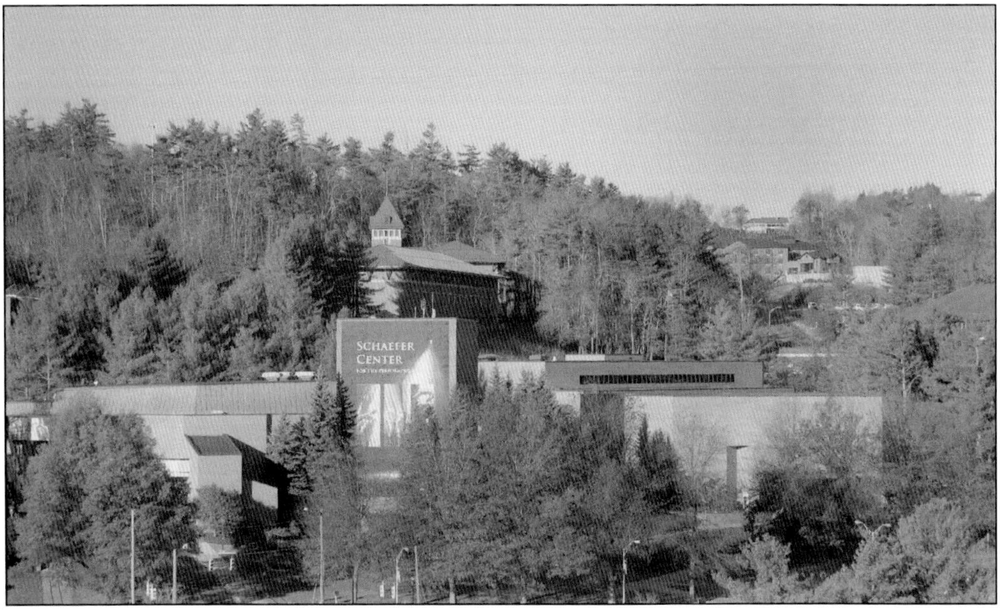

The Schaefer Center for the Performing Arts, formerly Farthing Auditorium, was recently renovated and renamed for Bonnie and Jamie Schaefer, who donated funds for the renovations and have been longtime supporters of An Appalachian Summer Festival. The building dates to 1976 and serves as the main performance venue for the campus.

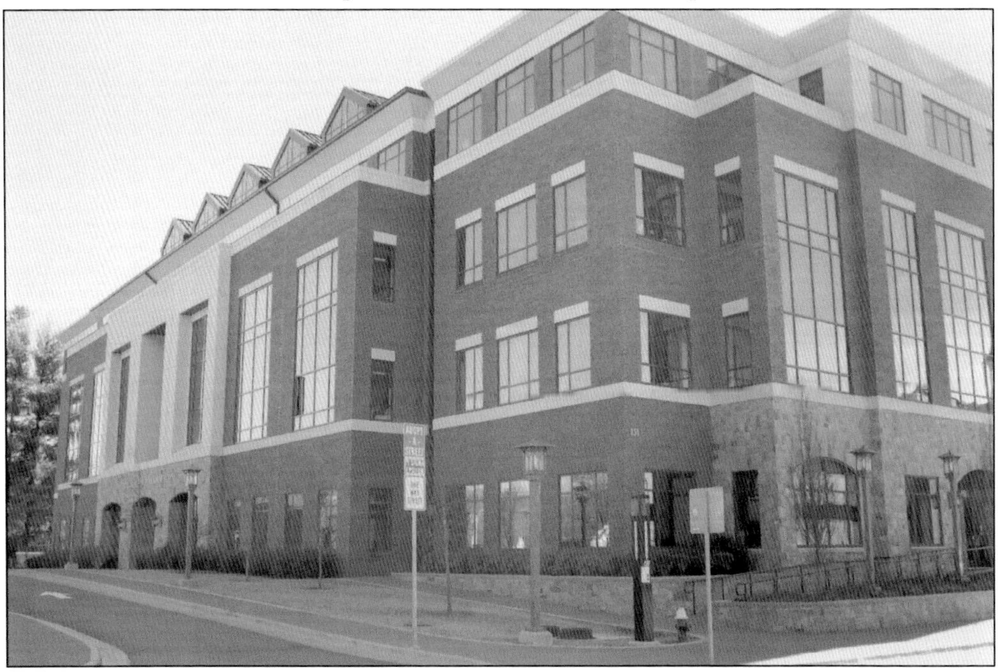

The new education building, which houses the Reich College of Education, opened its doors in 2011. A five-story building located at the corner of College and King Streets, it houses not only classrooms and offices, but also computer labs, counseling rooms, and reading clinics, as well as conference and seminar rooms. It also boasts a 24-foot-diameter mural by artist Brenda Council on the first floor.

BIBLIOGRAPHY

Books, Newspapers, and Bulletins:

The Appalachian. Student Newspaper. Boone, NC: Appalachian State Teachers College, 1934–2013.

Appalachian State University Bulletin. Boone, NC: Appalachian State University, 1930–2013.

Bell, John L. *History of Education in Southern Appalachia*. Cullowhee, NC: Western Carolina University, 1990.

Corbitt, Tom. *The Development of Public Education in Watauga County, North Carolina*. Self-published: s.n, 1976.

Dew Drop. College Bulletin. Boone, NC: Appalachian State, 1900–1929.

Howe, Richard D. *The Appalachian Faculty Emeriti*. Boone, NC: Appalachian State University, 2009.

Lanier, Ruby J. *Blanford Barnard Dougherty, Mountain Educator*. Durham, NC: Duke University Press, 1974.

Mellott, Jack, Mike Rominger, Charles Shoffner, and Ruth Douglas Currie. *Appalachian State University: The First Hundred Years*. Prospect, KY: Harmony House, 1998.

The Rhododendron. Student Yearbook. Boone, NC: Appalachian State University, 1922–2004.

Stam, Doris Perry. *Mountain Educators: The Dougherty Family and the First Fifty Years of Appalachian*. Boone, NC: Watauga Press, 2010.

Watauga Democrat, 1888–2013.

Archival Materials and Online Resources:

Appalachian State University Digital Collections. www.omeka.library.appstate.edu.

UA.5004: Blanford Barnard Dougherty Collection. Appalachian State University Archives, Boone, NC.

UA.5015: University Communications Records. Appalachian State University Archives, Boone, NC.

UA.5044: Division of University Advancement Records. Appalachian State University Archives, Boone, NC.

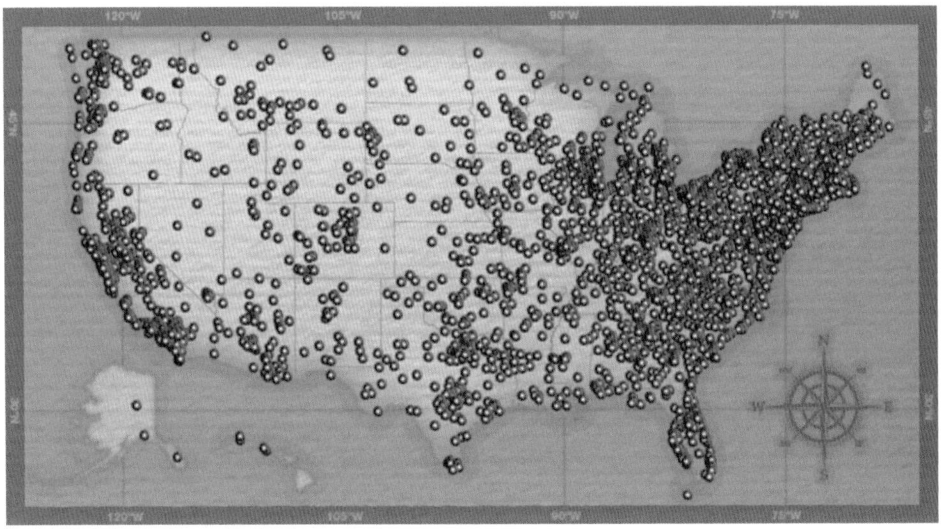